Dr. Ruth's PREGNANCY GUIDE *for* COUPLES

Love, Sex, and Medical Facts

Dr. Ruth K. Westheimer

Amos Grünebaum, MD, FACOG

Routledge

New York and London

Published in 1999 by
Routledge
29 West 35 Street
New York, NY 10001

Printed in Great Britain by
Routledge
11 New Fetter Lane
London EC4P 4EE

While every attempt has been made to make all the information in this book
as accurate and up to date as possible, conditions, medications, and human
knowledge change. Before making a final decision on any substantive matter
covered in this book, you should seek the advice of an appropriate professional.

Some of the product names, trademarks, and descriptive names used in this
publication are registered trademarks, proprietary names, registered designs,
etc., even though they may not be specifically designated as such. This does
not mean that such names, as described in the Trade Marks and Merchandise
Marks Act, are in the public domain.

Printed in the U.S.A.

10 9 8 7 6 5 4 3 2

LIBRARY OF CONGRESS CATALOGING-IN-PUBLICATION DATA
Westheimer, Ruth K. (Ruth Karola), 1928–
    [Pregnancy guide for couples]
    Dr. Ruth's pregnancy guide for couples : love, sex, and medical
facts / by Ruth K. Westheimer and Amos Grünebaum.
        p.   cm.
    Includes index.
    ISBN 0-415-91972-X (PB)
    1. Sex instruction.   2. Sex in marriage.   3. Pregnancy.
4. Conception.   5. Pregnant women—Sexual behavior.   6. Pregnant
women—Physiology.   7. Parenthood.   I. Grünebaum, Amos.   II. Title.
HQ31.W496 1999
    613.9′6—dc21
                                                        99-11384

I dedicate this book to the memory of my husband, Fred; to my children, Miriam Westheimer, EdD; Joel Einleger, MBA; Joel Westheimer, PhD; Barbara Leckie, PhD; and to my grandchildren, Ari; Leora; and Michal.

R.K.W.

I dedicate this book to my parents, Rachel and Freddie, to my wife Debbie, and to my daughter Emma. I am also grateful to my patients and colleagues, who over the years have pushed me and taught me that, at least in obstetrics, there is more than one way to do things right.

A.G.

$\mathcal{A}$CKNOWLEDGMENTS

THE authors wish to thank the following individuals for their help and encouragement. Each, in his or her own way, has made this a better and more valuable book for the reader. The following people, because of their special contributions, must be mentioned by name:

Peter Banks, MD; Rabbi Steven Bercovitz; Mem Bernstein; David Birnbach, MD; Barbara Brennan, CNM; Karen Brodman-Grimm, MD; Barbara Brummer, PhD; John Chiodi; Patricia Chiodi; Hersh Cohen; Marty Englisher; Gabriel Erem; Dennis Holt; Elliot Horowitz; Fred Howard; Michael Kafrissen, MD; Michael and Ronnie Kassan; Bonnie Kaye; Janice Klein, MD; Jeanne Kobritz, CNM; Robert Krasner, MD; Cantor Michael Kruk; Bill and Marga Kunreuther; Rabbi Bill Lebeau; Harry Lee, MD; Melinda Levine; Jo Leonard; John Lollos; Kara Minoui; Paul H. Minoui; Jacques Moritz, MD; Kai Q. Moy; Rebecca Nachamie, MD; Henry and Sydelle Ostberg; Bob Pinto; Ana Portzkova, CNM; Dan Present, MD; Sarita Sahni; Rose and Simeon Schreiber; Allan Schwartz, MD; Vickie Selzer, MD; Fred Rosenberg; Cliff Rubin; Amir Shaviv; Jonathan Sher, MD; John Silberman, Esq.; Helen Singer-Kaplan, MD; Nick Syrett; Haya Taitel, MD, RPh, MS; Malcolm and Barbara Thompson; Claire Wallick; Greg Willenborg; Bob Wilson; Sandy Woods, CNM

A very special thanks for Pierre Lehu for working with me like nobody else for the past 18 years, to Barbara A. Chernow, Ph.D., for her superb handling of the entire manuscript; and to the wonderful professionals at Routledge: Colin Jones, Kenneth Wright, Heidi Freund, Laura-Ann Robb, Ron Longe, Alli Hirschman, Ande Ciecierski, Zoisa Simmons, Shea Settimi, Alja Kooistra, Jennifer Askanazi, Meghan Quinn, Carrie Carlisle, and Luc Ferran.

$\mathscr{C}$ONTENTS

CHAPTER

3

Now That You're Pregnant

61

CHAPTER

4

The First Trimester:
The New You
81

CHAPTER

5

The Second
Trimester: Feeling
Like Yourself Again
103

CHAPTER

6

The Third Trimester:
Ready and Waiting
131

CHAPTER

7

Complications
of Pregnancy

155

CHAPTER

8

Labor: The Time
Has Come
169

CHAPTER

9

Delivery:
The Big Day
183

CHAPTER

10

Life after Childbirth

205

CHAPTER

11

Keeping the Romance Alive: Sex after Children

221

INTRODUCTION

IF a man is newly married, he shall not join the army . . . he shall be left free of all obligations for one year to cheer the wife he has taken.

Deuteronomy 24:5

"To cheer his wife"—And behold how great is this positive commandment . . . even when his wife is pregnant it is a *mitzvah* to bring her joy in this manner if he feels she is desirous.

Rabbi Isaac ben Joseph of Corbeil, 13th Century

THIS book is the result of a collaboration between an obstetrician and gynecologist and a sex therapist. We decided to work on this delightful endeavor because we found a common ground that we felt needed to be explored.

In many cultures, the belief is that sexual activity is solely intended for procreation. In this book, we would like to make it clear that the recreational aspect of sex should not be lost—not even during pregnancy. Although sex is the activity that (usually) results in pregnancy, doctors and other health care providers who treat and counsel pregnant couples learn very little about it during their training. For example, the leading textbook on pregnancy in the United States, which is read by nearly every obstetrician, says little about sex and has no index entry for the essential aspects of sexuality, such as orgasm, ejaculation, and masturbation.

Dr. Ruth's Pregnancy Guide for Couples offers helpful tips, case studies, and question and answer features about sexual activity, getting pregnant, being pregnant, delivering a baby, and keeping sex alive before, during, and after pregnancy. Whispering words of endearment, caressing each other, cultivating the joie de vivre (lust for life) in each couple's relationship is what this book advocates. Whatever we have written is based on scientifically validated data, but every couple should look at their own situation and discuss their concerns with their health care provider.

Let us suggest to everyone: Have great sex for the rest of your life!

1

GET READY, GET SET, BEFORE YOU GET PREGNANT

UNTIL recently, most books about pregnancy began with a traditional discussion of conception and ended with the birth itself—as if your pregnancy was unrelated to your lifestyle before conception or after delivery. In this book, the expecting couple will see pregnancy from a different perspective. We want to revolutionize the way you look at pregnancy, from the first moment the glimmer of the idea of becoming pregnant crosses your mind.

Our main focus is how to maintain a healthy relationship and stimulating sex life during pregnancy. To do this, however, the couple needs to understand what is happening to the mother's body and developing fetus during those nine months. The more you understand these changes, the more comfortable you will feel emotionally and physically, and the more the expecting couple can enjoy the experience of pregnancy together. A healthy relationship during pregnancy will also enable that relationship to grow after the baby is born. In the past, the father stayed in the background during pregnancy, but now he can no longer be viewed as a junior partner once conception occurs. Both parents need to be active and informed participants, whose needs and concerns are understood and addressed by each other and their health care provider.

Thus, this book includes information that every expecting couple will benefit from understanding, beginning with the importance of a healthy lifestyle for both parents before conception. We then take you through conception, a trimester by trimester explanation of physical changes and challenges, the birth itself, and what to expect once the baby is part of your lives.

Although many books about pregnancy discuss intercourse as a means of conception, we see it as far more than that. Getting pregnant may have been your ultimate goal in having sex before you got pregnant, but your sex life should remain active and fulfilling even after conception has occurred. In fact, sex is an important element in the whole experience of being pregnant.

Creating a family should bring two people closer together. However, it's hard for that closeness to develop if your sex life diminishes during the nine months of pregnancy and becomes just a dim memory once the baby is born. You begin this process of conceiving a baby as lovers; we want to see that you continue to be lovers through your pregnancy, parenthood, and grandparenthood.

This shouldn't be a revolutionary attitude, but sadly it is. Although your doctor or medical caregiver may expertly guide you and your developing child through a healthy pregnancy, he or she may not be as helpful when it comes to helping you maintain a healthy sex life. Medical schools teach doctors more about nosebleeds than about human sexuality. Even when prodded with questions about sex during pregnancy and childbirth, many doctors won't give more than superficial answers. That indifference may rub off on their patients. Couples begin to expect that sex during pregnancy—and for a long while after—is an aberration rather than the norm. As a result, many couples don't see the point of making the extra effort to keep it going. We feel strongly, however, that the opposite is true: Pregnancy without sex is the aberration.

We're not saying that pregnancy does not change your sexual relationship. Your sexual relationship during pregnancy will not be the same as it was before, nor will it return to the way it was before the pregnancy after the baby arrives. The very fact that your sex life is going to change, just as many other aspects of your life will change, is one reason you should focus on your sex life during pregnancy. The good news is that if you consider preparation for sex during and after pregnancy as vital to the overall process of having a baby—as essential, in fact, as going to Lamaze classes—then those changes need not mean a less rewarding relationship. They might even possibly improve your sex life significantly.

For these reasons, our book combines the expertise of a sex therapist with that of an obstetrician and gynecologist. We can offer you advice not only on the medical aspects of your pregnancy, but also on its

◈ Websites for Pregnancy Information

http://www.babydata.com
>This site has interactive tools that enable you to create a personal ovulation calendar that calculates the likeliest days for you to become pregnant. It also enables you to create a calendar for your particular pregnancy.

http://www.lalecheleague.org
>Sponsored by the Laleche League, this site provides information about breastfeeding.

http://www.lamaze-childbirth.com
>This site provides information about childbirth classes.

http://www.modimes.org
>Sponsored by the March of Dimes, this site provides information on how to have a healthy pregnancy and how to prevent birth defects.

http://www.nlm.nih.gov
>Sponsored by the National Institutes of Health, you can search for pregnancy-related information.

http://www.noah.cuny.edu
>This is a great site for reviewing most pregnancy information.

http://www.plannedparenthood.com
>Sponsored by Planned Parenthood, this site provides information on pregnancy and birth control.

http://www.pathfinder.com/ParentTime/Ask/dr_ruth
>Read and hear Dr. Ruth answer questions about sex and pregnancy.

sexual aspects. Although we may place a greater emphasis on sex than you might find in other books on pregnancy, we have no intention of neglecting pertinent health-related information. In the same way that good sex starts with foreplay, a healthy pregnancy starts with careful preparation. A wealth of information on pregnancy is available to couples in traditional and nontraditional formats. A sampling of Websites is given to complement the material in this book.

Although many of the discussions are about the transformations that a woman will undergo throughout her pregnancy, all the information is important for her partner as well. Our goal is to enhance your sex life during this period; obviously, we cannot neglect the male perspective. Although "you" interchangeably addresses either or both of you, every bit of information will be useful to both of you.

Thinking Ahead about Parenthood

In the days before easy access to birth control methods, it was assumed that soon after a couple was married, the first child would be on the way. Now, however, couples can choose when and if they are going to have children. Couples are faced with a decision-making process where once there was none, and most find that the process is not easy or simple, even if both partners are eager to have a family. Making a conscious decision to have a baby forces a couple to focus on the consequences of that decision—both practical and emotional. The decision to have a baby should include anticipating the changes that such a step will bring to your lives—not only during the pregnancy, but also nine months later—and trying to recognize and reconcile your attitudes and perspectives.

Financial considerations have always been a legitimate concern for a couple starting a family. Today, however, the financial issue has a new twist. Many more households require two breadwinners, but unlike previous generations, the woman is not just earning "extra income." She may now be a highly trained professional with a career she wishes to maintain. Thus, couples need to address the question of how to achieve a balance among their professional careers, the nurturing of the new child, and the needs of their personal relationship. The balance can be tricky and requires careful organization of one's time and possibly some financial sacrifices.

If both parents continue to work, the most basic questions become, "What reliable options are available for taking care of the newborn child, and how much does each cost? If one cannot afford full-time help at home, how does one choose a trustworthy and stimulating day care center?"

Then, in a world where employers expect increasing productivity from employees, working parents may not be able or willing to give the overtime necessary to stay on top. One or both parents may have to voluntarily give up opportunities for more lucrative positions rather than sacrifice time spent with the family. Or, one may choose to work part time or at home to spend more time with the child. Parents—particularly mothers—are often relegated to less demanding and less financially rewarding positions because employers see them as less reliable than someone unencumbered by children.

The financial considerations, however, are not the only, or even the most significant, impact of having a baby. Starting a family will change the fundamental nature of your relationship. For instance, couples who are planning to have a baby should ask themselves such questions as, "Will I be jealous of the time and attention my wife will give to the baby instead of to me?" and "Am I prepared to give up my quiet evenings at home?" The decision to have a baby is an even more far-reaching commitment than choosing to get married. You can walk away from a marriage if it goes bad, but you can never walk away from parenthood. Parenthood is a responsibility that the two of you will share for the rest of your lives.

Taking an Emotional Inventory

The very first step—one that you should absolutely take before you become serious about having a baby—is to test the status of your emotional well-being, both as individuals and as a couple. Most of the physical changes you will encounter during pregnancy will be temporary. If, however, you begin with a shaky relationship, the additional stresses of pregnancy may make it more difficult to repair. Such emotional difficulties could have long-term emotional effects on your child.

Although you might be joyous about the idea of having a child, the reality of this responsibility can cause concern even for couples with happy and secure relationships. For some, the reality sinks in during pregnancy. For others, it doesn't happen until after they take the baby home. And partners don't necessarily come to terms with the full ramifications of parenthood at the same time. Often, reality does not hit home until the baby arrives, but when it hits, there may be a moment of panic about having taken such an irrevocable step.

Admittedly, most people always have some family and financial concerns, but occasionally situations arise that appear to validate fears more than usual. Thus, expecting parents start to ask all kinds of understandable questions: "What will happen if everything goes wrong?" "What if I lose my job?" "What if the baby isn't healthy?" "What if we can't find another place to live?" If these fears become overwhelming, you may overreact, and this impacts both the child and your partner.

Although men and women have a long history of facing domestic crises together, traditionally their concerns were separate. Financial worries keep dad awake on his side of the bed, while household and family worries keep mom awake on hers. Now, however, dads and moms share many of the same family responsibilities. If they respond differently to those needs or disagree on the solution to a problem, small worries can trigger larger ones beneath the surface.

When emotions run high, talking about your feelings calmly is difficult. You know that compromises need to be made, so put them on the table as soon as possible. The closer you are to your baby's

ASK DR. RUTH

Q My husband and I met and married while we were in medical school. When we got out of school, we were very busy doing our residency training and began to drift apart. Now that our training is finished, we have a more normal life. Both of us have always wanted to have a family, and I've noticed that our friends who have had babies seem to find a renewed sense of closeness. I'm wondering if having a baby will draw us closer together again.

A That would be a big mistake! Having a baby will only intensify the pressures that already exist in your marriage. Once the baby arrives on the scene, you'll lose the freedom to just run out to the movies whenever you want, your financial situation will change dramatically, and you'll have relatives popping over all the time to see the baby. The hours you need to talk things out or see a counselor will diminish. As a result, not only might you end up losing your husband, you could end up being a single mother as well. What you must do is make the necessary repairs to your marriage first, and then if you are successful, you can make plans to have a baby. If necessary, seek the help of a marriage counselor. To find one, call a teaching hospital near you and get some recommendations for therapists. You may also ask your religious counselor to recommend someone. Interview a few of them and decide which one you like best.

---

arrival, the more excited and nervous you will become. By that time, compromise is difficult. Your fears make you more self-protective and less willing to reach out to the other person. Use the following guidelines to help you discuss your concerns about starting a family.

1. Before your first discussion, sit down separately and make a list of the issues each of you wants to raise. That way you won't forget something that is important to you. Don't shy away from the tough issues. They're the reason you're talking in the first place!

2. Choose a time to talk when neither of you will feel rushed and you won't be interrupted. There's nothing less conducive to a fruitful discussion than interruptions from telephone calls or visitors.

3. Don't expect to finish the job in one session. You'll probably find that talking about one concern raises others. You'll want time to think about new issues that come up, so plan to have several sessions.

4. Keep these talks upbeat. After all, you are lovers who are talking about bringing more love into the world through a child.

5. When you reach a compromise about a difficult point that works for both of you, write it down. You may need to refer back to your notes later on if a disagreement arises.

6. Be wary of the advice of family and friends. The perfect solution to a problem in one home may be a recipe for disaster in another. You need to sort through these issues with sensitivity to both of your needs as unique individuals.

From Our Files

Jackie and Jim, two professionals in their mid-thirties, were expecting their first baby. Jim was a stockbroker whose boss ran his department like a football team—everyone was expected to give 100 percent, whether selling shares or playing softball for the company team. Jackie manages the ladies' sportswear section at a large department store and was often called upon to work late. She is depending on Jim to leave work on time and relieve the babysitter once the baby is born. Although Jim was worried about how his boss would react the first time he had to leave at the stroke of five, he never shared his anxiety with Jackie. After all, she was carrying their child, and he wanted to protect her from as many worries as possible.

On the night that Jackie and Jim were being taught how to diaper a baby in Lamaze class, Jim was all thumbs. Every other father-to-be breezed through the exercise, but Jim just couldn't get the hang of it. During the class, Jackie tried to hide her frustration, but later she accused Jim of being clumsy on purpose so that he could avoid having to change a real dirty diaper.

Jim denied the accusation vehemently, but he knew in his heart that Jackie was partially right. He was faking clumsiness, but not because he wanted to avoid changing dirty diapers. Instead, he was trying to make Jackie lose confidence in his ability to care for the baby so that she would hesitate to ask him to leave work to relieve the sitter.

Their financial situation only made matters worse. They bought a house and a new minivan in anticipation of having a baby. As a result of the payments for these purchases, the budget for babysitting was very tight. Fortunately, they found a babysitter with reasonable fees, but even so, they could afford to hire the sitter only until six o'clock every night. This meant that one of them had to leave work by five o'clock sharp every day.

Now, however, Jim was worried that he would eventually have to choose between making his boss angry by leaving work early or making his wife angry by working late and forcing her to go home early to take care of the baby. With the baby only a few weeks away, Jackie and Jim were setting themselves up for a crisis if Jim could not live up to his side of the bargain.

Anytime you face an important decision, the possibility exists that some disagreement may arise between you. Having a baby is no exception. Discussions may become heated when trying to find a compromise about something important to both of you. If you have a secure relationship, you'll be able to sort through these disagreements, but if your relationship is tenuous, arguments about starting a family—a subject with enormous implications—can sometimes result in serious confrontations. It is therefore important for you and your partner to honestly communicate your fears, anxieties, thoughts, and feelings about this new stage in your lives.

Jim and Jackie could have avoided their crisis by talking openly about their feelings. If Jim had admitted his worries earlier, they could have made different financial decisions before the baby was born, so that more money would have been available for the services of a babysitter.

To guide your partner successfully over the emotional terrain of becoming a parent, you must be aware of each other's anxieties. If you are not, a sudden outburst by your partner will probably make you feel threatened rather than supportive. Your own fears will rise to the surface and exacerbate the whole situation. That's what happened to Jackie during the Lamaze class when Jim fumbled with the diapers. Instead of seeing her partner dealing awkwardly with a new situation, she saw her professional future on the line.

The key to handling the emotional upheaval of impending parenthood is to become attuned to each other's concerns. For that to happen, you need to talk about your fears and anxieties openly. Then you can work together to develop strategies to cope with and allay each other's worries.

Preparing Your Body

You are probably not surprised to learn that your health plays an important role in your pregnancy, but you also need to realize that some health factors need to be addressed before you become pregnant. This doesn't mean that you can't have a healthy baby if your pregnancy has already begun. It just means that you might improve the odds if you begin preparing for your pregnancy as early as possible. Preparation for a healthy pregnancy involves several stages.

During the first six to eight weeks of pregnancy, a baby's vital organs, such as the heart, kidneys, and brain are forming. Obviously, you'll want to do everything you can to ensure the healthy development of your baby during this time, but you probably won't even be aware that you are pregnant during most of these first critical weeks. And when you realize that you've missed your period, you could already be more than two weeks pregnant. By the time you visit your caregiver and go through the routine prenatal examination, another couple of weeks will have gone by. The only way to protect the child you are carrying in these early weeks is to take some precautionary measures even before you are pregnant. Rest assured that the vast majority of babies develop perfectly in these first few weeks when their mothers are still wondering whether or not they are pregnant. If you're still at the point of trying to get pregnant, we strongly suggest that you take steps to ensure a healthy pregnancy through preconception care.

Preconception Care

Preconception care is a growing and relatively new field that falls in the specialty called "preventive care." Preventive care anticipates conditions and prevents them from doing any harm even before they are

From Our Files

Rita was 17 weeks pregnant with her first child and continued to work half-time with the children in the nursery of her local church. When several children came down with a condition called "Fifth disease" (a condition brought about by a virus), Rita called her obstetrician to find out whether this could affect her. She became concerned when her obstetrician told her that approximately 50 percent of women are not immune and that if she became infected, her fetus could become infected too. The same day, Rita had a blood test to determine if she was immune. The next days were difficult, as she waited for the results, but she was happy to learn that she had had "Fifth-disease" before, was immune, and could not become infected again.

Rita could have minimized her concern by a preconception visit to her doctor. First, she would have learned that by working with small children, she was at risk for exposure to "Fifth disease." If she wanted to continue working, a simple blood test at that time could have told her that she was immune and safe. If she had tested negative, she could have been more cautious by decreasing her exposure to small children.

diagnosed. Research is finding that when put to proper use, preconception care can have a significant impact on the health of a mother and her baby by doing the following:

- identifying risk factors in both parents;
- testing for certain conditions that may affect the baby or the mother;
- educating prospective parents about conception and pregnancy;
- discussing and suggesting lifestyle changes before bad habits can harm the baby; and
- improving medical conditions and changing potentially harmful medications to reduce the negative impact on the pregnancy.

In addition to these steps, which emphasize the mother's health, other steps also take the father's health into consideration. These include reviewing the medical and family histories of both parents; taking a physical examination of the mother and father, if indicated; administering blood tests and any other necessary tests to both parents; and providing counseling regarding test results and suggested lifestyle changes. The goals of all these steps are to:

- help you become pregnant;
- decrease the risk of a miscarriage;
- decrease the chance of birth defects;
- improve your health;
- identify medical conditions that might affect your pregnancy;
- review prior vaccinations and update them if necessary;
- decrease any negative effects of preexisting medical conditions; and
- identify medications that might affect the fetus.

Although millions of babies are born every year to mothers who did not have preconception care, it is a good idea to take every possible precaution. If you are still in the planning phase of starting a family, seek out preconception counseling. To get you started, we've provided a "Worksheet for Preconception Evaluation" (Table 1) that you can fill out and bring with you to your health care provider.

Preexisting Conditions

The health risks caused by most preexisting conditions during pregnancy can be reduced if precautions are administered before conception. This section discusses common preexisting conditions that need to be considered and discussed with your doctor when a couple decides to have a baby.

INHERITED DISEASES

Inherited diseases are genetic conditions with which a person is born. Some are inherited from one or both parents, who may have the disease itself or may be "carriers"—people who do not have the disease, but carry the gene for the disease and can transmit it to their babies. However, it is possible for babies to be born with inherited diseases even if neither parent has the disease or is a carrier. With some inherited diseases, known as autosomal dominant disease, it takes only one parent to transmit the disease to the baby. In other diseases, known as autosomal recessive disease, both parents need to be carriers for the baby to get the disease. Screening of parents who are carriers is important, because these parents do not show symptoms of the disease and therefore may not know that they are carriers. This is particularly true if one or both parents belong to an ethnic group with a high prevalence of a certain condition, such as Tay-Sachs, sickle cell, and cystic fibrosis. If both parents are carriers, each has a 50 percent chance of transmitting the gene to the baby, and there is a 25 percent chance the baby may have the disease.

MATERNAL AGE

As a women grows older, the risk of having a baby with Down syndrome increases. Down syndrome, or trisomy 21, is a syndrome in which the baby has 47 instead of the normal 46 chromosomes, because there are three instead of two number 21 chromosomes.

Women under the age of 35 have approximately a 1 in 500 risk of delivering a baby with an abnormal number of chromosomes, of which approximately half are Down syndrome. This rate rises to approximately 1 in 200 by age 35, 1 in 66 by 40, and 1 in 20 by age 45. In addition, women over the age of 35 are also at an increased risk of developing certain medical conditions, such as high blood pressure or diabetes. This rate, however, has to be put into perspective. It means that 95 out of 100 babies born to women who are 45 years old will still be chromosomally normal.

TABLE 1 Worksheet for Preconception Evaluation

The following questions are a sample of some of the information your health care provider needs to assess the possible complications of a pregnancy.

     Certain risk factors may be found during this assessment. If you have one of these risk factors, there is a greater than average chance that certain problems will occur during the pregnancy or delivery of the baby. If you have preconception counseling before you become pregnant, you may be able to prevent some of the possible problems before you become pregnant. Therefore, you should answer the questions below and bring the form to your caregiver. Depending on your answers, further questions, exams, or tests may be necessary.

	YES	NO	N/A or Comments
Medical History			
Did you have or do you presently have any medical diseases, such as diabetes, hypertension, epilepsy, anemia, etc.?	YES	NO	
Do you presently take any medications (prescription or over the counter)?	YES	NO	
Have you had any infections?	YES	NO	
Have you had any X-rays?	YES	NO	
Have you had any surgery or accidents?	YES	NO	
Have you had any bleeding problems or blood transfusions?	YES	NO	
Have you ever had a blood clot (in your legs, lungs, or other parts)?	YES	NO	
Do you have any allergies?	YES	NO	
Have you been immunized against mumps, measles, and/or rubella?	YES	NO	
Do you have a history of herpes?	YES	NO	
Did you have chickenpox?	YES	NO	
Have you been tested for hepatitis, HIV, toxoplasmosis, parvovirus B19, or CMV?	YES	NO	
Gynecologic History			
How old were you when you began menstruating?			_____
How many days are there between your menstrual periods?			_____
How many days do your periods last?			_____
Have you used birth control pills or any other form of birth control?	YES	NO	
Have you had any problems getting pregnant?	YES	NO	
Are your menstrual periods painful?	YES	NO	
Have you had any vaginal and/or sexually transmitted (venereal) disease infections?	YES	NO	
Have you had pelvic surgery?	YES	NO	
Have you had any abnormal Pap smear results?	YES	NO	
Have you had any treatment for abnormal Pap smears?	YES	NO	
History of Previous Pregnancies			
Have you been pregnant before?	YES	NO	
If you were previously pregnant, how many times?			_____
Have you had any cesarean sections?	YES	NO	
How many living children do you have?			_____
Did your past pregnancies or deliveries have any complications, such as diabetes or hypertension?	YES	NO	
Have you had an ectopic pregnancy?	YES	NO	

	YES	NO	N/A or Comments
Have you had any miscarriages and, if so, how far along were you when you miscarried?	YES	NO	
Have you had any abortions and, if so, how far along were you when you had them? What method was used?	YES	NO	
Were any of your past deliveries premature?	YES	NO	
If you had babies before, did they have any problems?	YES	NO	
Have you breastfed in the past?	YES	NO	
Did you have any complications after previous births?	YES	NO	

Social History

	YES	NO	
Do you exercise at least 3 to 4 times a week?	YES	NO	
Are you at your optimal weight?	YES	NO	
Do you drink more than 2 cups of coffee per day?	YES	NO	
Do you drink alcoholic beverages?	YES	NO	
Do you use over-the-counter drugs?	YES	NO	
Do you or the baby's father use tobacco?	YES	NO	
Do you or the baby's father use drugs, such as cocaine, heroin, methadone, marijuana, amphetamines, or barbiturates?	YES	NO	
Do you have a stable home situation?	YES	NO	
Do you live with the baby's father?	YES	NO	
Do you have any financial problems?	YES	NO	
What kind of work do you do?			———
Are you exposed to any harmful substances or radiation where you work?	YES	NO	
Do you work with or are you often exposed to small children?	YES	NO	
Do you have any pets?	YES	NO	

Genetic History

	YES	NO	
Have you or the baby's father ever been screened for special diseases related to your ethnic background?	YES	NO	
Does anyone in the family have medical problems, such as high blood presure or diabetes?	YES	NO	
Does anyone in the family have a history of a genetic disease, such as cystic fibrosis, Tay-Sachs, or hemophilia?	YES	NO	
Has anyone in the family had a multiple pregnancy (twins, triplets)?	YES	NO	
Have there been any birth defects or mental retardation in the family?	YES	NO	
Did your mother take DES when she was pregnant with you?	YES	NO	
Did your mother have toxemia or high blood pressure during any of her pregnancies?	YES	NO	
Is there a family history of breast or ovarian cancer?	YES	NO	

Dietary History

	YES	NO	
Do you keep a healthy diet?	YES	NO	
How many meals do you eat each day?			———
Are you a vegetarian or do you follow any special diet?	YES	NO	
Do you take vitamins regularly?	YES	NO	
Have you had to follow a special diet in a previous pregnancy?	YES	NO	
Do you have any unusual cravings?	YES	NO	
Do you drink a lot of tap water?	YES	NO	

SEXUALLY TRANSMITTED DISEASES

No one ever wants to catch a sexually transmitted disease (STD), but every year 12 million people in the United States are infected with an STD. Many people think they are invincible and take all sorts of risks without considering the consequences. Some studies estimate that as many as one out of every two people might contract an STD at some point in their lives. We are living at a time when many people have been exposed to an STDs, so safety from these diseases is never a certainty.

If you have been with the same partner for a long time and neither of you has ever had sex with anyone else, you are probably safe. If you had sex with many people while in college, for example, an STD, such as herpes, can revive and cause symptoms at any time. Women, more than men, can harbor an STD without ever exhibiting any symptoms. The message is clear. If you have ever been diagnosed with an STD or if you have had unsafe sex, tell your doctor as soon as possible, preferably before you become pregnant.

Unlike other diseases, STDs are usually preventable, because they are transmitted through the close, intimate contact of sexual relations. If you take the proper precautions, you can lessen the chances of contracting these diseases. With the routine use of condoms, you can decrease your chance significantly. However, your baby does not have that opportunity, so the responsibility to protect yourself is even greater if you are considering a pregnancy.

If you do contract an STD, deal with it as soon as possible. Most are treatable, especially in their early stages. Therefore, if you notice one or more symptoms of an STD, don't bury your head in the sand and hope it will go away by itself. Head straight for the doctor. Of course, if you have an STD and become pregnant, there may be precautions you can take to keep from passing it on to your child, but again, you need to be aware that you are infected.

If left untreated, STDs can be especially troublesome in relation to pregnancy. In fact, some STDs do so much damage to the reproductive system that they make it impossible for you to become pregnant. Others can have a negative effect during the pregnancy. Finally, some can be transmitted to your baby during pregnancy or at the time of delivery, so that you have a newborn infected with a disease—one that might possibly be fatal.

Studies have shown that the most frequent STDs are HPV, chlamydia, gonorrhea, and HIV. Chlamydia and gonorrhea are routinely tested for in pregnancy, as are syphilis and hepatitis B. In addition, we strongly recommend that you be tested for HIV before or during pregnancy. The broader your knowledge of these diseases, the better you will be able to protect yourself. The possible effects of these diseases on pregnancy are listed in Table 2.

Planning for pregnancy is a good time for both partners to examine their pasts and visit a doctor, who will check and test for these conditions. Some require a blood test; others a culture of your genitalia. If an STD is discovered, your doctor will counsel you about its effect on your pregnancy and how to diminish your chances of passing the infection on to your child.

OTHER INFECTIONS

Some common infections, such as mumps, measles, rubella (German measles), chicken pox, toxoplasmosis, and CMV (cytomegalovirus), "Fifth disease" (parvovirus B19), and Lyme disease, are known to have serious implications during pregnancy. If you are planning to get pregnant, we strongly suggest that you discuss with your health care provider screening for any or all of these conditions before you stop using contraceptives. Your doctor can perform tests to see whether you have been previously exposed to these infections. The following is known about these infections:

1. If you have had mumps, measles, rubella, parvovirus ("Fifth disease") and/or chicken pox or were immunized against them before your pregnancy, you are immune for life and cannot transmit the condition to the baby.

2. If you were immunized and carry antibodies against hepatitis B, you are immune and cannot transmit it to the fetus. Most people previously infected with hepatitis B also become immune and make antibodies against that virus. Others, however, continue to carry the virus. They become what is called "chronic carriers" and may infect the baby or sexual partners.

3. If you become infected with these conditions for the very first time during your pregnancy, you are more likely to transmit them and infect the baby.

4. Women who have been previously exposed to CMV and toxoplasmosis may become reinfected during pregnancy and may still transmit the infection to the fetus, although to a much lesser

TABLE 2 Overview of Sexually Transmitted Diseases and Other Infections in Pregnancy

Organism/ Disease	Symptoms	Effect on Pregnancy	Diagnosis	Prevention and/ or Treatment
Chlamydia*	Often very few symptoms; vaginal discharge; burning on urination	Premature labor; infection of new-born at birth; new-born pneumonia and eye infection	Culture of vagina; culture of urine	Antibiotic; eye ointment for prevention to baby at birth
Gonorrhea*	Often none; discharge and burning from vagina and penis	Infection of new-born at birth; neonatal eye infection at birth	Culture of vagina	Antibiotic; eye ointment to baby for prevention at birth
Syphilis*	Often none; initially ulceration on labia or penis, then rash	Newborn infection; skin, brain, and bone lesions	Blood test and/or microscopy of lesion	Antibiotic
Hepatitis B*	No symptoms if chronic carrier	Newborn infection; increased chance of liver cancer when baby becomes adult	Blood test	Immunoglobulin and immunization of baby at birth
HIV+	Often none until symptoms of AIDS	Infection of fetus inside uterus and newborn at birth	Blood test	AZT or combined therapy before and during labor to prevent infection of baby inside uterus; also preventive therapy of newborn baby
Herpes	Primary vs. recurrent; painful blisters, but often no symptoms	Infection of newborn inside uterus or at birth	Culture of vagina/ cervix and/or blood tests	Drug therapy or cesarean section if there are lesions
Group B beta-hemolytic Streptococcus	Usually none	Premature labor and delivery; meningitis and pneumonia of baby	Culture of vagina and rectum	Either culture routinely at 35–37 weeks or treat with antibiotic if indicated. If the culture is positive treat with antibiotics during labor
Bacterial vaginosis (BV)	Vaginal discharge; itching, burning	Premature labor and delivery; premature rupture of fetal membranes	Microscopy; smell; check pH of vagina	Antibiotic
Genital warts	Warts on genitalia	Rare, but may grow	Culture; biopsy	None needed unless they grow and become very large; then surgery to decrease size and/ or cesarean section.
Trichomonas	Discharge	May be associated with preterm labor or rupture of fetal membranes.	Microscope	Antibiotic
Yeast	Itching; discharge	Little to none	Microscope, culture; pH of vagina	Local medication

*Routinely tested for in pregnancy.
+Testing strongly suggested.

degree and severity than women who become infected for the very first time during pregnancy.

5. The HIV virus may infect the baby notwithstanding that the mother has antibodies in her system. Testing for HIV before or even early in pregnancy helps you to receive proper treatment to decrease the risk of infecting the baby. It may also help you to receive better treatment.

CHRONIC MEDICAL CONDITIONS

If you suffer from a chronic medical condition, such as diabetes, hypertension, thyroid disease, lupus, or seizure disorders, consult your physician regarding what changes you have to make in your treatment before and during pregnancy. It may be beneficial to make some of these changes, such as altering medications, before you conceive, so discuss your intentions to become pregnant with both your personal physician and your gynecologist. The biggest risks to women who have diabetes are not only infertility and miscarriage, but also an increased risk of fetal malformation. The critical time period is the first four to eight weeks of pregnancy, because most abnormalities develop during this period. This is especially true if diabetes is not properly treated. Thus, we suggest that you become pregnant only if tests show that your diabetes is successfully controlled.

RH DISEASE

RH disease is a condition in which women who are Rh negative make antibodies that may affect the Rh positive baby. Your blood is either Rh positive or Rh negative. If you are Rh negative and the baby's father is Rh positive, there is a more than 50 percent chance that the baby will be Rh positive.

When an Rh-negative mother has a pregnancy with an Rh-positive baby, the baby's cells may stimulate certain chemicals in the mother's blood that may destroy the fetus's blood usually in the next pregnancy. This is called "sensitization" and can occur in any pregnancy, including miscarriages, abortions, and ectopic pregnancies. To prevent the mother from becoming sensitized, the mother usually receives an injection of a drug called RhoGam during and after pregnancy.

Medications to Avoid

What you put in your body while you're pregnant will eventually find its way into your baby. Therefore, you need to be careful about what substances you take into your body to ensure that your baby is not exposed to substances that could cause problems. Discuss any prescription and nonprescription medications you are taking with your physician while you are still thinking about getting pregnant.

PRESCRIPTION MEDICATIONS

If you are taking any prescribed medications while you are trying to get pregnant, discuss their use with your doctor or midwife. Don't stop taking any prescription medication without first consulting your doctor. Why? Because it can be dangerous to stop taking medication that you need. Your health care provider will determine first if you should stop the medication. If so, she will tell you how and prescribe an alternative medication.

You should be aware of a few routinely used medications that may potentially lead to birth defects. These are:

- certain anticonvulsants (seizure medications)
- Isoretinoin (Acutane) (an acne medication)
- lithium
- high doses of vitamin A (over 10,000 IR)
- imipramine (Tofranil) (used to treat depression)
- warfarin (Coumadin) (used to prevent blood clotting)
- propylthiouracil (used to treat thyroid disease)
- ACE inhibitors (used to treat hypertension)
- chemotherapy medications
- tetracycline (an antibiotic)

If you are taking any of these medications and want to have a baby, discuss alternatives with your doctor. Until you've gotten the go ahead from him or her that it is safe to conceive, continue using contraceptives.

OVER-THE-COUNTER MEDICATIONS

Many women automatically stop taking all over-the-counter, or nonprescription, medications as soon as they begin trying to have a baby. This healthy respect for the possible side effects of such medication is prudent. Although many of these drugs have been used without consequence during pregnancy, use your judgment before reaching for something in the medicine cabinet. Is there a chance that you're pregnant? If there is, give your gynecologist a call to see if the drug you're about to use is safe.

Perhaps more important than the medications you take for occasional illness are the substances you use habitually to wake up, calm down, or socialize. Caffeine, tobacco, alcohol, and prohibited substances, such as cocaine, heroine, and marijuana, all have a negative effect on a pregnancy. Many women use the health of their developing baby to firm up their resolve to kick a habit. We can't overemphasize the importance of breaking these habits now, before you become pregnant. Remember, the major organs of a baby are formed in the first few weeks of pregnancy. If you continue to use these substances until a pregnancy test confirms your condition, it may be too late to protect your baby from their harmful effects.

ALCOHOL

Planning for pregnancy is a good time to assess your alcohol use. Although there is no proof that an occasional drink will have a negative effect on your ability to get pregnant or on your pregnancy, it is prudent to avoid alcohol if there is even a chance that you're pregnant.

Heavy use of alcohol in men has been associated with decreased fertility as a result of a low sperm count or abnormal sperm formation. A woman who continues to drink heavily after she is pregnant may give birth to a baby with fetal alcohol syndrome (FAS), a condition associated with birth defects and mental retardation.

If you or your partner has a drinking problem, contact your doctor to find out where you can get help, or call Alcoholics Anonymous (http://www.alcoholics-anonymous.org), a national organization that offers programs to help you control your alcoholism.

TOBACCO

Women who smoke are less likely to become pregnant, so any woman wanting to conceive has an incentive to stop. Smoking during pregnancy also increases the risk of certain complications, such as the incidence of low-birthweight babies. Smoking is a tough habit to quit, but many new products are available to help you do so successfully. Find out from your doctor which product would be safe and effective for you to use, and whether or not you can use it safely while you're trying to conceive.

T I P

A lollipop or hard candy makes a good substitute when you want to reach for a cigarette, so keep a stash on hand. We'd also like to add a calorie-free way for you to satisfy an oral craving that is a lot more fun for you and your partner—oral sex!

CAFFEINE

Some studies suggest that pregnant women who drink more than two cups of coffee a day may have an increased risk of miscarriage. Caffeine was thought to be the ingredient in coffee responsible for this association. Other studies, however, have failed to show a relationship between caffeine intake and either birth defects or low-birthweight babies. Although some people find it difficult to break their regular "caffeine fix," it is probably wise to avoid caffeine while you try to conceive and during pregnancy. Let us suggest that if you need a daily "fix," you find other, healthier fixes to keep you going.

T I P

The male hormone, testosterone, is at its highest level first thing in the morning, so if you've given up that cup of wake-up coffee in the morning, why not start your day with a little lovemaking. A strong orgasm will wake you both up, that's for sure.

COCAINE, MARIJUANA, AND OTHER ILLEGAL DRUGS

We don't need to tell you that these substances are dangerous to use at any time, but during pregnancy you are also affecting the life of your unborn child. Obviously, neither parent should use illegal drugs, especially while you're trying to conceive.

You're Ready, You're Set . . .

In addition to giving up bad habits, you should seriously consider developing or continuing good ones, such as maintaining a healthy diet and exercising. You've made the decision and taken the necessary first steps toward your goal of having a baby—you both agree that you want a baby, you've prepared yourself emotionally for pregnancy and parenthood as much as is possible, you've gone for preconception counseling, and you are preparing your body for the coming months by being healthy, eating healthy foods, taking vitamins, and exercising. You are ready for the next exciting step—conceiving the baby!

2

Go! MAKING THE MOST OUT OF MAKING A BABY

NOW that you've decided to have a baby, the next step should be a cinch, right? If you've been sexually active for some time, you probably think that you know just about everything you need to know about the actual process of making a baby. Considering that there are approximately three million unintended pregnancies in the United States every year, how hard could it be to become pregnant when you intend to?

But having a baby is more than just having sex. And having sex can definitely be much more than having intercourse. This is one of the few times in your lives when you'll be able to enjoy spontaneous lovemaking with no worries about reapplying contraceptive gel or putting on a condom. Now's your chance to replace your stoic habits of contraception with the spontaneity and abandon of unprotected sex. So splurge a little to make the time special. Think about getting away for long romantic weekends at a country inn or a Caribbean club. If that's too rich for your budget, weave a magic spell in more subtle ways, like buying your partner sexy lingerie or making reservations for a lunchtime tryst at a hotel. Use your imagination!

Enriching your sex life is important not only for the physical pleasure you share, but also for deepening the emotional bond between you. That way, you will be able to express your feelings openly to each other as the pregnancy progresses. This is a time when your body will experience numerous changes, many of which may be difficult. Taking the time to be physically close will give you opportunities to express your hopes and fears about having a baby. Now is a good time to work out your understandable feelings and concerns about practical considerations and the effects that having a baby will have on your social and sexual lives. By talking through your fears and expectations, you may be able to find solutions before the baby is born. That way, when the baby arrives, you will not be overwhelmed by the changes and will be better prepared to create a loving and supportive environment.

One of our goals is to help you become attuned to each other's deepest concerns as you make these important decisions. We also hope to improve the odds of your getting pregnant sooner, rather than later, and to make sure that the parents-to-be have all of the information necessary to make this the healthiest pregnancy possible for mom and dad and their baby.

TIP

Talk about concrete ways to handle issues that are important to each of you. For instance, if one of you is worried that there will be no money for the two of you to go out anymore, set aside a special "togetherness" fund for babysitters and nights out. If finding time to be alone together is the issue, create a specific parent night out and plan to line up a regular babysitter.

Taking the Plunge—Putting Away Your Contraceptives

The decision to become pregnant will bring about welcome changes for those who have been using the barrier method of birth control, such as condoms and diaphragms. Sex without condoms or diaphragms is something to look forward to. If you've been using the rhythm method, you will now have the pleasure of having sex anytime, anywhere. What possibilities!

If you're using other contraceptive methods, such as the pill, it will often take no more than finishing your last pack and putting away your contraceptives before you can get pregnant. If you're on the pill, you may not be able to get pregnant right after you stop taking it. It will take some time before you start ovulating again. On average, ovulation resumes one to three months after you stop taking the pill. And ovulation is necessary because your body will have to produce the egg that needs to be fertilized by a sperm to form a fetus. However, it is not true that you have to wait three months after stopping the pill before trying to get pregnant. This recommendation was based on the unfounded belief that the hormones in oral contraceptives may linger for some time after you stop taking them and do harm to the developing fetus. There is no proof that getting pregnant immediately after discontinuation of oral contraceptives, or even while you're on the pill, is harmful to the fetus.

If you've been using injectable birth control, a form of birth control in which a contraceptive is injected every three months to inhibit ovulation, it is important to understand that its effects won't wear off instantaneously. Even after its effectiveness has worn off, several months may have to pass before normal ovulation begins again. This doesn't mean, however, that you cannot enjoy the pleasures of spontaneous and unprotected sex while waiting for your body to return to its natural rhythm.

As with injectable contraceptives, the effects of contraceptive implants, the small flexible hormone sticks implanted under your skin, may not wear off immediately after they are removed. These implants work by slowly releasing a certain progestational drug into the blood, thereby influencing ovulation, changing the lining of the uterus, and causing the mucus in the cervix to thicken, making it difficult for the sperm to penetrate and eventually reach the uterus. Because these implants remain effective for five years, they need to be removed by a doctor if you change your mind within those five years. Again, it may take some months before normal ovulation begins again.

The exact mechanism by which IUDs, or intrauterine devices, prevent pregnancy is not known. They are thought to prevent the egg from implanting, change the motion of the fallopian tubes, or even kill sperm. IUDs don't chemically disrupt the normal cycle of ovulation, so pregnancy is possible during the first cycle after removal. Some experts, however, suggest that you wait for one menstrual cycle to pass before trying to conceive in order to flush out the endometrial lining in your uterus that was exposed to the IUD. This is done to improve the likelihood of pregnancy rather than to decrease any risk to the fetus. You can get pregnant right after having your IUD removed without known harm.

Some women who have been using the pill or long-acting hormone contraceptives, such as injections, often worry that they will have a difficult time conceiving when they decide to get pregnant. If you don't get pregnant in the first months after the effects of the contraceptive have worn off, it doesn't mean that you are infertile. Contraceptives are designed to be a temporary means of preventing pregnancy and should not prevent you from conceiving after they're discontinued. Although it may take some time for your body to reestablish its normal ovulatory cycle, you have every reason to feel confident that you'll be able to get pregnant once the effects of the contraceptive wears off.

There is no evidence that babies conceived after the discontinuation of birth control have an increased risk of problems over babies conceived by women who have not previously used birth control. If you have any questions or worries about the long-term side effects of your birth control method or about any other possible problems related to discontinuing the use of your contraceptive, contact your doctor or caregiver, who will provide you with information to put your mind at ease.

ASK DR. RUTH

Q We've been using condoms because my husband had a lot of sexual partners before we got married. I'm really worried about catching a sexually transmitted disease if we stop using condoms in order for me to get pregnant. What do we do?

A You're right to be concerned. Once you stop using condoms, you and your partner are susceptible to catching or transmitting sexually transmitted diseases. And either of you could be carrying a disease without necessarily knowing it, since some symptoms are very subtle. Before you stop using condoms, you and your husband should be tested for common sexually transmitted diseases by your doctor. If either of you tests positively, consult him or her about how you can be treated without potentially infecting your baby.

Having Second Thoughts?

From Our Files

It felt so strange to Nancy to be drinking her morning orange juice without also taking a birth control pill. She'd been on the pill since she was 17, faithfully observing the daily routine of popping one into her mouth for eight years. Now, she and her husband had decided that the time was right to have a baby. As she took one last sip, Nancy hesitated a moment before pushing her chair away from the table. It wasn't that she didn't want to have a baby. She did. But she was anxious about the idea at the same time. She felt a little like she did on the morning that she first went away from home to college. Part of her felt very mature and couldn't wait to be on her own. But another part of her wished she could just continue going to school around the corner and live at home where she felt safe and secure.

Nancy knew she needed to discuss her feelings with someone close to her, preferably her husband Paul, but he was so excited about having a baby that she did not want him to think she had changed her mind. Finally, she raised the question with her older sister, who already had two children. Her sister explained that she had experienced similar feelings before her first pregnancy, but now wished she had aired them with her husband. Once Nancy understood that her feelings were natural, she found it easier to open up the subject with Paul. She discovered that he too had concerns, but together they affirmed that having a baby was the right thing for them.

Like Nancy, you too may have second thoughts. If so, don't be alarmed. Having a baby is a monumental step. It is not as simple as putting away your contraceptives or stashing your diaphragm in a dresser drawer. It's only natural that your desire to bring a baby into the world may be accompanied by anxiety about what your life will be like after he or she is born. It doesn't necessarily mean that you don't want to have a baby. It is just a natural expression of the anxiety that people feel when faced with a decision that will permanently change their lives.

If you have second or even third thoughts about having a baby, don't try to push them out of your mind. If you bury them in your subconscious, they'll just surface in other ways. You may find yourselves arguing over every little thing, when these anxieties are really the root cause. Or you may subconsciously start avoiding sex, especially around the time when you are most likely to conceive. If indeed you realize that you really don't want to have a baby, it is better to realize it now than after you're already pregnant.

On the other hand, you don't want to become so mired in your worries that you lose out on the novelty and excitement of having unrestrained and unprotected sex. How can you resolve your anxieties and prevent them from dampening your happiness?

One way is to establish a limit on the time during which you will allow yourselves to worry about how the new baby will affect your lives. Give yourselves 5 minutes to worry about it alone, or, better yet, 10 minutes to worry together. You'll find that sharing your worries and concerns about raising children will provide both of you with comfort and reassurance, as well as bring you closer together. This closeness will also make you better parents. When your predetermined worry time is up, say, "Enough," and push those thoughts out of your mind. How can you control what thoughts are in your head? It's not as hard as you may think. Try focusing on the positive side of your decision. Revisit the reasons why you decided to have a baby in the first place.

Experiencing Sex in a New Way

You may assume that you know what it feels like to have intercourse with your partner, but you're in for something wonderfully different now that you've decided to have a baby. We're not claiming that the earth will move and a procreative aura will enshroud the two of you, but sex will not be the same. After years of making love with the fear of becoming pregnant in the back of your mind, you'll definitely notice a psychological lift when you have sex with the aim of creating a new life. Your orgasms may not be stronger or longer, but the knowledge that this intimacy could result in a child will heighten your overall pleasure and intimacy. Some ways to take advantage of this special time are:

- Be spontaneous. Make love anytime and anywhere.
- Be giving. Think of new ways to give physical pleasure to each other. If you always wondered what multiple orgasms are like, this is a good time for you to find out about them!
- Be romantic. Go out to dinner. Light candles. Take a shower together. Wear edible underwear!
- Be loving. Talk to each other (and don't fall sleep as soon as you're done)!
- Be gentle. Give each other massages. Wash each other's backs. Sit in the tub and give each other a foot rub.

There's no guarantee that passionate lovemaking will get you pregnant faster, but terrific sex can't hurt. In fact, it may help. Some experts feel that your chances of conceiving improve when you're relaxed. Feeling secure in your relationship certainly will help to keep you relaxed, as will great sex. And great sex, in turn, is a wonderful way of reinforcing the emotional bond between you.

Don't Worry, Be Happy

What are the chances of getting pregnant when you make love? The numbers would seem to be on your side. A man's ejaculate, or the semen released in one ejaculation, typically contains more than 100 million sperm. It takes only one to fertilize an egg. Because a man could easily ejaculate once a day, he can produce three billion or more spermatozoae per month, all aimed at a single target—the one egg (in most instances) that a woman produces each month.

But even those overwhelming odds don't guarantee the desired result. Under ideal circumstances, only approximately 20 percent of women who are trying to have a baby get pregnant each month. It may take a few months before that exciting moment when your pregnancy test is positive.

Although you may not be able to herd those sperm in the right direction at first try, one way to increase your chances of getting pregnant is to stay relaxed. There is some evidence that stress can have a negative effect on your efforts to conceive a baby. How? Stress can interfere with the normal ovulatory cycle, making it less likely for an egg to be available for fertilization. It can also have an impact on the hormones that affect implantation of the egg in the womb, reducing the likelihood of a successful pregnancy. A man's fertility can also be affected by stress, which can decrease the sperm count and increase sperm defects.

TIP

If you have vacation days coming to you, instead of one long vacation, plan to take several long weekends over the next few months that coincide with the days you anticipate ovulation. Then, you and your partner can go away together or just create a romantic atmosphere at home. Print out the ovulation calendar at http://www.babydata.com and find out which days are best.

ASK DR. RUTH

Q I made the mistake of telling my mother that we were trying to have a baby. Now every time she sees me, it's like the Spanish Inquisition. She never asked about our sex life before, but now she wants to know everything. How can I get her to stop?

A It sounds as if your mother is very anxious to become a grandmother, which means that she'll probably also do her share of meddling after the baby arrives. While you may not be able to stop her altogether, you can find an opportunity to clear the air and help her understand your feelings. Take her for a walk or a drive or even a cup of coffee at the local diner. Start off by telling her how much you love her and how much you appreciate everything that she has done and will do for you as a grandmother, but then let her know that there are some things you have to do on your own. Tell her that her constant questions are putting even more pressure on you and that this is making you nervous and interfering with your enjoyment of her company. Promise that you will call her as soon as you find out that you are pregnant. Make sure to call her the next day and then thank her for her good behavior if she doesn't bring up the subject.

Obviously, you cannot eliminate all the stress in your life and couples can and do get pregnant while they're under stress. But there's no reason why you should not optimize your chances for conception. To give yourself the best odds, take a look at your lives before you put away your contraceptives. Try to reduce major stressors looming in the near future. Are you preparing for Medical or Law boards? Are there unusual pressures at work? Is there illness in the family? Keep in mind that even a happy occasion, such as a big family reunion or holiday party that you're hosting, can be stressful. Try to reduce stressful activities that are under your control, especially during the time of the month when you're fertile. For example, if you've never thrown a huge party or a sit-down holiday dinner for the whole family before, now isn't the time to start. Or, if new career opportunities come your way, consider them in the light of your new family project. Tackling the demands of a new job at the same time that you're trying to get pregnant is a perfect recipe for stress overload.

While you're trying to get pregnant, you'll probably get advice— solicited and unsolicited—from friends and relatives who already have children. The comments may be helpful, but they also can be alarming. Some parents may tell you that your life will come to a screeching halt as soon as the baby is born and that you'll be little more than indentured slaves for 18 years. Keep in mind that all of this is an exaggeration.

Life will change and a great many adaptations will have to be made when you become parents. However, those adaptations will not all be sacrifices. Most of the changes that parenthood brings with it enrich rather than detract from your life. Parenthood is much like any other part of life: part luck, but mostly what you decide to make of it. And, as most parents will tell you, the rewards are so much greater than the sacrifices.

When Timing Is Everything: Determining When You Ovulate

Once you've decided to have a baby, do not turn this joyful time into a stressful time by setting a timetable for conceiving the baby. This could delay, rather than encourage, conception. Instead, you should fully enjoy the freedom that comes from having sex without a worry in the world.

TIP

Try not to put yourself on a schedule in an effort to become pregnant during a particular window of time, such as between school semesters or right after a particularly busy business season. Despite all of the advanced technology surrounding pregnancy and birth, there still is no scientific way for a couple to plan intercourse that will guarantee pregnancy at a specific time. In fact, the stress caused by putting yourselves on a timetable may actually make it harder for you to conceive. Research has shown that couples who have regular intercourse two to three times per week are more likely to achieve pregnancy than those having intercourse fewer than two times per week on average.

If you are trying to get pregnant, you should know that there are only about five to six days or so in your cycle during which you can become pregnant. These are the day of ovulation and the four to five days immediately preceding it. How do you find out which days are best? Some women feel that they know exactly when they ovulate because they feel a small, sharp twinge in their abdomen, called *mittelschmerz* (middle pain), when the egg bursts through the ovarian wall. Other women feel bloated and achy during the few days in the middle of the cycle when ovulation occurs. Others have no symptoms of ovulation at all. Whether or not you have midcycle symptoms, there are ways of anticipating when you will ovulate; some are more scientific than others.

Your Menstrual Cycle

Your menstrual cycle is the time between the first day of one menstrual period (the day when bleeding begins) and the first day of the following menstrual period (Figure 1). Try to get a sense of how long and how regular your menstrual cycle is. To do this, you'll have to monitor it for several months. And write down those days, preferably in a calendar, because it might be difficult to remember them after several months.

Step 1: Calculate your menstrual cycle. Essentially, to calculate your menstrual cycle, you need to know when it starts and how long it lasts. For example, if the first day of your period begins on April 2 and the following period begins on April 30, your menstrual cycle would be 28 days. Keep in mind that it's perfectly normal for your cycle to vary a little from one month to the next—a 28-day cycle in March, a 29-day cycle in April, and a 27-day cycle in May. The average cycle lasts 28 days, but a normal cycle could last anywhere between 21 and 35 days.

Although the length of your period is of lesser importance, the information is helpful, because a menstrual period that is too short (less than 4 days) or one that is too long (more than 7 days) may indicate a problem. A short period may suggest too little hormones, and a period that lasts too long may indicate the presence of fibroids or polyps.

Step 2: Calculate the approximate day when you ovulate. Although the length of your whole menstrual cycle may vary, the number of days from ovulation until the beginning of your next menstrual period is always the same: a finite length of 14 days on average. This is called the luteal phase, and it corresponds with the life span of the corpus luteum, the collapsed follicle that remains after the egg is released.

Let's assume that you've tracked your period for three months and found that your cycle is always 28 days long. Assuming that it will continue on that schedule, you can anticipate that you will ovulate on day 14. If your cycle is 32 days, you will ovulate on day 18. In other words, if you subtract 14 days from the length of your whole cycle, you will

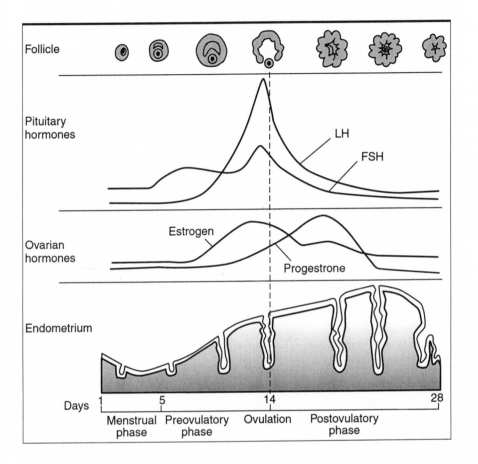

Follicle

Pituitary
hormones

LH

FSH

Ovarian
hormones

Estrogen

Progestrone

Endometrium

Days 1   5   14   28

Menstrual Preovulatory   Ovulation   Postovulatory
phase   phase   phase

FIGURE 1

*Typical menstrual cycle. Days 1-14: Follicular phase; Days 15-28: Luteal phase. Day 1 is the beginning
of the cycle, the day on which menstrual bleeding begins. The cycle ends when the next bleeding begins. The
influence of certain hormones from day 11 on causes the egg to ripen and to be released usually on day 14 of a
28-day cycle. If the egg is not fertilized, hormone levels drop, leading to a breakdown of the uterine lining and
menstruation usually 14 days after ovulation.*

arrive at the approximate day of your ovulation, starting to count on the first day of your menses or bleeding.

The longer you keep track of your cycle, the more accurate your calculations will be, so the earlier you begin, the better. Of course, you can still try to get pregnant while you're charting your cycle. Who knows, you may get pregnant even before you've had a chance to figure out exactly when you ovulate. If you have access to the Internet, you can get a printout of your ovulation calendar at http://www.babydata.com (Figure 2 is a sample calendar).

Sun	Mon	Tue	Wed	Thu	Fri	Sat
May 17	May 18	May 19	May 20	May 21 *First Day of Last Period*	May 22	May 23
May 24 *Missed Period? Check It Out!*	May 25	May 26	May 27	May 28	May 29	May 30
May 31	Jun 1 *A Little Fertile*	Jun 2 *Fertile*	Jun 3 *Really Fertile*	Jun 4 *Expected Ovulation Last Chance!*	Jun 5	Jun 6
Jun 7	Jun 8	Jun 9	Jun 10	Jun 11	Jun 12	Jun 13
Jun 14	Jun 15	Jun 16	Jun 17	Jun 18 *Expected First Day of Period*	Jun 19	Jun 20
Jun 21 *Missed Period? Check It Out!*	Jun 22	Jun 23	Jun 24	Jun 25	Jun 26	Jun 27
Jun 28	Jun 29 *A Little Fertile*	Jun 30 *Fertile*	Jul 1 *Really Fertile*	Jul 2 *Expected Ovulation Last Chance!*	Jul 3	Jul 4
Jul 5	Jul 6	Jul 7	Jul 8	Jul 9	Jul 10	Jul 11

FIGURE 2

A sample of a completed ovulation calendar. (From http://www.babydata.com)

Your Cervical Mucus

Most women are unaware that changes in the consistency of their cervical mucus (mucus that coats the cervix) coincide with the menstrual cycle. These changes are easy to recognize and serve as an excellent way to anticipate ovulation.

The cervical mucus functions as a barrier that prevents bacteria from migrating from the vagina into the uterus and causing an infection. When the mucus is thick and viscous, it is also more difficult for sperm to swim through and enter the uterus, thus decreasing the chances of conception.

Just before ovulation, the mucus undergoes a dramatic change. It becomes thin and watery, allowing any sperm that are deposited near the cervix to easily penetrate the cervix and the uterus. Once the sperm passes through the cervix, it can continue swimming toward the egg that is about to be released.

It's easy to tell the difference between the two types of mucus. To examine the mucus, wash your hands and then find a comfortable position in which you can gently insert your index or middle finger inside your vagina and reach up to touch the cervix. You can do this standing with one foot propped on a chair or lying in bed on one side with your knees bent. After you remove your finger from your vagina, you'll find a drop of cervical mucus on your fingertip. Put your thumb and finger together and then slowly pull the fingers apart. Under normal circumstances, the mucus will be creamy. However, in the days before you are about to ovulate, the consistency of the mucus will be much more elastic and will stretch between your two fingers for several inches in a stringy fashion. This is called *spinnbarkeit* (ability to spin). When your cervical mucus stretches between your thumb and index finger, you can be fairly certain that ovulation is just around the corner. If you're trying to conceive a baby, it's time to get going!

Basal Body Temperature

Another way to calculate your day of ovulation is to track your basal body temperature (Figure 3). This method is based on the fact that a woman's temperature rises slightly (approximately 0.4 to 0.8 degrees Fahrenheit) within 12 to 24 hours *after* she ovulates. The temperature remains elevated for 14 days and goes down again when she menstruates.

To get accurate readings, you'll need to use a special basal body thermometer and a special graph paper, available at most pharmacies

Table A (blank)

Days of Monthly Cycle	1	2	3	4	5	6	7	8	9	10	11	12	13	14	15	16	17	18	19	20	21	22	23	24	25	26	27	28
Date of Month																												
Day of the Week																												
Intercourse																												
Menses																								'				
LH Testing																												
Medication																												
Illness																												
Irregular Bleeding																												
Sleeplessness																												
Cramps																												
Breast Self Exam																												
Cervical Fluid																												
Exercise																												

Basal Body Temperature scale: 99.2°, 99.0°, 98.8°, 98.6°, 98.4°, 98.2°, 98.0°, 97.8°, 97.6°, 97.4°, 97.2°, 97.0°, 96.8°

A

Table B (completed)

Days of Monthly Cycle	1	2	3	4	5	6	7	8	9	10	11	12	13	14	15	16	17	18	19	20	21	22	23	24	25	26	27	28
Date of Month	5/8	5/9	5/10	5/11	5/12	5/13	5/14	5/15	5/16	5/17	5/18	5/19	5/20	5/21	5/22	5/23	5/24	5/25	5/26	5/27	5/28	5/29	5/30	5/31	6/1	6/2	6/3	6/4
Day of the Week	S	Su	M	T	W	Th	F	S	Su	M	T	W	Th	F	S	Su	M	T	W	Th	F	S	Su	M	T	W	Th	F
Intercourse						X			X		X		X		X		X			X				X			X	
Menses	X	X	X	X	X																							
LH Testing																												
Medication														(cough suppressant)					X	X								
Illness																		(cold)		X	X	X	X					
Irregular Bleeding					X																							
Sleeplessness																												
Cramps																												
Breast Self Exam						X																						
Cervical Fluid																												
Exercise					X	X			X		X			X	X								X	X				

Basal Body Temperature scale: 99.2°, 99.0°, 98.8°, 98.6°, 98.4°, 98.2°, 98.0°, 97.8°, 97.6°, 97.4°, 97.2°, 97.0°, 96.8°

B

FIGURE 3

A blank (A) and a completed (B) graph to track your basal body temperature and other factors that are important in determining when you are ovulating.

or from your doctor. Take your temperature every morning before you get out of bed and note it on the graph paper. Do this first thing in the morning before you get out of bed, because any activity may affect the reading. Make sure that you get enough sleep when taking your temperature and that you don't have a cold or other infections. These factors may raise your temperature and give you a false temperature reading.

After several months, you'll be able to identify a pattern by plotting your temperature on the graph paper. With the help of your doctor, you can analyze the pattern of your basal body temperature and determine when you ovulate in a given month. However, since a rise in temperature indicates the period *after* ovulation, you can use the pattern only to predict your fertile periods in the future. The 24- to 48-hour period just before the increase in temperature is your fertile period and the right time to have sex. The sperm needs to be there before you ovulate, and the day of ovulation and the days before it are the best to get pregnant.

Ovulation Detection Kits

As the name implies, an ovulation detection kit is a tool that helps you predict when you are ovulating. Available without a prescription from a pharmacy, it contains either a strip or a vial to collect and test urine for the presence of luteinizing hormone (LH). Different types of kits are available involving either a single step or several steps to detect ovulation.

Start using the test about five to seven days before you think you're going to ovulate and do it every day until you detect ovulation. A change in the color of your urine sample is your signal that you are about to ovulate. This can happen any time from 12 to 48 hours before ovulation. If you want to get pregnant, you should definitely have sex. These tests, however, are not infallible. False positive results can occur, for example, at the onset of menopause, when the level of LH also can rise.

You may use all or some of these methods in combination. However, even if you ovulate on the perfect day of the perfect month and even if you get pregnant at that perfect time, babies don't always come on the day they're supposed to. Even if your due date turns out to be the one you hoped for, the baby may decide to come into the world a little earlier or a little later.

It Takes Two

Maria and Pete had been trying to have a baby for more than a year. They had been to a doctor, and the test results showed that Pete's sperm count was low. Maria read that a man could increase his ability to produce sperm by eating fried bull's testicles (called Rocky Mountain oysters), so she put Pete on a steady diet of these delicacies. After a month, Pete could not stomach their sight, smell, or taste any longer. They returned to the doctor to see if there was anything else they could do to improve Pete's sperm count.

Like Maria, you may have heard that certain substances, like oysters, bull testicles, or rhinoceros horn, can improve a man's sex drive or ability to make sperm. Even though we don't want to discourage you from your enjoyment of exotic foods, we should also inform you that we have no confirmation that they actually help.

Of course, knowing when ovulation occurs isn't the only important factor in getting pregnant. As the saying goes, "It takes two to tango." As important as the egg is in the fertilization process, there must be sperm to fertilize it if you're going to get pregnant. So, let's not forget the male side of this equation.

The Ejaculate

The ejaculate consists of the spermatozoa—or sperm for short—and the seminal plasma, the fluid surrounding the sperm. The sperm are produced within the testicles. The seminal plasma is composed of secretions from several glands—the prostate, seminal vesicles, epididymis, and Cowper's. It is very high in a sweet chemical called *fructose*—a vital component of the ejaculate produced by the seminal vesicles.

Sperm are not necessarily uniform, and only high-quality sperm are able to fertilize an egg. Sperm quality is measured in terms of count, mobility, and morphology, or shape.

The sperm count refers to the number of sperm in the ejaculate. The ejaculate, on average, contains 100 million or more sperm. This does not mean that all men produce 100 million sperm each time they ejaculate. Some men do not have as high a sperm count as other men. If a man produces fewer than 20 million sperm per cubic centimeter (cc) of ejaculate, the likelihood of pregnancy is low. For fertilization to occur, there should be at least 2 cc to 2.5 cc of ejaculate.

Not only do you need a lot of sperm, but they also have to be good swimmers. The scientific term for the swimming ability of sperm is *sperm motility*. Sperm motility is necessary for the sperm to reach and fertilize the egg. The sperm have to look good, too. This is called *sperm morphology*. A malformed or irregularly shaped sperm cannot fertilize an egg.

Producing Quality Sperm	As with women, men can take some steps to prepare for conception. One is to improve the quality of their sperm. Sperm production takes place in the testes over a period of 10 to 11 weeks. Even though sperm are produced on a daily basis, the final sperm is the result of a three-month developmental process. The following practices will contribute to sperm production during the months leading up to conception:

- Do not wear tight-fitting underwear, pants, or exercise gear.
- Wear boxer shorts rather than briefs.
- Spend time at home without any clothes on, or at least without clothes from the waist down. A perfect time to do this is when you sleep.
- Avoid saunas, steam rooms, jacuzzis, and hot baths. Increasing the temperature of the testes during production of spermatozoa may have a negative effect both on the number and quality of sperm being produced. You do not have to put your testicles on ice, although such a measure has been suggested to improve male fertility!
- Women who either think they might be pregnant or who are pregnant are routinely advised by their health care providers to avoid toxic chemicals, alcohol, and drugs that may have a negative effect on the developing baby. Men also need to be wary of noxious substances that can have a negative impact on sperm production. However, the critical time for men to practice care is in the few months before and while the couple is trying to conceive rather than during the pregnancy.

The Youth Factor	Sperm are produced in the testicles 24 hours a day, 7 days a week, 365 days a year. If a man does not ejaculate, accumulated sperm will age. As sperm ages, its ability to impregnate probably decreases. It is therefore a good idea to flush out old sperm approximately a week before

you expect ovulation. That will leave only the most potent sperm to make their way up the fallopian tubes toward the descending egg.

There's no reason why this can't be fun, so be creative about ushering out those old sperm. Fellatio, or oral sex, is a welcome departure from vaginal sex for most men, so that's one option. But good sex that gives you both a delicious orgasm is an equally satisfactory solution. You can use a condom or any other form of birth control if you're not quite ready to start making a baby.

Quantity as Well as Quality

While sperm is produced every day, it may take some time to produce the large amount of sperm needed for fertilization. As already mentioned, it takes 10 to 11 weeks for a complete sperm to develop. Even the most virile man may experience a drop in sperm count below the level needed for fertilization if he ejaculates several times a day.

To make certain that there are a sufficient number of sperm to fertilize the egg when you ovulate, some experts suggest that you have intercourse not more than once a day during the fertile part of the woman's cycle. (Your partner, however, can have as many orgasms as she would like and as often as she would like.) As promoters of orgasm, it pains us a little to ask one of you to give up this delightful gift of nature. But the reward you'll receive far outweighs this sacrifice.

The Final Step: Fertilizing the Egg

From Our Files

Jerry had a problem with premature ejaculation. In fact, he had a very serious problem. When he had intercourse with his wife, Gina, half the time he ejaculated even before entering her vagina. Since their lovemaking always included Gina being brought to orgasm either orally or manually, the couple never felt it was necessary to do anything about Jerry's problem. However, after nine months of trying to have a baby, Jerry and Gina came to see me. They realized that in order to impregnate Gina, Jerry needed to deposit his sperm inside her vagina, so he needed to overcome his premature ejaculation. Luckily, Jerry's problem was not biological, but psychological, in nature—something that can readily be treated by any competent sex therapist.

Of course, for pregnancy to occur, the ejaculate needs to be deposited inside the vagina. The closer to the cervix the sperm is deposited, the better the chances of your getting pregnant. That's not always as easy as it sounds.

This does not mean that you can't ever get pregnant if the man ejaculates close to the entrance of the vagina. In fact, a healthy, strong sperm can swim all the way up the vagina, through the cervix, and impregnate a fertile woman, as many unsuspecting women have found out (Figure 4). Nonetheless, if the male has considerable problems with either premature ejaculation (i.e., if he ejaculates before he enters the vagina) or suffers from erectile difficulties (i.e., if he cannot sustain an erection that will allow him to penetrate the vagina), conception is going to be a difficult process. If you have these difficulties and have determined with your doctor that they are not caused by biological problems, it's time to consult a sex therapist, who will provide you with various methods and techniques for correcting these problems or to discuss other options, such as intrauterine insemination (IUI), with your doctor.

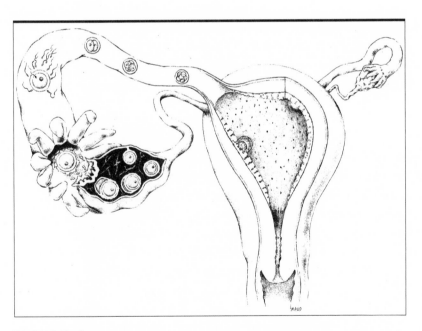

FIGURE 4

The fertilization of the egg by the sperm, and the route of the fertilized egg into the uterus.

Getting Ready for the Big Day

So your calendar says that the big day is almost upon you. All the tests point to the fact that you're ovulating. If you're right, a mature egg is just about to be released from one ovary and make its way down one of your fallopian tubes and remain viable for about 12 hours. Sperm can survive in the woman's genital tract for an average of 24 to 48 hours, so to get pregnant, ideally you must have sex in the 12 to 24 hours before that egg is released. But, before you go ahead, we have a few words of advice.

First of all, we suggest that you don't make too big a deal out of any one sexual episode. There are no guarantees that one particular sexual interlude, even on the right day at the right time in the right position will definitely result in conception. If you start thinking this way, you'll be disappointed every time sex during your ovulation period does not result in a pregnancy. This can only lead to anxiety and stress which, as already mentioned, are not conducive to conception.

> **TIP**
>
> *Try making conception an adventure. Have you tried having sex on the dining room table? Well, here's your chance. What about outdoors? Or perhaps in the backseat of your car.*

Whatever you do, don't make this into a chore. Yes, you may be following a schedule of sorts, but you're not laboratory rats. You're still two people who love each other and who are trying to give each other utmost pleasure. If one of you isn't quite ready to make love, wait a little while. Better yet, take some time for an old-fashioned seduction. The hour or two you spend in foreplay won't necessarily make a difference to your fertility schedule, but will make all the difference in your enjoyment. And it also can tip the scales in favor of conception. A dry vagina is a hindrance to pregnancy (and pleasure), whereas a very wet one helps the process and increases the fun.

The Best Positions for Conception

There is no doubt that certain positions increase the odds of getting pregnant by facilitating the entry of the sperm into the vagina. This makes it easier for the sperm to find their way through the cervix. If nothing else, adding a little variety to the equation can't hurt your relationship, although you should never try to force your partner into trying something that he or she does not feel comfortable with.

MISSIONARY POSITION

The most common position for intercourse in Western societies is to have the man lying on top of the woman, both facing each other (Figure 5). This is called the missionary position, possibly named after missionaries who tried to impose it on natives, who preferred other positions that the missionaries found sinful. This turns out to be a very good position for getting pregnant, because the woman's vagina is upside down, forming a perfect cup in which to receive the semen. To improve conception, the woman may tilt her pelvis upward by putting a pillow or cushion under her pelvis. This causes the vagina to tilt even further backward and facilitates the entry of the sperm into the uterus. Also, after ejaculation, we suggest that the man keep his penis inside of the vagina as long as possible to ensure that as much of the ejaculate as possible reaches the cervix. The woman should continue to lie on her back with her pelvis slightly tilted upward for some time, maybe 20 to 30 minutes afterward, to improve the movement of sperm up the vagina into the cervix and uterus. Your partner could also assist in preventing the sperm from leaking out by gently pressing the labia closed.

From Our Files

Alma and Henry came to see me for a second opinion because they had been trying to get pregnant for eight months, without success. They had gone to see an infertility specialist, who had suggested several tests, including a surgical procedure. Among the many questions that I asked was which position for intercourse they preferred. They replied that she straddled him, sitting on top while he was lying on his back. They had been using this position for many years because they found it very pleasurable and it gave her the best chance to achieve orgasm. They hadn't even considered (nor did their other doctor) that the sexual position might play an important role in becoming pregnant. I explained that in the woman-on-top position, much of the ejaculate would come out of the vagina once the woman got up. Although this would not totally prevent pregnancy, it certainly wouldn't improve the chances for pregnancy. I advised them to try the traditional missionary position, with him on top and her lying on her back. Three months later she called with the good news that her pregnancy test was positive.

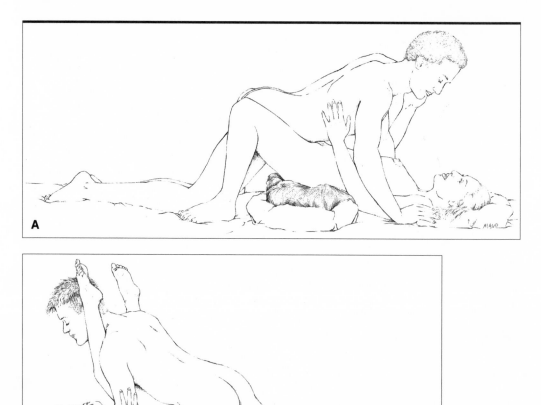

FIGURE 5

(A) The traditional missionary position with the man on top of the woman. (B) A variation of the traditional missionary position, with the woman's legs raised in front of the man's chest.

REAR-ENTRY POSITION

In the rear-entry position, the man enters his partner's vagina from behind, as she lies either with her knees to her chest or her head facing down toward the bed, either on her knees or supported by pillows (Figure 6). It is a position that might be especially successful for women who have been told that they have a retroverted uterus, a

FIGURE 6

The rear-entry position, with the woman's head facing down and her pelvis supported by pillows.

uterus that is tilted backward. Having sexual intercourse in the rear-entry, knee-to-chest position deposits the sperm closer to the cervix because the penis can achieve deeper penetration of the vagina.

What to Avoid If You Want to Get Pregnant

If you are trying to become pregnant, any position that might prevent sperm from reaching the cervix should be avoided. We are not saying that these positions absolutely, totally prevent you from getting pregnant, but that they won't make getting pregnant easier. These include standing, sitting, bending over, and hanging from a chandelier (especially if it is not well secured).

If the women gets up right after her partner ejaculated, the sperm might flow out and prevent fertilization. We therefore suggest that the woman remain on her back for 20 to 30 minutes to ensure that enough spermatozoae reach the cervix. The woman should also empty her bladder beforehand, so that she doesn't have to get up because her bladder is full. Never have anal sex before introducing the penis into the vagina, because this may introduce harmful bacteria.

Having sex under water in a tub or jacuzzi may introduce chlorinated water that may kill sperm. The hot water may also increase the male's body temperature, thereby lowering his sperm count. As with other positions to avoid, if the woman moves into a vertical position too soon, she could lose valuable sperm. Douching is also not a good idea, whether or not you are trying to get pregnant. Douching may change the vaginal pH and thus create a hostile environment for sperm. In fact, research has shown that women who regularly douche are decreasing their chance to become pregnant. The vagina is self-cleansing and does not need any special cleansing agents. Douching, in fact, may kill the "good" bacteria, called "Doederlein's bacteria," which are responsible for maintaining a healthy balance in the vagina. If you feel there is an unusual odor or discharge, you might have an infection that needs specific treatment, so we suggest you see your doctor to determine its cause. Treating specific infections will improve your chances of getting pregnant.

Vibrators and other devices used for stimulation can introduce an infection if they are shared with others or if they are not properly cleansed. Using a clean vibrator on your clitoris when trying to get pregnant is okay.

Lubricational Foreplay

Sufficient lubrication, the secretion of fluid from the vaginal walls and glands, is an essential part of enjoying sex. Now, many couples who can't achieve sufficient natural lubrication are using artificial lubricants, such as KY Jelly, Vaseline, or Astroglide. And that's fine if you are not trying to get pregnant. But did you know that any of these artificial lubricants may potentially kill sperm? If you are serious about getting pregnant, avoid all of these artificial lubricants.

There is a very important alternative if you can't get sufficient lubrication: foreplay. First, allow sufficient time for foreplay, which should be an essential part of your interaction every time you have sex. But, did you know that when you are trying to get pregnant, it might even improve your chances? Sperm actually move better in a moist vagina than in a dry one. Let us make some suggestions:

- Start with a romantic dinner.
- Send her flowers the day before.
- Talk sweetly to each other.
- Touch each other in parts other than your genitalia.
- Massage each other.

Some women become sufficiently aroused without direct contact with the clitoris, but most require direct stimulation of the clitoris. Both of you need to have excellent communication so you know what the other expects. She may like it if he stimulates her clitoris with his finger, or even with a vibrator. But use a soft touch, because the clitoris is very sensitive. Kiss her and let her guide you to maximize her pleasure.

Even with foreplay, some couples still find it difficult to obtain enough vaginal lubrication. To fix this, some have suggested using saliva, while others feel that even saliva might have a negative effect on sperm. Yet others have suggested the use of egg white, because it is natural and closely mimics the cervical secretions. However, there is a theoretical risk (never proven) of an infection from the egg. If you have problems with insufficient lubrication and you are trying to get pregnant, we suggest that you ask your doctor for advice.

Oral Sex and Pregnancy

FELLATIO

Fellatio is when the women puts her partner's penis into her mouth and stimulates him (Figure 7). She can do this either until he ejaculates or she could stimulate him until they continue with vaginal intercourse. Another term for fellatio is "blow-job." Many men like to have fellatio performed on them and it can be a perfect alternative to vaginal intercourse. However, for pregnancy to occur, the sperm has to be deposited inside her vagina. If he ejaculates inside her mouth or far away from her vagina, she cannot get pregnant. Even if she swallows his sperm, she cannot get pregnant.

FIGURE 7
In fellatio, the woman stimulates her partner by putting his penis into her mouth.

FIGURE 8

In cunnilingus, the man stimulates the women's clitoris with his tongue.

CUNNILINGUS

Cunnilingus is when the man stimulates his partner's clitoris with his mouth (Figure 8). For many women, it's a wonderful part of foreplay that can culminate in an orgasm. Some couples like to stimulate each other orally, and before they come he might insert his penis into her vagina until they both have an orgasm.

PREGNANCY

Can you have oral sex before vaginal intercourse and still get pregnant? There is really no indication to the contrary and, in our experience, couples have become pregnant after stimulating each other orally. In fact, some experts suggest that saliva be used as a lubricant if the vagina is really dry. However, a few conflicting reports suggest that saliva may have a negative effect on spermatozoa. We recommend that if you are serious about trying to get pregnant, it is a good idea to avoid mixing saliva and sperm.

Orgasms

Obviously, for pregnancy to occur, the man has to have an orgasm and ejaculate inside the woman's vagina. But is it important for the woman to have an orgasm as well? There's no positive proof that a woman's orgasm will improve the odds of her getting pregnant, but the physical changes that the female body experiences during an orgasm would seem to create a conducive environment for conception.

When a woman has an orgasm, she experiences a certain type of contraction that can result in her cervix dipping down, putting it right into the pool of semen deposited by her partner at the end of her vagina. This may help additional sperm to swim up through the cervix and into the uterus, increasing the chances of pregnancy.

Determining the Baby's Sex

If your heart is set on having a baby of a certain sex, you may end up being disappointed. Such feelings of disappointment will cast a pall on what should be a joyous moment in your life. While it's alright to try to have a child of a certain sex, don't invest very much of yourself in the outcome. If you look at this as a lark, then it won't spoil your enjoyment of having a baby.

A Short Lesson in Genetics

The nucleus of each of the trillions of cells in our bodies contains our genes. They are located in chromosomes, which consist of a chemical called *deoxyribonucleic acid* (DNA). Each chromosome carries many genes. Genes provide the creative directions that make us who we are. They determine the color of our skin, eyes, and hair; our height; and every single other physical aspect about us, as well as a few emotional and psychological traits.

Human cells have 23 pairs or sets of chromosomes to make a total of 46. Twenty-two of these pairs are equal pairs in men and in women. The twenty-third pair is called the sex chromosome, and it is different in men and in women. In women, the twenty-third pair has two X chromosomes, whereas in men, the twenty-third pair has one X and one Y chromosome. This pairing of chromosomes, two X chromosomes or an X and a Y chromosome, takes place during fertilization and determines whether the baby will be a girl or a boy. The deciding factor rests within the sperm. Each sperm and each egg carries 23 chromosomes. The 23d chromosome of the egg is always an X chromosome, while the 23d chromosome of each sperm can be either an X or a Y chromosome. Combined, they will make 46 chromosomes. So, the sex of the baby will be determined by dad's sperm.

If the sperm that fertilizes the egg has an X chromosome, then the resulting embryo will have two X chromosomes and become a girl. If

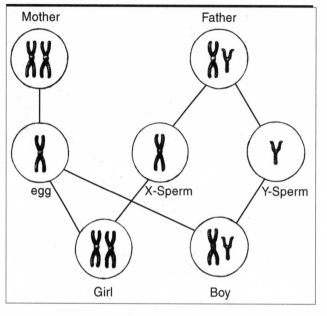

FIGURE 9

A chart showing how the 23 chromosomes combine to produce either a boy or a girl.

a sperm with a *Y* chromosome fertilizes the egg, then the embryo will have an *X* and a *Y* chromosome, and will become a boy (Figure 9).

Helping Nature Choose the Sex

With all the millions of sperm swimming toward the egg, you might assume that there's nothing you can do to influence whether your baby is going to be a girl or a boy. You're probably right, but many people try nonetheless by using either traditional folk methods or so-called scientific methods. We include some techniques here that might be helpful. Before giving you any specifics, however, we have a word of caution. None of these methods is guaranteed to let you actually determine the sex of your child.

How to Choose the Sex of Your Baby by Landrum B. Shettles describes prevailing strategies for the selection of your baby's sex. Before we list some of them, let us acquaint you with the scientific bases of these methods.

1. Given normal conditions, sperm with *Y* chromosomes, or male sperm, move faster than sperm with *X* chromosomes, or female sperm.

2. Male sperm are less resistant to hostile environments (such as inhospitable vaginal secretions) than female sperm.

3. Female sperm survive for longer time periods than male sperm.

4. *Y*-bearing sperm are smaller than *X*-bearing sperm.

FEMALE ORGASMS

One of the oldest methods of sex selection involves orgasms. It has been suggested that the chances of the baby being a boy will be improved if the woman has an orgasm before or while her partner ejaculates. In fact, in the Jewish tradition, it is said that if a woman "ejaculates" first (which we take to mean having an orgasm first), the baby will be a boy. An unofficial survey of his patients by Dr. Grünebaum shows that there might be some truth to this theory.

Additional evidence that might support this tradition shows that the more acidic the vagina is, the more likely it is that the baby will be a girl. The more alkaline the vagina is, the more likely it is that the baby will be a boy. This theory seems to be borne out by the fact that a woman's vagina becomes more alkaline during and after an orgasm. An alkaline vagina will increase the odds of the baby being a boy, because a male sperm will survive longer in an alkaline environment. Therefore, to increase the odds of having a girl, the woman should delay her orgasm until after her partner ejaculates, because it will be harder for a male sperm to survive an acidic environment.

MALE AND FEMALE SPERM

It is believed that *X*-bearing sperm (female sperm) live slightly longer than *Y*-bearing sperm (male sperm). For that reason, if you have intercourse 48 to 72 hours before ovulation, the likelihood is that many of the male sperm will have died by the time fertilization takes place, increasing the chances for a baby girl. Making love as close to ovulation as possible, that is, within 12 hours before ovulation, may increase the chance for a baby boy, because male sperm move faster, and thus will most likely reach the egg ahead of the female sperm.

POSITIONS AND THE SEX OF THE BABY

Some people claim that sperm deposited close to the cervix is more likely to produce male babies, and sperm deposited in the vagina, but not as close to the cervix, is more likely to produce female babies. This theory is based on the fact that male sperm swim faster than female sperm, and so will get to the egg faster. The rear-entry position, with the tip of the penis being closest to the cervix during ejaculation, may be an ideal position in which to conceive a baby boy.

To try for a girl, use the traditional missionary position, with the man on top of the woman. This will result in shallow penetration, with the sperm deposited in the vagina rather than at the cervix.

SPERM FILTRATION

Finally, some laboratories claim that they can filter out one type of sperm to improve your chances of having either a boy or a girl. For such a system to work, the sperm would have to be placed in the vagina by means other than sexual intercourse. If you already have four or five children of one sex and really want one of the other, giving up intercourse, the pleasurable system of depositing semen in the vagina, for an artificial one may be worth it. But in general, we favor orgasms over laboratories.

What about Twins?

There are two kinds of twins: identical twins, known as maternal or monozygotic twins, and nonidentical twins, known as fraternal or dizygotic twins.

Identical twins develop from a single egg that is fertilized by one sperm. If the developing egg, called a blastocyst, splits in two within 12 days after fertilization, two separate fetuses (identical twins) will grow. Identical twins are always the same sex and share the same genetic material. Half of identical twins are boys and half are girls. The incidence of identical twins is the same all over the world, approximately one in 250 pregnancies. The mother's age, race, and genetic background do not play a role in the development of identical twins.

For the development of nonidentical, or fraternal twins, the mother releases two separate eggs either from one or both of her ovaries at one time, and the eggs are fertilized by two different sperm. In general, approximately one half of the nonidentical twins are boy–girl or girl–boy pairs, one quarter are boy–boy pairs, and the other quarter are girl–girl pairs.

The incidence of nonidentical twins varies significantly in different ethnic groups. It can be as high as 1 in 20 pregnancies in some African groups, and as low as 1 in 150 pregnancies in Asian groups.

The incidence of nonidentical twins is genetically determined, and differences are probably the result of the different levels of hormones that induce ovulation.

Over the last several years, the incidence of nonidentical twins and even triplets or more fetuses has significantly increased. This is in large part a result of the use of fertility drugs that enhance the production of ova and because of the increased use of in vitro fertilization (IVF), in which several fertilized eggs and embryos are simultaneously implanted in the uterus.

Superfecundation and Superfetation Because this is a book about sex and pregnancy, another question about twins needs to be answered: Can twins be conceived by different fathers? Although it's rare, it can happen. If a woman has intercourse with different men during the same ovulation cycle, it is possible for each man to fertilize a different egg. This is called superfecundation. It is also possible for one egg to be fertilized during one ovulation cycle and another egg during the next cycle. This is called superfetation and can happen as a result of intercourse with either the same man or different men.

We know this can happen because occasionally we have reason to be suspicious about the parents of twins. Such suspicions may be aroused if twins look totally different or vary significantly in size or development. A blood test may show if the twins were conceived by different fathers. Twins conceived in different cycles (superfetation) are extremely rare, but twins conceived in the same cycle by different fathers (superfecundation) are probably more frequent than we previously thought.

Infertility and Treatment

You've been trying to get pregnant for several months, but your pregnancy tests have been disappointingly coming up negative. What should your next step be? For couples who have used birth control conscientiously for years, it is particularly ironic when they finally try to conceive and cannot. Usually, your caregiver will not suggest that you see a fertility specialist until you've tried to get pregnant for at least six months. Conception takes time even when both partners are healthy.

If you decide to consult a fertility expert, he or she will begin by getting an overview of your process of fertilization to see where the problems might be. You will be advised to have intercourse when ovulation is likely to occur, which means that the prescription might be to have sex on a certain day of the month. For the purposes of your evaluation, it will be the ovulation calendar, ovulation kit, or your basal body temperature chart that instigates sex, not a sudden rush of passion.

One of the first steps in looking for the cause of infertility is to test the ejaculate. If a low sperm count is found, it may be necessary to maximize the sperm by having sex within a day or two of ovulation. You may want to abstain from ejaculating and save the sperm for the day when your partner is fertile. Or, you might have to ejaculate into a jar for the ejaculate to be injected by the doctor into the uterus.

This is not the way sex was meant to be, without any spontaneity or passion. When you undergo fertility therapy and sex is scheduled, measured, and examined, intercourse can become a chore. This may cause problems in the marriage. As long you remind each other of how much you want this baby and view this as a joint effort, the problems are usually short term and can be overcome. However, if the fertility treatment drags on, having your sex life dictated and dissected may seem like a violation. It's not uncommon for one partner to tire of the process and ask to end treatment after one last effort, whether it is successful or not. At such a moment, despair can make you focus on the one point of contention to the exclusion of other options that might meet both your needs, such as the possibility of adoption. Instead, a cycle of blame and recrimination may surface that can lead to more distance and distrust between you.

The first step we recommend if and when you reach this point is to take a break from your efforts to conceive a child. Put the charts and thermometers and tests out of your minds and return to life as usual. Often, after a few months of normal interaction, you can patch up your differences and then decide how to proceed. If you are dedicated to proceeding with fertility treatments, make sure you've both discussed openly what feelings were driving you apart and what measures will help you avoid the same problems in the future. Here are some suggestions for avoiding problems:

- Share information. Make sure both of you are in the information loop. If the woman is keeping track of her cycle privately and then demands sex when her chart says she is fertile, her partner may feel pressured—and possibly resentful. If, however, he is made aware of his partner's cycles and knows in advance when her fertile period is coming, he'll feel more a part of the process and probably be more willing to cooperate.

- Fantasy can help. By now you know that minimizing stress is important when you're trying to conceive. But when you have been trying to conceive for a long time, each passing month without the result you desire only increases feelings of stress. One way to reduce the stress and put some playfulness back into your lovemaking is with fantasy.

Fantasy can be very stimulating. What starts out as play acting might actually turn into one of the best sexual adventures you've had in a long time. If you feel you need help to weave a fantasy, by all means, use whatever works for the two of you. For example, instead of calling him upstairs to bed and finishing the crossword puzzle while he's undressing, try putting on some dance music and luring him upstairs with a striptease. Or offer her an all-over massage. Borrow videotapes of sensuous exercises from your video store. After a few minutes of exercising together in the nude, you should feel revitalized and ready to burn some calories making love.

When It's Time to See an Expert

If infertility reaches a crisis point and your bedroom becomes a battlefield, you may not be able to resolve these issues yourselves. Before your despair and frustration undermines the loving and secure home you want to offer your child, seek professional help. Several available methods can help you in your quest to have a baby.

INDUCING OVULATION

If the cause of infertility is a problem with ovulation, certain medications are available to enhance or induce ovulation. Often, the woman will conceive within several months after taking such a medication.

REMOVING TUBAL OBSTRUCTIONS

A diagnostic test, such as a laparoscopy (in which an optical scope is passed into the abdomen) or a hysterosalpinography (an X-ray film of the uterus with a contrast medium) may indicate that the fallopian tubes are blocked. If so, the blockage could be preventing the egg from being fertilized or implanted in the uterus. In such cases, surgery can open up the tubes, or reattach them, as needed to get pregnant. Another alternative is to use ART (see below) to get pregnant.

ADVANCED TECHNIQUES FOR BECOMING PREGNANT

Sometimes, more drastic techniques are necessary to help a couple become pregnant. They include "low-tech" techniques, such as obtaining the ejaculate and then depositing it with a small catheter into the cervix or uterus at the time of ovulation (intrauterine insemination or "IUI"). To improve the chance that the sperm will fertilize the egg and to prevent the surrounding seminal fluid from adversely affecting the uterus, the ejaculate is sometimes washed and most of the seminal fluid removed before injection.

"High-tech" techniques for becoming pregnant are called "ART," which stands for "assisted reproductive technology." These techniques have been developed over the last decade and go by such names as GIFT, IVF, ZIFT, or ICSI. In essence, despite the strange sounding names, they are just different variations on similar techniques. With ART, the sperm are obtained from the man's ejaculate and eggs are removed from the ovary, usually by inserting a needle into the ovary under sonographic guidance. The eggs and sperm are then mixed in a culture dish, left incubated for some time, and the fertilized egg or embryo is then placed into the woman's uterus or fallopian tube.

OBTAINING THE EJACULATE AND SPERM

One step in this procedure is collecting what doctors refer to as "the specimen," or the ejaculate (Figure 10). How do you get the ejaculate? Since the man's ejaculate must reach the laboratory rather quickly, he is usually asked to masturbate at the laboratory facilities, either in the bathroom or, in most advanced facilities, in a room that has been designed specifically for this purpose. Such a room is usually well stocked with erotic literature and perhaps even some X-rated videos. Between the antiseptic setting, the pressure that comes from knowing that a technician is waiting outside the door to accept the sample, and the lack of desire, it is not always the easiest place for a man to have an orgasm.

On the face of it, this process doesn't sound romantic at all. But, perhaps we can help you change that. While we don't want to interfere in the medical treatment of a couple dealing with infertility, we do have some suggestions that might be helpful in making the production of the specimen more enjoyable.

FIGURE 10

One way to obtain the man's ejaculate is for the woman to stimulate the man with one hand while holding a jar in which to capture the ejaculate in the other hand.

If you have a choice among equally reliable infertility specialists, try to choose one close enough so that you can collect the specimen from your home and immediately take it to the fertility clinic. Then, you can collaborate on collecting the specimen and make the moment, if not romantic, as sexy (even funny!) as possible. At least, working together in the privacy of your own home, you could, if not look forward to the event, certainly not dread it as much. Don't forget to keep the container with the ejaculate at body temperature, because sperm are very sensitive to cold and die off easily.

If the infertility specialist is too far from your home to make this practical, ask about going to a nearby motel or hotel. There you could have privacy, and who knows what the added excitement from this illicit meeting with your partner in a rented motel room could lead to?

Either of these settings will give you the privacy you need to make this special act of masturbation as romantic and pleasurable as possible. Bring props, like music, pillows, and candles. If the room has a waterbed, that's a plus. However, if there's a hot tub, don't use it. Remember that high temperatures have an adverse effect on sperm production.

The important point is to make this experience as intimate and loving as possible. This may not be the usual way of conceiving, but it is the way that your child will be conceived, hopefully, so try to make it loving and memorable.

If fellatio is part of your sexual repertoire, begin that way. Just be careful not to miss the opportunity to deposit his ejaculate directly into the container and make sure that saliva and ejaculate do not mix. If you want to obtain the sample through sexual intercourse, ask for a special condom in which to collect the ejaculate. To make you less nervous, you could practice this procedure at home with your own condoms. However, ask your fertility specialist how many days you must abstain before collecting the specimen in order to have the maximum number of sperm.

If you have to provide the specimen at the clinic, try to stay as light-hearted about the procedure as possible. Remember, if this works, you're going to have a baby. Keeping that in mind may lift both of your spirits.

If depositing the sperm in a container is not the most romantic process, injecting it into the uterus may seem even less so, no matter what method is used. The woman is usually alone with her fertility doctor and with other personnel while this is done. Some women may prefer it that way. Feel free to ask that your partner be by your side if it makes you more comfortable. Maybe you can even ask for the lights to be dimmed and to have some music playing. You might even be able to do this by candlelight. Your emotional needs count, too, so don't be intimidated about making your requests.

It may be technically feasible for your partner to actually perform the injection, so find out if that's possible and discuss the option with your partner. Don't be shy about making other requests that will not only improve your relationship with your partner, but may also improve your chances of getting pregnant. Many times, artificial insemination is done early in the morning, but that's not necessarily because the procedure is more successful during daylight hours; it is because it's more convenient for the clinic to do it during the day.

If the only way the two of you can be at the clinic at the same time means the insemination has to occur after working hours, make sure to ask in advance if the procedure can be performed after work, so that you both can share in the experience. Your specialist may be able to ask the clinic to say open late one night to allow the two of you to share in the insemination procedure.

Such infertility techniques are not like making love and the woman is definitely not going to want to have an orgasm to accompany it, but the psychological and emotional components of becoming pregnant should not be ignored. The more pleasant the experience, the better. And, unless your doctor prohibits it, there is nothing wrong with making love and both partners having orgasms the natural way right after the insemination. So go home, or back to the hotel room, relax, and enjoy each other. You've just taken a big step toward your future as a family. And if you are successful that day, you can always remember it as one that was full of intimacy and love, not just mechanical intervention. One final reason for making artificial insemination as pleasant as possible is that it might have to be repeated, and you don't want to dread having to go through the experience another time.

The Next Step

Once you've done everything and feel that you've covered all the bases toward your goal of getting pregnant, waiting to see if you are pregnant can be filled with anxiety, excitement, and other emotions. In the next chapter, we hope to help you sail through this very exciting time of your life.

CHAPTER

3

$\mathcal{N}$OW THAT YOU'RE PREGNANT

ARE you absolutely sure you're pregnant? If so, spread the good news. Call family and friends, go to dinner, have sex—celebrate.

$\mathcal{F}$rom Our Files

Judie and Mark had been trying to have a baby for the last few months. When her period was a week late, they thought that they might have been successful. Judie bought a home pregnancy test on her way back from work, and the next morning, she and Mark woke up early to find out if "they" were pregnant. The test was positive, but a few days later, Judie started spotting. She called her gynecologist and was able to get an appointment that day. The doctor ordered a pregnancy test to confirm what she suspected. Based on Julie's history and the findings of the internal examination, Julie was pregnant. The doctor explained that it wasn't unusual to experience some spotting or bleeding in the first month or two of pregnancy.

But, be sure before you make the announcement. Today, with home pregnancy kits, you can verify your suspicions quickly, easily, and painlessly. Don't base your announcement on a missed period. Remember a missed period does not automatically mean you're pregnant, no matter how regular you may be. At the same time, vaginal bleeding does not always indicate a period. Two out of ten women who are pregnant experience enough vaginal bleeding to mistakenly think they're having a period.

What other physical signs of pregnancy might you experience? One you've definitely heard about is morning sickness—that nausea and vomiting that many women feel when they wake up. But you may also note greater fatigue, frequent urination, food cravings, enlargement and tenderness of the breasts, and darkening around the nipples. As your pregnancy progresses, you will see more definitive indicators, including increased darkening of the abdominal midline between the pubis and the navel, enlargement of the abdomen, and movement in your belly. If you haven't guessed that you're pregnant and gone to see a doctor by the time you feel your baby kicking inside of you, then we suggest that you start paying a lot more attention to your body . . . and buy a full-length mirror!

It is true, however, that until recently, women—and their partners—experienced weeks, and sometimes even months, of anxious waiting to find out if they were pregnant. But you can purchase a home pregnancy test at your local drug store that will give you a reliable answer as early as the first day of a missed period. This greatly benefits the mother and the baby she is carrying, because prenatal care can begin during the critical early weeks of the development of the fetus.

Taking the Pregnancy Test

You suspect you're pregnant, and you've purchased a home pregnancy kit. Should you perform the test alone? Or should you share the moment with your partner? There is no right or wrong answer to this question. Discovering that you are or are not pregnant can be an intensely emotional experience for both of you. Whether or not to take the test together is a personal decision that only you can make. A primary factor that will determine how you'll handle the pregnancy test is whether or not the pregnancy was planned.

Planned Pregnancies

If you're both looking forward to having a baby, then you'll be thrilled to know for sure that you're pregnant. You may be surprised, however, to find yourself experiencing a host of unanticipated emotions as well.

You may have daydreamed about snuggling up in bed with your partner and watching the results of your pregnancy test together, and this dream may come true. But you may find that when the time comes, you prefer to take the test alone. Why? Perhaps you're not sure how you will respond to the result and want some privacy to sort through your feelings before sharing the result with your partner. Or, you may choose to take the test in private to avoid disappointing your partner if the result is negative. In either case, make the decision after talking with your partner about both of your concerns and preferences, so that you'll plan for the important moment in a way that meets both of your needs.

DOING THE TEST ON YOUR OWN

If you let your partner know that you want to do the test by yourself, he may not only understand your need for privacy, but might even prefer it that way. Maybe he'd rather hear the big news the way it was given in old movies—with you making the announcement during a special candlelight dinner you've prepared for him.

You'll want to plan the best moment to give your partner the news. You've already experienced the moment of discovering you're pregnant when you took the test, so you probably know that the joy is mixed with anxiety. That's natural! It's one thing to dream about having a child—to imagine each time you make love that your deep, passionate connection to one another is creating a new life. It's another thing altogether to face the fact that you are now responsible for another human being.

> **TIP**
>
> *A fun way of letting your partner know that he's going to be a daddy is by placing a teddy bear with a sign that reads "You did it!" on his pillow. You can also use a doll with a rubber ball underneath its dress to make it look pregnant. Watch his reaction.*
>
> *Another way is to wrap up a book on sex and pregnancy, just like this one, and leave it at his place at the dinner table. Not only will he find out that you're pregnant, but he'll also get the message that you are definitely still interested in sex.*

Choosing to have and care for a baby is, perhaps, the only irrevocable decision you'll make in your life. You can always change where you live, what you do for a living, who your friends are, and, if worse comes to worse, to whom you are married. But when you have a child, you become a parent for the rest of your life.

Having a baby is one of the few sure things left in today's transient world. No one can take away the deeply rooted love you have for your child or the love that is returned. And no one can take away the joy of seeing your child's innate gifts develop as he or she matures. But the great joys of having a child are matched by the demanding challenges of raising him or her. You don't just watch a child grow; you nurture, cajole, support, protect, and direct a child into adulthood.

When you find out that you're pregnant, you will experience many, sometimes conflicting, emotions. You will certainly be excited, but at the same time, scared. What is pregnancy going to be like? Will I feel physically well enough to work the same way that I do now? After the baby is born, will we be able to balance both parenthood and careers? Will my boss see me in the same light? What if there is something wrong with the baby? These are only some of the questions that will race through your mind—not only at the moment when you find out you're pregnant, but perhaps throughout your pregnancy. Hopefully, you will have discussed these anxieties with your partner. In addition, a friend, sister, or mother to whom you can talk about your worries and who'll reassure you that everything will be okay is a great support.

Your partner will also go through a variety of emotions when you tell him the big news. He may have some worries of his own, so do not be surprised and offended if his initial reaction is not as excited as you expected him to be. If the first words from him are thoughts such as, "How can we afford a baby? We barely get by ourselves," do not be alarmed. Before breaking the news to him, send out feelers to gauge what type of day he has had. A call to him at work before leaving the office for the day is one way to find out. Better yet, you can snuggle with him on the couch after the two of you get home and ask him about his day. This will give him a chance to unburden himself of any troubles, so that he can be more receptive to the big news. Or, if he's had a really bad day and can't seem to shake it off, postpone sharing your secret until a more opportune moment.

What if you want to do the test alone, but your partner wants to participate? One easy solution is to perform the test twice—once in private and once together. Some pregnancy tests even come two to a package, so you won't have to buy a second one.

DOING THE TEST TOGETHER

If you agree to do the test together, make sure you do it when neither one of you has to run off to work or an important appointment. If the result is positive, you'll want time to savor the joyous moment together. If the result is negative, you'll want to have time to reassure and comfort each other and perhaps, plan another month of delicious procreative sex!

Whether the test is positive or negative, whether you do it by yourself or together, the highly emotional moment can ignite romantic feelings, and along with them, desire. What better way to respond to a negative result than by trying again right away? And if the result is positive, what better way to celebrate than by making love?

Unplanned Pregnancies

Pregnancy carries with it some very strong emotions, and they're not always positive. This is particularly true if the pregnancy was unplanned, but then planning a pregnancy is a fairly recent development. For both partners, an unplanned pregnancy may mean that feelings of guilt and anxiety can take over the relationship. For recently married couples, who have not yet established a secure emotional and financial

ASK DR. RUTH

Q My wife just found out that she's pregnant and she's overjoyed. I have to admit that I'm a lot less enthusiastic. Although we had talked about wanting to have children some day, we hadn't planned this pregnancy. I've just started my own business, and the extra responsibility of having a child, not to mention the sleepless nights, on top of the 15 hours a day I'm already working, will be overwhelming. I sometimes wish she wasn't pregnant, but I don't have the guts to bring it up. I'm putting up a good front now, but inside I'm starting to panic.

A I can understand why you're so upset. Even when two people have decided it's the right time to have a baby, they feel overwhelmed when they find out it's actually going to happen. Modern contraception gives us the illusion that we can pinpoint the perfect moment to have a baby. In reality, there is no perfect moment. No one can really be sure when conception will occur. And so much can happen during the nine months of pregnancy that what seemed like a good time may become an inconvenient one, and vice versa.

My advice, therefore, is to tough it out and support your wife's decision to have this baby. Let her support you too—tell her your concerns. Children are going to interrupt your lifestyle whenever you have them. But they also will bring with them so much love and joy that soon you'll feel that it is your work that is interrupting your time with your baby!

base, the prospect can be frightening. At the other extreme, older couples must deal with the medical realities of a high-risk pregnancy and the responsibility of caring for young children at a time when contemporaries are experiencing a rebirth of freedom as their children become more independent.

But an unplanned pregnancy is not necessarily an unwanted pregnancy. If you discover you are unexpectedly pregnant, the first step is not to panic. Evaluate your feelings. Consider whether there really ever is a perfect time for a baby. Then, talk honestly with your partner; understand that his first reaction may be fear and anxiety, but he may come to accept—and even welcome—the news.

Miscarriages

The sensitivity of new pregnancy tests also means that many women now find out that they are pregnant even before they have missed a period. What used to pass as a late period is now often recognized as a miscarriage. In fact, miscarriages can occur in up to four out of ten pregnancies, especially if you include the very early ones, which, in the past, were not recognized as such.

More than half of miscarriages occur because of an abnormal chromosome count. Nature sometimes makes mistakes, and a miscarriage is how nature amends them. If you suspect a miscarriage, contact your caregiver immediately. Remember that a great majority of women who have a miscarriage go on to have a perfectly healthy pregnancy the next time.

The Announcement

Eventually you will want to let people beyond those intimates on your short list know about the new development in your lives. This is one secret, after all, that will eventually reveal itself. Once people know, you will receive lots of advice and be asked many questions. So, be prepared and announce the good news when you are ready. You and your partner may want some time alone to enjoy and adjust to the news. In addition, many expectant parents choose to wait to spread the word about their baby's pending arrival until later on in their pregnancy, when they are more confident about the news about the pregnancy. They worry that if something unexpected happens, they'll have to go through the agonizing process of telling a lot of people the bad news. Some couples choose not to breathe a word about a pregnancy to anyone until they've passed through the first few months of pregnancy and there is less risk of miscarriage. This is a natural reaction, and you needn't feel worried or ashamed of it. You don't owe anyone a first edition of your announcement. It's perfectly reasonable to wait until you're comfortable about sharing the news with other people, even your parents or other close relatives.

Sharing the News with Your Children

If you already have children, you need to decide how and when to inform them about your pregnancy. Your decision will depend in part on how old they are, but the best way is to announce the news simply and straightforwardly. Then, let them ask questions. That way, you will know what information they need to understand the changes that will take place. Today, expectant parents can find lots of books appropriate to different age levels that help explain pregnancy to children at different age levels. For young children, a simple picture book that shows how mommy will look and how the baby is growing is probably enough.

Ask for their help and understanding. Let them know you may be more tired than usual or feel uncomfortable at times, but reassure them of your love and try to prepare them emotionally for a new sibling. Buy a doll and use it to teach them about babies—how to hold them, bathe them, and feed them. Let the child feel like a participant, not an outsider.

Sharing the News at Work

When should you tell your employer? This is a difficult question to answer. The majority of women can continue to work through their pregnancies; some even work until their due date. However, you need to review your work activities to determine if there might be a negative effect on your pregnancy. For example, does your job involve long periods standing on your feet; carrying heavy loads; exposure to potentially harmful substances, such as lead or anesthetic gases; or exposure to high temperatures? In addition, certain medical conditions may make certain types of work hazardous. If you have a preexisting condition or if your workplace poses any potential problems, discuss the situation with your health care provider, preferably before you become pregnant, and certainly as soon as possible after you've conceived.

Keep in mind that pregnancy, by itself, is not a disability, although you may qualify for short-term disability benefits after the birth occurs. But an employer or supervisor cannot discriminate against you just because you are going to have a baby. Telling people at work early in the pregnancy might, in fact, help you in those cases where the workplace may present some of the hazards discussed. You may be able to request a reassignment to prevent potential problems.

If you plan to return to work after the baby is born, you may want to think through your plans before announcing your pregnancy. Consider if you might want to return part time, if you would like to take advantage of flexible working hours, or if your schedule will permit any necessary overtime. Once you know what you want, you will be better able to answer the inevitable questions your employer will ask. Keep in mind that some women who plan to return to work right after the pregnancy when they first learn that they are pregnant may change their minds after the baby is born.

First Things First

Now that you know you are pregnant, the next step is to decide where to deliver your baby and who you want as your health care provider. If you make these decisions before becoming pregnant, you already know what to do. If you haven't chosen a provider yet, we suggest that before you select one, first decide on the hospital where you want to deliver your baby. Once you've made that decision, look for the right person to provide prenatal care and deliver your baby.

Choosing a Hospital

Just as all doctors are not equal, all hospitals are not either. Hospitals range from large university medical centers, which join teaching facilities with a hospital, to small community hospitals, which provide basic care with a personal touch. Some hospitals have strict policies that set guidelines that providers have to follow for labor and delivery; others allow women and their providers to follow their own preferences.

T I P

How strict or lenient a hospital's policies are will be of concern to those who want to follow a particular method of labor and delivery, so make sure to ask whether or not the hospital you are touring allows for personal preferences during birth.

In general, hospital policies are changing with the times. In the past, most hospitals had very strict, traditional policies about labor and delivery; today, many are more flexible about allowing providers and women to implement individual practices. Many more hospitals are allowing midwives to deliver babies and provide rooms where women can labor and deliver in the same bed instead of being moved from a labor area to a delivery room.

How many options you have to consider for your birth will depend on where you live and with what institutions your provider is affiliated. Obviously, a large metropolitan area like Chicago or Los Angeles will have many options, large and small, while a smaller community will have fewer. Some practitioners are affiliated with several hospitals; others work at only one. It is perfectly legitimate to decide that you want to deliver at a specific facility and choose a doctor who can deliver there, rather than the other way around.

BIRTHING ROOMS

Although you'll probably give birth in a hospital, you're not going there because you are sick. The only reason you're in a hospital setting is in case of a last-minute problem. Giving birth is perfectly natural, and more and more hospitals are taking this into account when designing their maternity wards. Modern hospitals are designed to make your experience as pleasant as possible. For instance, many now provide birthing rooms that look like bedrooms, where a woman can go through labor and delivery in one bed, and where family members can visit and even be present for the birth.

ANESTHESIA

Chief among fears of pregnant women is being in too much pain during labor and delivery. Today, many options for pain relief, both traditional and nontraditional, are available. Make sure to inquire about what options will be available to you. Find out if the hospital has an anesthesiologist—a specialist in pain relief—who has had training in caring for pregnant women. Ask if 24-hour support is available for your choice of anesthesia. This is also a good time to inquire about the percentage of women who receive specific types of anesthesia during labor, and whether the hospital offers the so-called walking epidural, the latest kind of anesthesia that provides pain relief while allowing women to walk around during labor.

NEONATAL INTENSIVE CARE UNITS

In most cases, the baby you deliver will be perfectly healthy. Sometimes complications arise that require swift intervention, such as when a baby is born prematurely. The neonatal intensive care unit, or NICU, is usually the place where high-risk newborns are transferred for care and observation after birth.

Hospital neonatal intensive care units are graded according to the depth of care they provide—Level I for low-risk care and Level III for high-risk care. You'll want to know what level of NICU, if any, is available in each hospital you tour and whether a pediatrician is available to deal with any problems.

Birthing Centers

A birthing center offers an experience in a home-like setting, rather than in a traditional labor and delivery room. Only women who have low-risk pregnancies should consider having their babies in birthing centers. Birthing centers are small, intimate settings in which the rooms look more like bedrooms than hospital rooms. These centers offer the minimum of intervention (i.e., no intravenous procedures, epidural anesthesia, electronic monitoring, and so forth) for the optimal natural childbirth process. They often have jacuzzis and other amenities and are staffed by midwives or doctors.

Some birthing centers may be located inside hospitals, separate from the traditional labor and delivery units. Others are free-standing facilities, separate from hospital buildings.

The advantage of hospital-based birthing centers is that facilities are available to handle a problem on site, so if a crisis arises during a delivery, the mother can easily receive the necessary care. In a free-standing birthing center, a mother experiencing difficulties has to be transferred to the nearest hospital, often with precious time lost for transportation.

Childbirth at Home

Although millions of women around the world still deliver healthy babies at home, we do not recommend it. We have seen many unexpected emergencies turn out well in a hospital that would have been problems at home. That being said, some women may consider their home an alternative to in-hospital childbirth. If you should decide to deliver your baby at home, we suggest you find a provider who is experienced in home birth and can determine if you are a good candidate for this option.

Choosing a Health Care Provider

After you've chosen a facility in which to give birth, your next step is to choose your health care provider and set up your first appointment. We use the word health care provider rather than doctor because in this field, you have a few alternatives. However, we may use the terms doctor, health care practitioner, health care provider, caregiver, and numerous other terms interchangeably throughout the book when referring to the professional who is helping you through your pregnancy. Table 1 lists different professionals who are capable of helping

TABLE 1 Health Care Providers

	Training	Board Certification	Expertise
Obstetrician/gynecologist	Four years medical school followed by four years of residency in obstetrics and gynecology.	Yes. Written and oral examination required. Recertification required every ten years.	May handle all kinds of pregnancies, from the routine to complicated. May consult a specialist for unusual complications.
Maternal-fetal medicine (MFM) specialists (also known as perinatologists)	Four years of medical school, plus four years of residency in obstetrics and gynecology, plus two to three years specialized training in high-risk obstetrics.	Yes. Written and oral examination required. Additional subspecialty written and oral examinations. Required to write a thesis.	Oversees part or all of prenatal care for high-risk pregnancies, such as multiple births, high blood pressure, diabetes, lupus, or some other medical or surgical conditions.
Family practitioner/ general practitioner	Four years of medical school, followed by three to four years of residency in family practice.	Yes.	Routine pregnancies.
Midwives	Four years of training as a registered nurse, plus one to two years of formal education in approved programs. Usually affiliated with an obstetrician, who is available in case of complications or emergencies.	Yes. Written National Boards with requirement by ACNM to maintain continuing educational credit.	Low-risk, uncomplicated pregnancies and those who prefer the least medical intervention.

you through your pregnancy and provides information about the training and expertise required for each category.

Your relationship with your caregiver during your pregnancy will last at least last nine months, if not more. Therefore, it is critical that you choose someone you both trust and with whom both of you feel comfortable. That's why we suggest that you interview your top candidates in person.

Whether you're entitled to choose from the entire universe of providers or are limited to those affiliated with your health insurance company, you should definitely interview your primary candidates before choosing one. You're going to be spending nine very intense months with your health care provider, leading up to the most intimate moment you'll probably ever share with a "stranger"—giving birth to your child. You want to be as certain as you can that your relationship is going to work.

During your interviews, listen to your inner voice at least as much as to the cold facts you gather from each practitioner. Some intangible issues cannot be addressed in a question and answer session. Only your intuition can tell you if a professional is rushing you; is not giving you his or her full attention; or is at ease talking about any subject—even something as private as sex. These intangibles are as important, if not more so, at crucial moments than the nuts and bolts information, so let your intuition guide you.

You probably already have many questions on your minds that you're eager to ask your caregiver. Before you meet with him or her, think carefully about what you want to know. To help you organize your thoughts, we've listed some questions you should ask. We hope it will encourage you to think of other issues that are particularly important to you.

1. What is your training?
2. How long have you been in practice?
3. How many babies have you delivered?
4. Are you board certified?
5. What hospital are you affiliated with?
6. Do you have partners in your practice? What will your partner's role be in the pregnancy?
7. If you do not have partners, who covers for you when you are not available? Will I get to meet that person during my care?

8. What is your cesarean section rate? (The overall average cesarean rate for American women is approximately 24 percent).

9. Do you have any special philosophy about pregnancy and birth?

10. What routine procedures do you follow during labor and delivery and why? (For example, do you administer enemas, attach an intravenous line [to put medications directly into your blood stream], perform a routine episiotomy, allow walking during labor?)

11. What are your office procedures regarding billing, appointments, and phone calls?

12. What is your fee, and what services are included?

T I P

These days many doctors work in a group. You may see one doctor for your office visits, but if he or she is not on call when you're ready to give birth, the doctor who is on call will deliver your baby. For that reason, it's a good idea to learn something about the other providers in the group, for instance, do they all share similar practice philosophies? If not, what differences exist among them?

Of course, if you prefer a specific method of labor and delivery, ask if the practitioner will support your decision. Ask if the practitioner thinks there are any risks associated with the type of birth you are considering.

A note for the future dad: It may be a little unorthodox to suggest that you make a list of your own concerns about your partner's caregiver, but he or she is going to play a critical role in your pregnancy, particularly during the delivery. Because you are going to be your partner's mouthpiece and advocate, especially during delivery, you need to feel comfortable dealing with the provider. You may want to read ahead in this book to become familiar with what will be happening over the next nine months. That might help you formulate your own list of questions.

Aside from evaluating your interaction with the provider, you'll also want to take into consideration other aspects of the practice. Were the nurse and administration staff pleasant, informative, and responsive? You should come away feeling that you're encouraged to call with any question or concern, no matter how minor.

If you have access to E-mail, ask your provider if he or she can be contacted by E-mail. This will give you access to your provider, although you should not expect an immediate response. And you should definitely not use this method of communication for emergencies!

One of the factors to weigh when choosing your provider is the hospital or birth center where you'll be delivering your baby. It's a good idea to tour the maternity areas of the facilities with which your candidates are affiliated.

T I P

Make a written list of questions each time you see your caregiver, not just for the initial interview. How many times have you left a doctor's office and said to yourself, "Darn, I wish I had asked about such and such." It's easy to forget concerns that you have at home or work when you're in a different environment. That's especially so when there's an exciting development during your office visit, such as hearing your baby's heartbeat for the first time. So keep a notebook at hand and write down your questions as they come up. You might also want to write down the answers to your questions so that you can refer back to them later.

Your Medical Insurance

The kind of medical insurance you have is likely to have a significant impact on your choice of health care practitioner. Many women today belong to health maintenance organizations (HMOs), a prepaid medical service in which members pay a monthly or yearly fee for all medical services, or an insurance plan. HMOs usually allow women to have two primary care physicians—a general practitioner and an obstetrician/gynecologist, who can be chosen from a list of participating physicians. This is good if you feel that you have received quality care from the doctors who participate in your HMO.

What happens, however, if you have your heart set on going to a doctor about whom your best friend has been raving, but he or she is not affiliated with your HMO? Under these circumstances, you have several options. Find out if your HMO provides an out-of-plan option, which allows plan participants to use doctors outside of the HMO. Or ask the doctor if he or she would consider joining the plan to which you belong. Doctors are constantly expanding the number of HMOs with which they are affiliated. You may even find out that the doctor you prefer is already in the process of joining your plan. If not, ask the doctor to do you a favor by reviewing your HMO listings and referring you to any like-minded practitioners. If these don't work, you can always go the traditional route of asking the doctor what his or her fees are and paying the fee as you would if you were not part of an HMO. The most significant expense in having a baby is hospital care, which is a separate fee that is covered by most HMOs even if your caregiver is not affiliated with the HMO. You should find out how many nights you and your baby can stay in the hospital. There is controversy about the fact that HMOs and insurance carriers are "rushing" mothers and their newborns home too quickly. What happens if there is a problem and you or your child need to stay longer? A simple call to your HMO or insurance carrier will answer these questions.

> **TIP**
>
> A word about advice from friends and relatives concerning the choice of a doctor. Bear in mind that what works for your friend or relative may not work for you. You wouldn't necessarily have married your best friend's husband, for instance, or chosen the same wedding dress as she did, so don't assume that her choice of provider is the right one for you.

The Other Health Care Provider—You

Once you have chosen your health care provider and a hospital, you have nine months to prepare for the big event. During this time, you are your most important health care provider. It's up to you to take care of your body and your baby and make sure that you're in top shape for the big event.

Weight Gain

Having a baby is going to cause changes in your body. That's a fact. With all the emphasis on skinniness in our culture, it's hard for most women to accept the added padding—particularly on the hips and backside—that is a normal and healthy part of pregnancy. You need a

From Our Files

Cathy had been trying to get pregnant for almost a year, so she was thrilled to discover that after all of this time she really was going to have a baby. The first resolution she made was not to allow this pregnancy to result in her gaining back all of the weight she had lost a few years ago. It was too much of a struggle to get it off and keep it off, and she didn't want to go through it again.

Her doctor had told her that she should expect to gain between 25 and 30 pounds, but she thought she could get away with less. She knew she had to eat healthy foods, which she did anyway. Since she was taking her prenatal vitamins religiously, she figured that she could skimp a little on the meat and milk and fill up on salad and fruit, like she was used to.

Cathy's husband was concerned that his wife's diet was not the healthiest for the baby. He had read that a pregnant woman requires protein, calcium, and other nutrients found in some of the very foods she was avoiding. They decided to ask this question of their caregiver, who then worked with Cathy to establish a healthy diet for both mother and baby.

healthy diet to build a healthy baby. Most women should gain between 25 and 30 pounds. Those who are underweight should gain slightly more, and those who are overweight slightly less. Some women gain a lot of weight early in their pregnancy, and some put on more weight in the last few months. You don't need to go to the other extreme, however, and literally eat for two. Nor can you build a healthy baby on a diet of rich desserts. Remember, when it comes to food, it's nearly the same as sex. Quality is usually better than quantity. Table 2 shows how these pounds should be distributed during pregnancy.

A Healthy Diet　In order to get the additional nutrition you need, you'll need to increase your intake of food by approximately 10 to 15 percent (that is, from approximately 2200 to 2500 calories a day for the average woman). That's only an additional 200 to 300 calories, which you can get from one extra portion of lean meat or low-fat cottage cheese.

The biggest change in your diet will probably be what you eat, not how much. If you usually don't keep track of how much you are eating from each food group, now's the time to start. Table 3 shows the changes in recommended dietary allowances for pregnant women and lists possible food sources for each group.

TABLE 2 Average Distribution of Pounds Gained by a Woman During the Nine Months of Pregnancy

Baby	7 pounds
Mother's storage of fat and protein	5 pounds
Blood volume	5 pounds
Breasts	1 to 2 pounds
Increased body water	2 to 3 pounds
Uterus	2 pounds
Placenta	1 pound
Amniotic fluid	2 pounds
Total (on average)	26 pounds

TABLE 3 Summary of Recommended Dietary Allowances for Women Aged 25-50 Years, Changes from Nonpregnant to Pregnant, and Food Sources

Nutrient	Nonpregnant	Pregnant	Percent Increase	Food Sources
Energy (kcal)	2,200.0	2,500.0	+ 13.5	Proteins, carbohydrates, fats
Protein (g)	50.0	60.0	+ 20.0	Meats, fish, poultry, dairy
Calcium (mg)	800.0	1,200.0	+ 50.0	Dairy
Phosphorus (mg)	800.0	1,200.0	+ 50.0	Meats
Magnesium (mg)	280.0	320.0	+ 14.3	Seafood, legumes, grains
Iron (mg)	15.0	30.0	+100.0	Meats, eggs, grain
Zinc (mg)	12.0	15.0	+ 25.0	Meats, seafood, eggs
Iodine (µg)	150.0	175.0	+ 16.7	Iodized salt, seafood
Vitamin A (µg RE)	800.0	800.0	0.0	Dark green, yellow, or orange fruits and vegetables, liver
Vitamin D (IU)	200.0	400.0	+100.0	Fortified dairy products
Thiamin (mg)	1.1	1.5	+ 36.3	Enriched grains, pork
Riboflavin (mg)	1.3	1.6	+ 23.0	Meats, liver, enriched grains
Pyridozine (mg)	1.6	2.2	+ 37.5	Meats, liver, enriched grains
Niacin (mg NE)	15.0	17.0	+ 13.3	Meats, nuts, legumes
Vitamin B_{12} (µg)	2.0	2.2	+ 10.0	Meats
Folic acid (µg)	180.0	400.0	+122.0	Leafy vegetables, liver
Vitamin C (mg)	60.0	70.0	+ 16.7	Citrus fruits, tomatoes
Selenium (µg)	55.0	65.0	+ 18.2	Whole grains, peas, beans

Source: National Academy of Sciences

Be sure to drink enough fluids. The recommendation is 8 to 10 cups a day. Water is good, of course, as are herbal teas without caffeine, plain or flavored (but unsweetened) seltzer water, and fruit juices.

Keep in mind that everyone benefits from a healthy diet, so your need to eat nutritious meals should not make you an exception. With your partner, plan weekly menus that include all the food groups in the proper amounts. That way, you buy exactly what you need and avoid temptation or ill-advised choices as you rush through the supermarket trying to create a meal at the last minute.

T I P

Natural fruit juices are full of vitamins that are good for you, but they are full of calories, too. If you like to drink a lot of juice, try making a juice spritzer by combining 1/3 juice with 2/3 plain seltzer, or 1/4 juice with 3/4 seltzer.

Exercise

Eating a nutritious diet is one important way to keep you and your baby healthy. Staying physically active is another. If you weren't exercising regularly before you became pregnant, now is not the time to start a strenuous routine. If you have been playing sports regularly, we suggest that you continue with those that are safe, as long as you don't overextend yourself. Keep the following guidelines in mind while you exercise:

- Monitor your heart rate regularly and slow down when it reaches 140 beats per minute.
- Keep yourself hydrated by drinking plenty of water, especially if the weather is hot and humid.

T I P

One way to make sure that you're not exercising too hard without stopping to check your pulse every few minutes is to exercise at a level where you can carry on a conversation with someone (or sing to yourself if you're alone) without catching your breath.

- Wear layers of loose, comfortable clothing, and remove layers to prevent overheating.
- Stop playing or exercising long before you become exhausted.

KEGEL EXERCISES

This is one type of exercise that you can't overdo, and its benefits will last you well beyond the birth of your child. Kegels are designed to strengthen the pubococcygeal, or PC, muscle. Strengthening these muscles will not only help you deliver your baby, but also give you better control over your bladder and (best of all) give your lover extra pleasure during intercourse.

The great thing about doing Kegel exercises is that no one can tell when you're doing them. You can do them while sitting at your desk at work, behind the wheel of your car, or while waiting for the bus at a bus station. The hardest part of the exercise is locating the muscle.

To identify the PC muscle, sit on the toilet and begin to urinate. Voluntarily stop the stream and release it. The muscle you use to do that is the PC muscle, and the contraction and release you've just done is the Kegel exercise.

To feel the effect of your PC muscle, lie on your bed and relax all of your muscles. Then, place your finger in your vagina and contract your PC muscle. The squeezing on your finger is your PC muscle working.

Once you've identified the PC muscle, you can begin an exercise program. It's very simple. Contract the muscle, hold for 10 seconds (or as long as you can), and release. Repeat the exercise 10 times, and do the whole routine six times a day. As you develop strength, you'll be able to hold the contraction for longer counts and do the routine more often.

> **TIP**
>
> *To make it more fun, put your partner's finger in your vagina as you perform your Kegel exercise! Who knows, this could lead to something exciting. Or, you could do Kegel exercises using his penis. We can assure you that he'll enjoy being your Kegel coach!*

By the way, men have the same muscle, which they can discover in the same way by voluntarily stopping and releasing their urine. This exercise will help them achieve greater control over their ejaculation.

You're All Set

You've both begun one of the most wonderful and challenging adventures of your lives. You will now be beginning the next phase. And we're going to be with you every step of the way.

$\mathscr{T}$HE FIRST TRIMESTER: THE NEW YOU

THE first trimester is a special time because you know you're pregnant, but the good news is still yours to tell. Although you may have made some minor changes to your lifestyle, such as drinking decaffeinated beverages instead of coffee, your pregnant state is not yet noticeable. That's good. As joyous as expecting a baby might be, it's going to take you and you partner a little getting used to. It's a lot easier to adjust without the rest of the world looking on.

Strengthening the Bond

The ability to ease into your pregnancy gives you and your partner a wonderful opportunity to strengthen your relationship with each other. And a strong relationship is more important than ever. Pregnancy, delivery, and the months afterward are challenging, The closer the two of you are at the start, the better you'll come out at the end. So, while life is still relatively normal, make time to be alone together to talk about your feelings.

No matter how happy or busy you are, some anxieties about your new condition are natural. Even the father may undergo some physical changes. In addition, he has his own concerns. He may be worried about losing his partner's attention after the baby is born, about financial responsibilities, and even about how his partner will change physically. Pregnancy has its difficult moments for him too. So, share

From Our Files

Jim, a freelance writer and his wife, Maryanne, a lawyer, are expecting their first child. When Maryanne started experiencing morning sickness and the tiredness that comes with early pregnancy, both of their mothers tried to help as much as possible. Jim knew that he shouldn't be jealous of all the attention Maryanne was receiving, but he couldn't help himself. He resented the fact that nobody seemed to care about the emotional changes he was undergoing.

In addition, Jim had another concern. Both he and Maryanne wanted to continue their careers after the baby was born. Because Jim worked at home and his hours were flexible, they agreed that after a few months, she would go back to work and he would take care of the baby. Jim, however, wasn't as confident as he pretended to be that he could juggle both taking care of a baby and writing.

At this stage, Jim is a bit overwhelmed by the experience of pregnancy and the commitments he has made. He is realizing that helping his wife through the pregnancy and then taking care of a newborn, while still writing creatively, is overambitious. He needs to lessen the pressure he has put on himself. First, he should admit his concerns to Maryanne, so that they can find a solution together or discuss the problem with a therapist. One suggestion is that Jim use the baby's first few months as a wonderful opportunity to do some reading that is relevant to his writing and think through some of his ideas for new works. However, he should hold off producing new material of his own until the baby is on a less demanding schedule. This way, he will be contributing toward his professional goals in a less demanding way that will enable him to meet the needs of his newborn.

your feelings with each other. Just knowing that you have each other to count on will boost your courage. Talk about your expectations for the future. Are you uncertain about returning to work full time once the baby arrives? Do you feel a need to move to a new home or a different neighborhood? In discussing your concerns, remain flexible about your options. Remember that not all changes have to be made before the baby is born and that most decisions aren't forever. If you make a choice that doesn't turn out as you expected, such as deciding to work at home part time, you can always change your mind.

From Embryo to Fetus

A normal pregnancy lasts on the average 40 weeks from the first day of the menses until the due date. It is usually divided into three-month periods called trimesters. You may find, however, that your doctor divides the pregnancy into halves or weeks or even five parts that include three months each before and after the pregnancy. Whatever divisions you or your caregiver use to follow the progress of your pregnancy, you should know about the various changes that will occur during the different stages. For our purposes, pregnancy is divided into the traditional trimesters.

During the first week of the pregnancy, the fertilized egg, or the embryo, starts to divide rapidly and implants itself in the uterus. The following six to seven weeks are crucial because it is the time when most of the organs are developing. During the first three weeks, the spinal canal is open. It closes 26 to 28 days after fertilization. After the fourth week, the heart starts to beat. Although the beat is irregular at first, within a week it becomes regular. Approximately six weeks after fertilization, the extremities begin to form as short fins, eventually growing into arms, legs, hands, and feet. At this point, the embryo has developed into a fetus.

Beginning a Healthy Pregnancy

We cannot overemphasize the importance of maintaining your health before and during pregnancy to ensure a healthy pregnancy and a healthy child. A woman who is physically fit, follows a nutritious diet, is at her optimal weight, and avoids harmful substances gives herself and her baby a head start. As soon as you suspect you may be pregnant, immediately see your caregiver. The earlier a high-risk pregnancy is detected, the more doctors can do to protect it.

Recent research has shown that adding a supplement called folic acid to your diet might prevent birth defects, such as neural tube defects (NTDs), including spina bifida, in which the neural tube in the embryo fails to close completely.

Exercise

The first trimester can be well under way before a woman is aware of her pregnancy. Because the fetus undergoes so many crucial changes during these months, women who are trying to conceive are well advised to maintain a healthy lifestyle even before they're sure they're pregnant.

Once they are pregnant, the majority of women can continue their usual activities. There is no proof that regular activity, such as jogging, playing tennis, swimming, or engaging in sex, leads to problems such as miscarriages or fetal malformations in the majority of normal, healthy women. Most caregivers recommend against starting a new exercise program while your're pregnant, except for prenatal exercises designed specifically for pregnant women.

The exercises that are most beneficial for pregnant women are those that strengthen the abdominal wall to help support the growing uterus and the pelvic muscles that you'll need for pushing. Leg exercises are also important to improve circulation and avoid the muscle cramping that is common in pregnancy.

You should, however, use common sense in selecting your activities. Avoid activities that involve a high risk of injury, such as downhill skiing, horseback riding, and contact sports. Women should also avoid activities that raise the body temperature above 100.4 degrees Fahrenheit, because it may increase the risk of the fetus developing certain problems. Such activities include exercising too vigorously for more than thirty minutes, particularly in hot, humid weather, and sitting in a hot tub, sauna, or steam room for too long. In addition,

From Our Files

Georgette and Burt weren't planning on having children just yet. They had been married only a year and wanted to savor married life a few more years before taking on the added responsibility of a child. But they were not as conscientious about using birth control after they were married, and Georgette unexpectedly became pregnant.

By the time Georgette made her first appointment with her doctor, she was already ten weeks pregnant. She was alarmed to see horseback riding on the list of things a pregnant women should not do. She had been horseback riding just two weeks earlier while chaperoning a group of high school students on a trip to a dude ranch. Georgette was worried that she might have injured her baby, but her doctor reassured her that there was very little likelihood that she had caused her baby any harm.

Now that she has been reassured, Georgette should be careful not to focus on the timing of the pregnancy. As the months pass, her concerns should be replaced by feelings of joy, happiness, and anticipation. With a good relationship, Georgette and Burt should reassure each other that even after the baby arrives, they will make time for each other. In fact, they can even arrange now for a babysitter to come once a week so they know they will have time to go out together.

women with a history of difficult pregnancies or those with special problems should consult their caregivers about which activities are appropriate.

Women whose pregnancies are unplanned should not be overly concerned that their activities during the first few months before they knew they were pregnant have harmed the fetus. The odds are no harm has been done.

What to Avoid In the past, the embryo and the fetus were believed to be safely protected within the uterus. In the 1960s, however, a drug called thalidomide radically changed prevailing thought. Thalidomide, which was given to pregnant women with sleeping problems, was subsequently found to have potentially devastating effects on the developing embryo. Since then, other harmful agents, called *teratogens,* that cause malformations in the fetus or embryo have been identified. Teratogens include specific drugs, viruses, or radiation. Fortunately, only a few teratogenic drugs that are commonly used must be avoided during pregnancy. They include certain male hormones, chemotherapy drugs, anticoagulants, and anticonvulsants.

Chapter 1 listed some of the substances, such as alcohol, tobacco, and illegal drugs, that should be avoided completely before and during pregnancy. In addition to these, substances mentioned below should be avoided not only throughout your pregnancy, but also during the first trimester.

TOXIC SUBSTANCES

If you work with potentially hazardous substances or chemicals, discuss them with your caregiver to determine whether or not they pose a risk to the baby. Avoid prolonged exposure to certain household products, such as cleansers, pesticides, paints and paint removers, and products that cause fumes, such as oven cleaners and aerosol sprays. Consider using alternative natural products if they are available. Make sure there is plenty of ventilation, no matter what cleansers you use. If you want the baby's room painted, pick out the colors and leave the painting to someone else. Open the windows and leave the house for a few hours while the room is being painted and the fumes air out. If you want any furniture refinished, ask someone else to do it in the basement or outdoors. If your water pipes are old, check your water supply for lead. In certain areas, you should also check for radon inside your home.

HAIR GROOMING AIDS

Although no conclusive evidence links hair dyes or curling chemicals to birth defects or miscarriages, it is safer to avoid using these products during pregnancy. If you must color your hair, ask your hair stylist to use a natural, vegetable-based dye. If you use an aerosol hairspray, consider switching to a pump spray instead.

EMISSIONS FROM HOUSEHOLD AND OFFICE EQUIPMENT

There has been some concern about exposure to certain emissions from office and household equipment, which have been reported to be linked to problems in pregnancy. These reports have been inconclusive, and although most office and household electronic equipment is considered safe to use, you can take steps to minimize exposure. Some suggestions for avoiding exposure to emissions from household or office equipment are:

- Check the seal around the doors of microwave ovens to make sure that it is intact. Don't stand in front of the microwave oven when it is on.
- There are screens available from your office supply stores that protect against emissions from video display terminals (VDTs), such as computer monitors and television screens. However, most radiation comes from behind computers. If you sit directly behind a VDT, move your desk to a different position.

X-RAYS

X-rays are used either to treat cancer (therapeutic X-rays) or to diagnose certain conditions (diagnostic X-rays), such as a broken bone. There is a tremendous difference between the two. Diagnostic X-rays usually emit low-level radiation that poses little risk, while therapeutic X-rays can be damaging. If you need to have an X-ray taken, tell your caregiver that you're pregnant. Maybe there is an alternative, such as an ultrasound test, that can be used. Take appropriate protective measures, such as putting a lead apron over your abdomen, while taking an X-ray. (This precaution should be taken whether or not you are pregnant to protect the eggs in the ovaries from exposure).

Your First Visit and Physical Exam

The moment you know you're pregnant, make an appointment with a health care professional. Hopefully, you have already seen your health care provider and had preconception care. If you have not had regular gynecological examinations until now, you may be squeamish about having some stranger looking into your vagina. Try to remember that your gynecologist is examining your vagina, cervix, and uterus as functioning parts of your body that are now in the process of creating another life. Focusing on your procreative, rather than on your sexual self, may help you to feel less uncomfortable about all of the prodding and probing that will be going on during the next nine months.

In Chapter 1, we describe your first visit for preconception care. Your first visit to your gynecologist or caregiver as a pregnant woman will be very similar, with further tests to determine if you have any problems that might negatively affect your pregnancy or the developing infant. Are all these tests really necessary? Yes! Why? First, because you are now responsible not only for your health, but also for that of the child you are carrying, and second, because pregnancy is a very in-

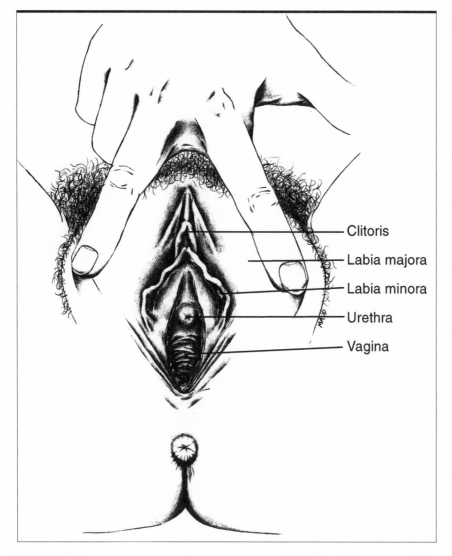

— Clitoris
— Labia majora
— Labia minora
— Urethra
— Vagina

FIGURE 1

During your first visit, your health care provider will examine your external genitalia.

tensive activity that stresses your body in many ways. It is vital for your doctor to know whether you have any problems that might negatively affect your pregnancy or the developing child. With advance knowledge of any potential difficulties, your health care provider can take appropriate steps to give you the best medical care.

Routine procedures at a first visit will include a complete physical examination as well as an examination of your genitalia (Figures 1 and 2). At that point, your doctor will also take a Pap smear (a screening test of your cervix) and a test of your vagina to check for chlamydia and gonorrhea. Your doctor will also carefully examine your cervix, which undergoes changes in appearance during pregnancy. He or she will also examine your ovaries and uterus by pressing on your abdomen.

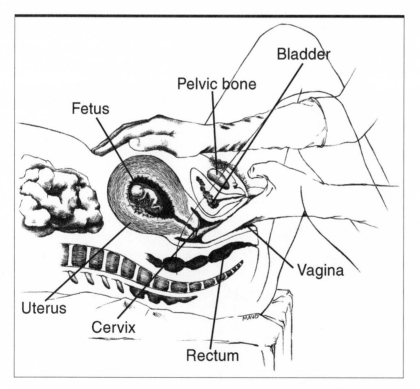

FIGURE 2

Your health care provider will also perform a pelvic examination, which enables her to check your cervix, uterus, and ovaries.

If you feel pain while this is being done, tell your doctor. This could be an indication of an ectopic pregnancy, which is a pregnancy that occurs in the fallopian tubes. Your doctor also will assess the shape and size of your pelvis to determine whether a normal-sized baby will fit through the birth canal during delivery.

Other procedures include urine and blood tests. Your urine will be checked for the presence of glucose, protein, blood cells, and signs of dehydration and infection. A blood test will determine your red cell, white cell, and platelet count. Other tests may also need to be done, for example, African-American women should be screened for sickle cell anemia and those of Ashkenazi Jewish descent for Tay-Sachs disease. The blood test will screen for syphilis; identify blood type; screen for antibodies; and determine if you are immune to rubella (German measles) or are carrying the hepatitis B virus. In addition, your doctor should also recommend that you be tested for the presence of antibodies against HIV, and she may also suggest additional tests, such as checking antibodies against cytomegalovirus, toxoplasmosis, and chicken pox.

During the first visit, many doctors might also do an ultrasound to take an image of the uterus and ovaries (Figure 3). A sonogram will enable your doctor to better assess how far along in your pregnancy

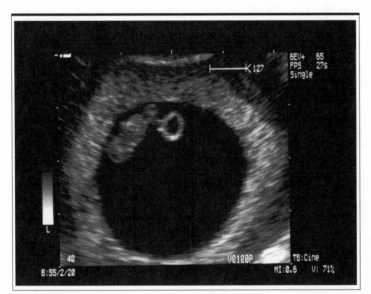

FIGURE 3

An example of an ultrasound image of a seven-week pregnancy.

you really are, where the pregnancy is located, and if there is more than one fetus. Often, the prospective parents can receive a sonogram photo of the baby to show to family and friends. Although often blurry, it can become the first entry in your photo album.

Estimating Your Due Date

On your first office visit, you'll finally ask that all important question: When is the baby due? You will want to know for several reasons—you will want to measure your progress; you will need to make arrangements at work; your friends will want to organize a baby shower. And, of course, both of your parents will want to know when they'll officially become grandparents.

But, the answer to your question will not be an exact date, but an estimation. The length of a pregnancy is calculated from the first day of your last menstrual period, which is called the menstrual age. You may ask, "How can the menstrual age be reliable if everyone's cycle is slightly different?" The answer is that it isn't meant to be exact. The menstrual age assumes that every woman's cycle is 28 days, and that every woman conceived two weeks after the first day of her last menstrual period (which is when you would have ovulated). Your due date is usually 266 days (38 weeks) after fertilization or, if you add 14 days, 280 days after the first day of your menstrual period, assuming a 28-day cycle. On the other hand, the due date for women with a 35-day cycle is still 266 days after fertilization, but 287 days after the first day of the menstrual period. Because most people find it hard to add days to a date on a calendar, there is a simple formula that most practitioner's use, called Naegele's rule. Take the first day of your last menstrual period, add seven days, and add nine months. Or, you can do it backward: From the first day of your last menstrual period, add seven days, subtract three months, and add a year.

If, for example, the first day of your last menstrual period was July 11, adding 7 days brings you to July 18. Now, add 9 months and you will get April 18. April 18 will be the estimated due date for your baby's arrival. By adding exactly 280 to July 11, you will also arrive at April 18, unless the next year is a leap year. Then, the date would be April 17. If you have a menstrual cycle longer than 28 days, you must add to that date the difference on days between your cycle and an average 28-day cycle. If your menstrual cycle is shorter than 28 days, subtract from that date the difference in days between your cycle and an average 28-day cycle.

If your cycle is 25 days and the first day of your last period is April 1, add 7 days. That's April 8. Subtract the three-day difference between your cycle of 25 days and 28 days and your due date is January 5.

But don't bet your house that the baby will definitely be born on the estimated due date. It is just an estimate. On average, only about five percent of babies are born exactly on the due date, but more than 80 percent are born in the period called *term,* which is within three weeks before and two weeks after the due date or between the 37th and 42nd weeks of the pregnancy. The due date is a range of five weeks within which the baby is expected to be born. A baby born more than three weeks before the due date, or before 37 weeks, is a preterm or premature baby. A baby born two weeks after, or after 42 weeks, is a postterm baby.

Even this calculation isn't foolproof, however. There are other factors that can throw it off by several weeks, such as if you have an irregular cycle, if you missed a period without being pregnant, or if you bled early in your pregnancy and mistook that for a period. Such a miscalculation probably won't last for the duration of your pregnancy. Thanks to modern science, it is likely that your due date will be confirmed, and adjusted if need be, based on ultrasound examinations, which are far more accurate at determining the age of the baby and the probable due date.

The New Pregnant You

Compare a picture of a woman just beginning her pregnancy to a picture of her just before she begins labor. You probably will have difficulty recognizing her. That's because a woman's body changes quite significantly through the nine months to adapt to her pregnancy.

The dramatic changes that your body is undergoing are caused by an intricate interplay of hormones that begin the moment you conceive. Interestingly, many of the same hormones that cause your monthly period, such as estrogen and progesterone, are also responsible for the changes that your body will go through during pregnancy. Although it is your abdomen that will eventually do most of the stretching, your breasts will begin to increase in size much earlier. In

T I P

Because our culture puts so much emphasis on women being slender, it's not uncommon for a pregnant woman, especially during a first pregnancy, to feel uncomfortable about her appearance. This is especially in the early months when her waist thickens, but she is not obviously pregnant. Trying to squeeze into clothing that no longer fits will only exacerbate those feelings. Rather than wait until the last possible moment to switch to maternity clothing, go out and buy a couple of outfits as soon as you have trouble zipping or buttoning your regular clothes. Any woman knows that not fitting into one's clothes can be very deflating. The solution? Buy clothes that fit!

fact, for some women, it is the tingling and tenderness in their breasts that are the very first signs of pregnancy. In addition, your breasts may secrete a light discharge. This is not unusual, unless there is blood in the discharge. If the tenderness in your breasts disappears early in your pregnancy or if you have a bloody discharge from your breasts, inform your caregiver immediately. These could be indications of problems, and you should have them checked out.

Aside from your growing stomach and fuller breasts, you will notice other visible changes in your body caused by other hormones. Melanocyte-stimulating hormones (MSH) may cause darkening of the skin in specific areas, particularly in women with darker complexions. Skin that is already pigmented, such as the nipples, is likely to become darker. You may notice a dark line called the linea nigra developing from the pubic hairline upward. This is a darkening of the ordinarily white midline, the linea alba, which you may not have noticed before.

Some women develop what is called a "pregnancy mask," or chloasma or melasma gravidarum, wich results in light patches on dark-skinned women and dark patches on light-skinned women. This discoloration will fade gradually after delivery. In the meantime, protect your face from the sun with a sunblock (SPF 15) and a hat, because sun exposure increases the pigmentation. You can also use make-up to even out your complexion. Bleaching, however, is ineffective as well as inadvisable.

Many women experience what is called morning sickness. This is a misnomer because the feelings of nausea that often last through the first trimester can occur any time during the day, and sometimes all day. Of the 40 percent to 50 percent of women who experience morning sickness, 75 percent actually vomit. It is not known exactly what causes morning sickness, although many explanations have been proposed. The most widely accepted cause of morning sickness is that increased hormone levels irritate the digestive system.

There are as many remedies for morning sickness as there are mothers, and it's worth trying as many as appeal to you. The tried-and-true method of eating bland crackers before getting out of bed does help some women avoid feeling queasy first thing in the morning. And many moms-to-be swear that nibbling on a cracker quells a wave of nausea in the office, so keep a snack bag in your purse. Strong odors; heavy, greasy, spicy foods; cigarette and cigar smoke; stress; and an empty stomach also are frequently mentioned triggers for nausea that should be avoided. Make sure to give yourself extra time to do everything to keep your level of stress down, and get plenty of rest. Even if you can't eat, make sure to drink plenty of fluids to prevent dehydration. If you can get down a fortified milkshake or fruit shake, all the better.

Most women today are aware of how important it is to the health of their baby to gain enough weight. They also know how vulnerable the fetus is in the first trimester, so they worry when morning sickness prevents them from eating more than soda and crackers for days on end. There's no need for anxiety, because morning sickness rarely affects a woman's nutritional intake enough to harm the fetus this early in pregnancy. Many women don't gain weight during the first trimester—and some even lose weight—because of morning sickness, but they make up for lost time later on and their babies turn out fine.

Many pregnant women, even those who are usually quite energetic, feel very tired in the early months of their pregnancy. This is probably caused by the increased level of progesterone, which has been documented to have a sedative effect. Don't worry. These doldrums will pass, usually after the first trimester, and you'll revert to your old energetic self.

Pregnancy hormones also cause your vagina's pH to change. There may be an increase in vaginal secretions and a change in the odor of your vagina. This discharge may increase as your pregnancy progresses and can become quite heavy toward the end.

A few adaptations in your personal hygiene can make you more comfortable with the changes in your vaginal discharge. For instance, wear a panty liner and change it frequently. Also, freshen up during the day with mild soap and water to keep the genital area clean and dry. In addition, avoid close-fitting clothing and fabric, such as spandex, because these materials don't breath. Cotton or cotton-crotched underwear is helpful. Many couples find the increased lubrication makes sex more pleasurable. Enjoy it!

One of the inconveniences that pregnant women have to endure is frequent urination. At least two reasons explain why you get the urge to urinate every five minutes. One is that the baby is pushing against your bladder. Second is that as a result of the increase in blood volume, your kidneys have a higher blood flow and consequently produce more urine. There's nothing much you can do about this. Cutting down on your fluid intake is not only useless, it is also not advisable because you need a lot of fluid. Fluids like water, fruit juices, and vegetable juices are important, so keep a glass of liquid nearby throughout your day.

Constipation is another common problem during pregnancy. This can be caused by hormonal changes that relax the bowel muscles, making them less efficient at elimination. To avoid constipation, include lots of fiber in your diet, such as raw or lightly cooked fruits and vegetables, and remember to drink 8 to 10 cups of water each day. Because most of the fiber in some produce is in the peel, don't remove it before eating and be sure to wash the produce thoroughly to remove any residue. If such natural measures don't give you adequate relief, talk with your health care provider and ask for other possible remedies. Natural stool softeners, such as bran or other fiber concentrates, may be recommended. Excessive pushing when the stool is hard can lead to or aggravate hemorrhoids.

Often, pregnant women experience mood swings. One day you feel elated and excited at the prospect of having a baby. The next day you may feel nauseous, tired, and depressed, and may want everyone around you to feel the same. You may have strange cravings—a cheeseburger at 2 AM—and conflicting emotions—feelings of deep love for your husband and resentment because he left the bed unmade before going to the office.

Some of these character alterations are the result of chemical changes in your body, but outside influences may also play a part. Research has shown that women who have a supportive partner, want the baby, and are financially secure are less likely to feel irritable than women who have less social support. Mothers, however, aren't the only people who have mixed feelings. Future fathers have been known to experience the mood swings and cravings commonly attributed to pregnant women. They may have difficulty coping with all the attention their partners are receiving and fear that they will be pushed aside once the baby comes. Both partners need to constantly reaffirm their commitment to each other and set aside time for themselves and for good sex.

Making Love

How your sex life is affected by these changes depends on how well your relationship is adapting to the prospect of becoming new parents. The more supportive you are of each other, the more your sex life will thrive. If the pressures are starting to get to one or both of you, sex can easily become a forgotten pleasure.

Completely stopping sex without medical reasons would be a mistake, because an important part of mutual support is the manner in which you make love. No matter how passionate and vigorous you normally are during sex, during a pregnancy, the gentle aspects of lovemaking must be brought to the fore. As we've said, you will be having feelings of insecurity at this time. You need to hear and feel that you are in this process together, and there's no better way of communicating this than by making love deliberately and romantically. Try to spend a little more time than you usually do and attempt to verbalize some of your emotions. Afterplay—those moments of closeness after you've made love—is always an important part of any sexual encounter; during pregnancy, it is a particularly important part of lovemaking. It is often during these moments that you will let your guard down and share feelings that you ordinarily bottle up inside.

Talking to Your Health Care Provider about Sex

We're going to try to address common questions about sex during pregnancy, but as with any other health issue, we can speak only in generalities. Specific issues may crop up that can be handled only by your health care provider. You may feel uncomfortable talking about sex, and in far too many cases, so may your doctor. It's pointless to tell someone not to be embarrassed, because that's not an emotion over which you have control. We can tell you, however, to do your utmost to overcome these feelings and ask whatever questions you want to frankly. Even if your health care provider isn't volunteering information, it is available to him or her, and your questions deserve to be answered. Keep in mind that your doctor knows that you and your partner had sex because you are pregnant, so there's no reason to feel ashamed of admitting that you're still having sex. Unfortunately, your doctor may only tell you, "Do this" or "Don't do that," without explaining why. If you press for an explanation, you may be able to get enough information to help you understand how to make your sex life better during pregnancy.

Sex:
What's Safe,
What's Not

You can enjoy sex in the first trimester in the same way as before you were pregnant, unless there are specific reasons for not having sex. We cannot guarantee your safety, however, if you are the type who likes to have sex hanging from chandeliers that are not well secured! That little embryo/fetus is buried deep within you where it is safe during intercourse. As long as you are comfortable with a position, rest assured that the baby inside of you is too. If, as your pregnancy advances, certain positions may suddenly feel uncomfortable, avoid them.

ORGASMS

We hope that an orgasm is a usual part of your sexual response. If you generally have trouble experiencing orgasm, or have never had one at all, you should consult some books on the subject or see a sex therapist. From a physiological point of view, an orgasm is brought on by changes in muscle tone and blood flow. These changes go through the following stages—excitement, plateau, orgasm, and resolution. Not everyone will experience these stages for the same amount of time. The length of each stage may even vary each time you have an orgasm.

While orgasms occasionally trigger some uterine contractions, these are not to be confused with labor. When you have an orgasm, many muscles in your body, including the uterus, contract. In addition, your toes might curl and your spine might arch. Under normal circumstances, you might not notice this, but when you are pregnant, it is understandable to worry about uterine contractions. Be reassured that there is nothing to be concerned about. Labor is a sustained series of very strong contractions needed to push the baby out, whereas the few contractions that you feel from an orgasm don't last long enough to affect the baby.

THE CLITORIS

The clitoris is the part of a woman's genitals that triggers orgasms in most women. In some women the clitoris becomes engorged when they are pregnant. It may even increase in size as a result of the hormones that increase blood circulation. For some, this heightens the sensitivity of the clitoris—and therefore the sensations—when they have sex. Other women find this uncomfortable.

ORAL SEX

As discussed in Chapter 2, not all sexual positions involve entry of the penis into the vagina. As the months pass, you may choose to engage in those sexual activities that do not involve vaginal penetration, assuming that both partners feel comfortable with them. Oral sex is an alternative that can offer the utmost in pleasure and safety.

There is, however, one caveat when performing cunnilingus. Forceful blowing into the vagina might cause an embolism because the pelvic vessels are distended during pregnancy and could result in injury or even death of the woman. You should never blow into the vagina during pregnancy

ANAL SEX

Anal sex, in which the man inserts his penis into the woman's anus, is not harmful during the first trimester. There is one cautionary note about anal sex, however, which applies at any time, but is particularly important to pregnant women. After the man has inserted his penis in the anus, to prevent infection he should never place the penis in her vagina or mouth without washing it thoroughly with soap first. To be extra careful, we suggest using a condom if you have anal sex. There are potentially harmful bacteria inside the rectum. If introduced into the vagina, they may cause an infection that could harm the fetus and mother.

CONDOMS

From our Files

During a visit to her doctor, Fran learned that her husband George had tested positive for herpes—a disease transmitted by contact with herpes lesions during intercourse, while she had not. Because the baby was at risk of contracting herpes from Fran during vaginal delivery, it was critical that she take precautions to not contract the disease. Her doctor emphasized the importance of using a condom for the length of the pregnancy to protect her from herpes. If Fran became infected shortly before going into labor, the baby could be infected during delivery and it might be necessary to perform a cesarean section. In fact, the doctor recommended that they continue to use condoms to prevent Fran from becoming infected with this sexually transmitted disease in the future.

Fran faced two dilemmas. First, how to deal with the unexpected knowledge that George was infected with herpes and second, how to convince him that using a condom would not diminish his sexual pleasure. George's first reaction was, "We never used them before. Why should I have to use them now when your're pregnant?"

Fran decided that they both needed to relax before discussing this problem. She began by preparing a romantic candlelight dinner. When they went to bed, she reached into her purse for a package of condoms. The condoms were of various colors that were selected to match the sheets. She hoped this touch would add interest and humor, thereby further breaking the tension between them. She slipped a condom on his fingertip and told him to scratch so he could judge whether the condom affected his ability to feel. When George realized how little impact the condom had and that his penis was at least as sensitive as his fingertip, he realized that his sensitivity would not only be the same, but would be heightened by the knowledge that he was preventing transmission of herpes to his baby. They began again with a fresh condom and had wonderful sex.

While it may not be apparent that a pregnant couple should use condoms when having sex, pregnancy can be a time when safer sex (to prevent transmission of sexually transmitted infections) is extremely important, because no prospective parent would want to transmit a sexually transmitted disease to his or her baby. If you are at risk, but are unaware of having a transmittable disease; if you have learned that you have an STD as a result of testing in early pregnancy; or if you are not monogamous and the possibility of infections from other partners might be introduced during the pregnancy, using a condom is critical to protect the health of your child.

VIBRATORS

Vibrators come in many different sizes and shapes and can be used to stimulate the woman's clitoris and external genitalia. Although some vibrators are made to be inserted into the vagina, do not use vibrators internally because changes during pregnancy increase the risk of injury to the vagina.

VIGOROUS SEX, VIGOROUS EXERCISE

Some couples really like to go at it, making sex an aerobic sport. Thus, the same care should be exercised as for all other potentially strenuous activities. For instance, a woman is more likely to suffer injuries to her joints when she is pregnant because the increased hormones loosen the soft connective tissue in her skeletal system. Because vigorous sex can increase one's temperature too much, turn on the air conditioner, remove blankets, and do it in the nude. Drink plenty of fluids before beginning any rigorous routine and stop for additional fluids when you feel thirsty, but make sure your bladder is empty.

BREASTS

No matter what size your breasts were before you became pregnant, they're going to increase in size as your pregnancy progresses. That change in cup size will be the most dramatic for small-breasted women. And like flowers to bees, your new breasts are going to attract your husband. The problem is, your new breasts may not appreciate his attention. If they're very sore, he may have to be put on notice that he can look, but not touch, until they are less sensitive. Will he be disappointed? A bit, but you can try to explain to him that anticipation will only heighten his appreciation when you are ready to have him fondle your breasts.

Keeping a Positive Attitude

There are some indulgences you should take full advantage of now. Most positions for lovemaking that you have been using can remain in your repertoire early in pregnancy. Make the most of them now. As your belly increases in size, some of your favorite positions may have to be abandoned temporarily until the baby is born.

During the first trimester, being amorous and romantic can prove difficult if you're feeling nauseated most of the time. If you are used to making love either in the morning or at night, but suffer from nausea at either of those times, initiate unexpected romantic trysts at the times when you are feeling good.

The first trimester is a kind of settling in period as you get used to being pregnant, both from the physical and psychological points of view. There may be some rough moments, but just keep in mind that the road will soon get a lot smoother.

THE SECOND TRIMESTER: FEELING LIKE YOURSELF AGAIN

FOR many women, the second trimester is the most comfortable time of a pregnancy. You often feel better because first-trimester symptoms, such as fatigue, nausea, and even lightheadedness, fade away, but you are not yet experiencing third-trimester concern about the delivery. Thus, you will have a sense of well-being and comfort that should reassure you and your partner.

Keeping the Bond Strong

As a woman becomes visibly pregnant, both partners need to be sensitive to how this impacts their relationship. Pregnant women often fear that their partners find them unattractive or fat when they are pregnant, but the problem is usually more complex.

As with any problem that arises between you, good communication skills are the key to a solution, but they can be used only if you keep the lines open and use them early and often. All problems are best solved sooner rather than later. Because issues in your relationship are all interconnected, a problem in any area, whether related to sex, money, issues of reponsibility, or respecting personal boundaries, can impact the others.

If one of you can't talk about what's behind the problem, or if you have never developed the skills to reach out to each other, or if you've

During the second trimester of her pregnancy, Julia felt terrific. Everyone could see that she was pregnant, and friends and family—sometimes even strangers at the mall—were particularly attentive and made such a fuss. Her husband Rick was pleased that Julia felt so much better, but the growth of her belly and the thrill of feeling the baby kick suddenly made him realize—in a way that he hadn't before—that this was all very real. They truly were going to have a baby, and all the physical signs proved it. Rick suddenly found himself facing conflicting emotions—he was excited, frightened, and, he admitted to himself, jealous of the attention Julia was receiving. Even his own parents made Julia the center of their world.

Julia and Rick had always been sensitive to each other's feelings. Julia noticed that Rick was excited about the baby but seemed withdrawn during family gatherings and was sometimes reluctant to touch her. Both knew that they needed to talk.

Julia and Rick arranged a quiet Saturday at home with no outside commitments. After discussing Rick's concerns, they decided to call their health care provider. She reassured Rick that Julia needed his touch more than ever and that sex would not harm the baby. Julia and Rick agreed to spend several weekends by themselves, away from family and friends, to enjoy each other's company and the baby they were going to have. Julia's attention made Rick feel much better.

already tried to talk to each other and just end up frustrated and more estranged, it is time to seek out a sex therapist, couples' counselor, or religious adviser. Such an adviser can help the two of you learn to communicate your problems in a way that will bring out your desire to support and help one another rather than to find fault and blame one another. In the first few months after your baby is born, it will be much harder to find the time to go for counseling and focus on your problems, so take advantage of your luxury of time now.

If your relationship is strong and you are eagerly awaiting the birth of your child, most of the problems can be handled by the two of you. Often, you can find the solution by taking a step back from the problem, listening to each other, and approaching the situation anew with an awareness of each other's feelings.

The Growth of Your Baby

In the second trimester, your uterus will grow significantly, as the baby undergoes a tremendous growth spurt. By the thirteenth week, the baby is completely formed. During the rest of your pregnancy, the baby will continue to grow until the organs are mature enough to sustain life outside the womb.

At the end of the second trimester, your baby will be able to move its limbs, make a fist, suck its thumb, and even hiccup. If you could snap a photograph inside the uterus, you would see hair beginning to grow on the head, the appearance of eyebrows and eyelashes, and a body that is better proportioned than in the first trimester (Figures 1 and 2).

At about the sixteenth to twentieth week, you and your partner will enjoy the long-awaited thrill of feeling the baby move. Now, you have

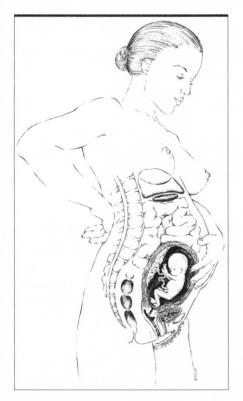

FIGURE 1
The pregnant you at 20 to 24 weeks.

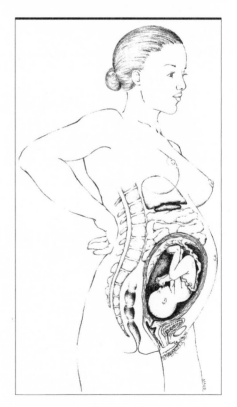

FIGURE 2
The pregnant you at 24 to 28 weeks.

your own proof that the person inside you is alive and kicking. From the twenty-fourth week on, the baby is considered viable, which means that he or she could survive, with proper medical attention, if born at that premature age.

Maintaining a Healthy Pregnancy

You will probably feel much more comfortable during the second trimester of pregnancy than during the first. But it is not just your outward appearance that changes. Your body continues undergoing significant internal changes as well. In response to the increasing blood volume, your blood vessels swell up. This, in turn, is responsible for some of the external signs of your pregnancy, such as varicose veins. Other changes—some of them welcome ones—will also occur as the early symptoms of your pregnancy slowly subside. The hormonal changes in your body will influence many functions other than the growth of your baby.

Welcome Changes

Some of the positive changes in your body during the second trimester will increase your level of comfort and enable you to feel the baby growing inside.

REDUCTION IN NAUSEA

This is a welcome change. Keep in mind, however, that it will not happen like clockwork at the end of the first trimester nor will it happen overnight. The nausea will subside gradually, and for most women, will disappear altogether. Believe it or not, food will even start to smell good again!

INCREASED ENERGY

Remember always feeling fatigued during the first trimester? This, too, will gradually change. In fact, many women get a surge of energy during the second trimester.

INCREASED HAIR GROWTH

Under normal circumstances, your hair grows in cycles—some are actively growing while others are dormant. However, during pregnancy, as a result of the presence or increase in hormones, almost all of your hair is actively growing, so your hair will often become thicker and more luxurious than usual, but it may lose some of its curl and body. For some, the increased hair growth may appear not only on the head, but also in less desirable areas, such as the face (chin, cheeks, upper lip), legs, arms, stomach, or even the back. This extra growth is temporary and most, if not all, of it will disappear after birth. However, if the extra hair bothers you, you can remove it by shaving or waxing.

QUICKENING

The first sign of fetal movement about the sixteenth to twentieth week is called quickening. For many women, it is both thrilling and a little unnerving. It can take a little while, after all, to get used to sharing your body with another living being.

Feeling the baby move for the first time makes the pregnancy concrete for many women and their partners. If you're like many expectant parents, you'll find yourselves talking to the baby and maybe using a nickname for him or her. (And there is good evidence that the baby will be able to hear you, too.) Now might be a good time to start making a list of names for the new member of your family.

T I P

Many pregnant women describe the first kicks as feeling like little bubbles or a fluttering in the stomach, rather than like true kicks. Having your partner feel your baby's kicks can be an exciting moment that will bring the two of you closer.

Continuing Adjustments

In addition to the above changes, you will also experience some new discomforts. Be assured that most of these are perfectly natural and will disappear after the baby is born. If you understand the cause of these changes and follow the suggestions listed below, most will be manageable. Of course, you should discuss any concerns you have about these conditions with your health care provider.

FREQUENT URINATION

The need to always go to the bathroom, which you experienced early during the first trimester, will continue. However, during the first trimester the cause was mostly hormonal. Now, the cause is the increasing

From Our Files

Sally was an executive who worked for an advertising firm. As it happened, she was the only woman in a group of men working on a particular account during her pregnancy. In her early pregnancy, she was embarrassed about having to leave meetings so frequently to go to the bathroom, and she was pleased when the frequent urgency seemed to subside at the end of her first trimester. As she approached the end of her second trimester, however, the frequent urges to urinate returned. Sometimes they were strong and sudden, making it necessary for her to make dashes for the bathroom. This embarrassed her, particularly since she believed that her male coworkers were uncomfortable, too.

Sally needs to understand that she is probably making more out of this than her colleagues. One approach is to accept the situation and not make an issue out of it with her male colleagues. Those who have children probably remember their own wives going through the same experience. If, however, Sally continues to feel self-conscious about her need to go to the bathroom, she could keep a box of chocolates or candy in her office to give out to her colleagues each time she returns from the bathroom. This should lighten the atmosphere for everyone.

pressure from your growing uterus on your bladder, which leaves less room for urine to accumulate. This can be a problem, but don't try to minimize it by cutting your intake of liquids. Your body needs extra fluid as a result of the increase in your blood volume, and cutting down on fluids could have a negative effect on your health. So, keep up the fluids—approximately 8 to 10 cups a day—and factor in your trips to the bathroom when you're out on the town, driving in the car, or working at the office.

Although it is sometimes difficult, you can help prevent urine from leaking when you laugh or cough by doing Kegel exercises to strengthen the pubococcygeal, or PC, muscle, which will help control your bladder.

HEARTBURN AND INDIGESTION

When the smooth muscle of the esophagus relaxes, stomach acids are able to splash back into the throat. This causes the burning sensation known as heartburn, which can be a hassle for many pregnant women. Another change is that the food you eat moves through the stomach more slowly, causing bloating and indigestion. As your pregnancy progresses, your growing uterus creates upward pressure on your organs, including your stomach, increasing the likelihood of heartburn. Some of the things you can do to avoid heartburn and indigestion are the following:

- Avoid clothing that increases pressure on your stomach, such as tight belts and waistbands.
- Eat several small meals throughout the day instead of three big meals.
- Eat slowly, in small bites, and chew food thoroughly.
- Refrain from eating fried, spicy, or fatty foods and drinking certain beverages, such as coffee, soda, or alcohol. These foods can cause heartburn. Stay with boiled or broiled food.
- Elevate your head when you are lying down.
- Instead of bending over at the waist, which encourages acid reflux (as well as strains the back), bend your knees and squat to reach for what you need.

If these suggestions don't help, your doctor may recommend a safe antacid for you to take.

CONSTIPATION

This is another problem caused by the slowing down of your intestines. As your pregnancy progresses, the pressure of your growing uterus on your bowels also may interfere with elimination and increase the likelihood of constipation. The same steps recommended earlier—lots of fluid and fiber in you diet and moderate exercise (if permitted)—can bring relief. If constipation becomes a chronic problem, consult your health care provider for advice. To help prevent constipation, consult Table 1, which lists foods high in fiber.

TABLE 1   Foods High in Fiber

Food	Serving Size	Fiber (in grams)
Pinto beans	1/2 cup	7.4
Oat-bran	1 cup	5.8
Raisins	3/4 cup	4.7
Whole-wheat bread	2 slices	3.9
Apples (including the skin)	1	3.7
Prunes	6	3.6
Oranges	1	3.1

BACKACHES

Many pregnant women complain about backaches, which may become worse as the size of your belly increases and your center of gravity shifts forward. To compensate, you may unconsciously change your posture to stand with shoulders back, neck arched, and belly thrust forward. It is this deeply sway-backed posture that strains the back muscles.

Some relief from backache can be had simply by standing up straight—just as your mother always told you to. To check your posture, stand with your back to a wall, heels together 3 or 4 inches from the wall. Now, press your lower back and shoulders against the wall. For additional help to reduce your physical complaints, try some of the exercises shown in Figure 3. Additional relief may come from massage.

> **TIP**
>
> When you're standing for any length of time, such as on a ticket line or at the kitchen sink, check your posture periodically to make sure you haven't settled into the pregnancy slouch. Imagine someone tugging on that imaginary string on top of your head and draw yourself up as tall as possible. Also, when you're working on your feet for any length of time, standing with one foot on a stool can ease back discomfort.

Most women know, too, that high heels are hard on the back, but it may surprise you to know that completely flat shoes also can aggravate back pain. A two-inch heel is recommended as the best height heel when your back is aching.

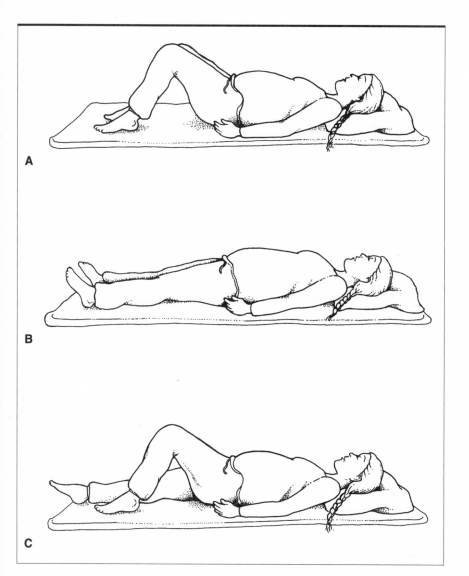

FIGURE 3

Illustrations A through C show exercises to lessen back pain and improve leg circulation that are appropriate during your pregnancy.

Although it might be more comfortable for your back if you sleep on your side, no one has control over how they move while they're asleep. You can rest assured that you didn't hurt your baby if you find yourself sprawled on your back when you wake up in the morning.

VARICOSE VEINS

Veins carry blood back from the extremities to the heart. Because the blood travel against gravity, a valve system in the veins prevents the blood from flowing back, or pooling. Varicosities develop when these valves don't close properly or are missing altogether, allowing the blood to pool in the vein and causing a bulging appearance. Varicose veins appear most often on the lower extremities, although some women may also develop varicosities on the vulva. (Hemorrhoids, in fact, are a kind of varicose vein.) Varicose veins appear to be a hereditary problem; thus, women with a family history of them are more prone to their development.

You can prevent or minimize varicose veins by avoiding pressure on the veins and improving circulation. Try some of these suggestions:

- Wear support pantyhose.
- Avoid tight waistbands, elastic-topped socks or stockings, and girdles.
- Avoid sitting or standing in one position for long periods. Take frequent breaks to move around, stretch out, and keep the blood circulating in your legs.
- When lying down, put a pillow under your feet to raise up your legs.
- When sitting, put a stool under your feet to raise your knees above your hips.
- Take a 20- to 30-minute walk every day to exercise and improve circulation and muscle tone in your legs.

If the area around a varicose vein becomes red, swollen, warm, and painful, it may be an indication of an infected vein, a condition called thrombophlebitis. If you develop these symptoms, don't massage or apply heat to the area. Call your health care provider and ask for advice about how to proceed.

LEG AND FOOT CRAMPS

Muscle cramps in the legs are common during pregnancy and often occur at night. One frequent cause is an imbalance of certain minerals, called electrolytes, including calcium, phosphorus, magnesium, and potassium.

To combat these cramps, ask your health care provider if you can take a calcium and potassium supplement that does not contain phosphorus (some experts believe that an excess of phosphorus can also increase the risk of cramping). You can also follow the instructions already given for improving circulation in your legs.

If you develop a cramp, slowly extend your leg and flex your foot backward from the ankle. Massage the area and apply a warm compress to soothe the muscles.

DIZZINESS

Dizziness occurs more often during pregnancy and is often aggravated by a sudden change in position. Because pregnant women have more relaxed blood vessels and an increased volume of blood, the heart has to work harder to pump the blood through your body. When your enlarged uterus presses on the vein guiding the blood to the heart, less blood is available for the heart to pump. This, in turn, lowers your blood pressure and causes dizziness.

To prevent dizziness, move your legs when you are sitting to encourage circulation. When you stand up, do so gradually. Put one hand on something to support you if you do feel lightheaded. If the dizziness persists after you stand up, lie down with your feet elevated for a few minutes to increase the blood flow to your head.

ITCHINESS

As your stomach begins to grow significantly in the second trimester, the skin covering it can become very itchy. This itchiness is caused by the skin stretching to accommodate the growing uterus. Frequent massages with moisturizing cream will help decrease itchiness.

STRETCH MARKS

Stretch marks occur when skin is stretched beyond its capacity and the collagen fibers in the skin (the elastic tissue that allows the skin to stretch) tear. Heredity plays a role in whether or not stretch marks develop. Excessive weight gain will force the skin to stretch even further and cause more stretch marks. Although these striations will be very visible now, after birth, they will fade considerably, becoming silvery lines that are not terribly noticeable.

HEADACHES

Headaches are a common side effect of pregnancy. They can last a few minutes or a few hours and occur once or twice during pregnancy or every few days.

For many headaches, simple remedies such as an ice pack at the back of the neck or on top of the head, fresh air, an hour or two in a quiet, dark room, or a nap can alleviate the headache. If you experience severe headaches that are not relieved by any of these remedies, call your health care provider. Occasionally, headaches may be caused by a more serious condition called preeclampsia, which is often associated with hypertension. In the absence of a serious reason for the headache, mild pain killers often can be taken without doing harm, but consult your doctor before taking any medications.

The same applies to migraine headaches, which may occur either less or more frequently during pregnancy. Try to use practical steps to avoid and treat them. Avoid common triggers, such as chocolate, nitrates, monosodium glutamate, alcohol, and stuffy, smoky rooms. If the migraine becomes unbearable, call your health care provider for advice on what you can do to alleviate the pain.

Your Physical Exams

At one time, doctors had very few tools with which to diagnose problems in the second trimester. Measuring the mother's weight gain and taking a blood pressure reading were the most important gauges available to evaluate how the pregnancy was progressing, but they had to wait until the baby was born to determine if it had developed normally. Although weight and blood pressure are still important indicators, you can now find out many things about the developing fetus that were unimaginable even a decade ago. Some things, however, you will not know until after the delivery, such as the color of the baby's hair and who he or she will look like.

Routine Procedures

During this trimester, you will see your health care practitioner approximately every four weeks. During each visit, the exam will consist of checking your urine; measuring your blood pressure; monitoring weight gain; measuring the size of the uterus; listening to the fetal heart beat; and answering questions you may have. Some additional tests may also be ordered by your doctor or health care provider.

Special Procedures

SONOGRAM

You may have already had a sonogram in the first trimester, but many practitioners believe that a sonogram should be done routinely in the second trimester—usually at about 18 to 20 weeks into the pregnancy—to monitor the health and development of the fetus. By using ultrasound, a sonogram can create images from inside your womb that will, among other things, check the fetus and verify your due date; measure different parts of the fetus; look for fetal anomalies; verify the location of the placenta; check for multiple gestation (i.e., twins, triplets, and so forth); evaluate the amount of amniotic fluid; and check the condition of the uterus, ovaries, fallopian tubes, and cervix.

During a sonogram, the technician and your provider may be able to tell the sex of your baby. By the fourteenth to sixteenth week of pregnancy, the external fetal sex organs have developed—the labia of girls and the penis of boys can be distinguished from each other. In many instances, the picture may not be clear enough because the legs of the fetus may be inopportunely positioned to block the view.

The question is, "Should you ask?" This is a personal decision that nobody can make for you. Many people stay with tradition. They prefer the mystery and surprise of not finding out until the baby is born. Some people also have the uneasy feeling that if you are told the baby's sex and pick out an appropriate name, buy the right color clothes, and paint the room accordingly, it will be the one time when a mistake was made. For some couples, having the doctor lift the baby and say, "It's a boy!" or "It's a girl!" is part of the childbirth experience.

If you want to know the sex of your child, ask your sonogram technician to take a peek and let you know. Conversely, if you don't want to know, make sure that the technician and your health care provider both know that you want to be kept in the dark.

MATERNAL-SERUM ALPHAFETOPROTEIN (MSAFP) TEST

Alphafetoprotein (AFP) is a chemical excreted by the fetus into the amniotic fluid, and from there into the mother's blood. The MSAFP test, which is usually performed between the fifteenth and twentieth weeks of pregnancy, determines the AFP level in the mother's blood. It is sometimes combined with two other blood tests, the estradiol and beta HCG tests, which are performed to gather additional information.

An increased amount of AFP in the mother's blood is sometimes, but not always, associated with various conditions of the fetus, such as the presence of twins; abnormalities of the fetal abdomen; neural tube defects; and certain blood diseases of the fetus. A low level of AFP is sometimes, but not always, associated with chromosomal abnormalities of the fetus, such as Down syndrome.

It is important for you to understand that the MSAFP is a screening test, not a diagnostic test. If an abnormal level of AFP is found, further testing, such as an ultrasound or an amniocentesis, will be ordered to determine if there is, in fact, any abnormality present. In the majority of cases in which there is an abnormal MSAFP test, further testing shows that the fetus is perfectly normal.

Why are so many results misleading? A major factor is the sensitivity of this test to the time it is performed during pregnancy. A woman's AFP level can be incorrectly diagnosed as abnormal if her due date was calculated incorrectly, and the test is performed too early or too late.

GLUCOSE SCREEN

At approximately the twenty-sixth week of your pregnancy, you are often given a glucose challenge test, which is a screening procedure for diabetes. Pregnancy increases your risk of developing diabetes. This is called gestational diabetes. A woman who has a history of diabetes in a previous pregnancy, has had twins, or has delivered a big baby in a previous pregnancy is at an increased risk of developing diabetes during pregnancy.

In a glucose challenge test (GCT), you will be asked to drink a small amount of a solution containing 50 grams of glucose. An hour later, a sample of your blood will be taken. If the sugar level in your blood is abnormally high, another test, the glucose tolerance test (GTT), may have to be performed to determine if you have developed diabetes.

In the glucose tolerance test, you will be required to drink a so-lution with 100 grams of glucose. Your blood will be drawn four times: before you drink the glucose, and then one, two, and three hours after. If the test results suggest that you have diabetes, you may be started on a special diet or given medication to control your blood sugar.

AMNIOCENTESIS

An amniocentesis is a prenatal diagnostic test that detects certain inher-ited or genetic conditions. During this test, the doctor removes some amniotic fluid, which is mostly baby urine. This test is suggested for women 35 years of age and older, because they are at greater risk of having a baby with Down syndrome; women who have already given birth to a child with Down syndrome; couples who are carriers of an in-herited disorder (for example, sickle-cell anemia, Tay-Sachs disease, and cystic fibrosis); women who have had a child with a spinal defect; women who are carriers of a sex-linked genetic disease, such as hemophilia; and women whose MSAFP test indicated abnormal levels of AFP.

To prevent complications, your doctor will first establish by ultra-sound the best possible place inside the uterus to insert a needle. Your abdomen is cleansed with a special solution to decrease the risk of infection. Most doctors like to keep the ultrasound next to the nee-dle, while it is being inserted through your skin into the amniotic cav-ity, to monitor its position and placement. Once the tip of the needle is inside the amniotic fluid, a small amount of fluid (approximately 1/5 of a cup) is extracted. The amniotic fluid contains cells from the fetal skin that can be used to detect the presence of certain conditions. Most doctors advise that you should rest for 12 to 24 hours after the amniocentesis. Although there is not much known about possible complications, we suggest that you wait at least a day or so before re-suming sexual intercourse. The results of this test take from one to three weeks to obtain, a wait that will feel interminable for most parents-to-be.

ETHICAL CONSIDERATIONS

The results of a sonogram or amniocentesis can present expectant parents with serious ethical questions. The purpose of these tests is to confirm that the fetus is healthy, which turns out to be true in the vast majority of cases. But, what will you do if any of the tests indicate that your baby has serious problems? Such news can create a very emotional and stressful period for both of you. What will you do if, as a result of a sonogram or amniocentesis, you discover that your child has a problem? Will you carry to term or choose to interrupt the pregnancy? What are the physical and psychological implications of these decisions?

To deal with these questions, we strongly recommend that you both meet with a genetic counselor before undergoing these tests, but definitely after you have learned the results. If the tests show that the fetus has a problem, the counselor or your doctor will explain the results and go over possible options with you. Although the final decision can be made only by the expectant parents, they can answer your questions about interrupting the pregnancy, as well as what support will be available to you if you decide to carry to term.

These tests, such as an amniocentesis, are only meant to provide you with the facts you need to make an informed decision. Performing an amniocentesis does not mean that any one outcome is predetermined. The test only tells you whether or not your child is likely to have an abnormal chromosome count, information that, should you choose to continue the pregnancy, will give you adequate time to prepare.

The Pregnant You

By the second trimester, you can no longer keep the news of your pregnancy quiet. Unlike the first trimester, when you experienced subtle physical changes that may have been obvious only to you and your partner, during the second trimester, you'll finally start to "show."

The Clothes You Wear

The change in your physical appearance will create some practical considerations. For a while, you're going to be in the awkward stage: too pregnant to fit into your old clothes, but not yet pregnant enough for maternity outfits.

You don't want to go out and buy a new wardrobe that's going to last only a few weeks, but you have to wear something. . . . Here are some wardrobe suggestions:

- Raid your partner's closet. Odds are that some of his shirts may fit you even if you have to roll up the cuffs.
- When you buy clothes, think of the future. The clothes you wear during the second trimester might well be the clothes you'll be

TIP

If you're planning on breastfeeding, choose loose shirts and skirts or pants rather than dresses. You'll want to be able to lift your shirt and have it double as cover while you're nursing.

wearing for a few months after you give birth when your body is in transition again. Think of what the season will be after the baby is born and purchase outfits that will work now and then.

- Consider buying second-hand clothes. It's a lot cheaper, and you can donate them to charity when you no longer need them.

- Borrow from friends and family.

- Buy a little at a time. Because your body is changing, it's better to buy one outfit with different accessories than to buy several outfits that might not be comfortable within a few weeks.

- Buy layered outfits. You may feel warmer than usual in the last months of pregnancy, so look for light, natural fabrics, such as cotton, that can breathe. Purchase outfits that can be layered so that you can remove a layer or two if you begin to feel too warm.

- Invest in bras that fit. Some women can use their regular bras during pregnancy because their breasts don't change dramatically in size. However, other women notice a significant increase in the size of their breasts, and their regular bra no longer offers adequate support. You can purchase nursing bras if you're planning on breastfeeding. However, the bras you buy before childbirth may not fit after your baby is born. Often, breasts enlarge again when they start producing milk. If your breasts increase in size significantly after you start to produce milk, you may have to buy yet another supply of nursing bras.

- If the shoe fits. . . . Your feet may become a whole size larger during pregnancy, and you may need to purchase a pair or two to get you through. Why do your feet become larger during pregnancy? Because it's common for the feet and ankles to retain some fluid, thereby causing swelling. Also, your feet may spread as your foot joints loosen because of the presence of relaxin. This

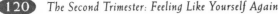

hormone, which loosens your pelvis in preparation for delivery, also affects other joints as well, including the joints in your feet. Excess weight gain can also lead to additional fat tissue in the feet, making them larger.

- Rent formal wear. Maternity formal wear is at least as expensive as regular formal wear. Unless you frequently attend formal functions, you might want to rent evening gowns from a local maternity or department store. Or, you can ask friends and relatives who have had children if they have a gown you might borrow. You also might consider buying just a long maternity skirt and wearing it with one of your partner's dress shirts and bowties.

Because of all these changes, you may feel distinctly different about your body once your pregnancy is obvious. Instead of just feeling thicker and heavier, you should feel pregnant and proud of it!

Sharing the News with Your Children

If you already have children, they will be interested in knowing what's going on. If you've been talking about your pregnancy a lot in the first trimester, then they may already know all about it, particularly if you experienced nausea, fatigue, and other symptoms.

But many parents wait until the second trimester to inform other children about the new baby. This gives the parents time to adjust and to reassure themselves that everything is okay. By the second trimester, however, you have little choice, as you can no longer hide the changes that are taking place. In fact, if you do not tell your children, they may—particularly the younger ones—think something is very wrong because of your changing shape.

No matter when you choose to tell your children about the new baby, your strategy will be the same. Very young children will not have a grasp of the changes that are in store, but need enough information to adapt to the consequences. Here, picture books may prove helpful.

Most parents' main concern, however, is that the elder child will be jealous of the baby. How jealous depends, to a great degree, on the child, but there are things that you can do to help ease the transition. For instance, you can talk about the baby to make the children excited about its arrival.

If an older child is going to be switched from a crib to a bed, make the transition now so that he or she won't feel that the baby has taken the crib away. Also, include your child in some decision-making, such as helping to choose the wallpaper in the baby's room. Finally, bring your elder child with you when you next see your caregiver. Let him or her hear the baby's heartbeat or look at the sonogram.

Making Love

There's one more change that often takes place during the second trimester that should compensate for the discomforts: an improvement in your love life. Many women report an increase in libido which, in the first trimester, may have taken a back seat to morning sickness and fatigue.

Sex:
What's Safe,
What's Not

Many expectant couples have concerns that sex might somehow interfere with the pregnancy. The most frequently expressed concern is that the baby may be hurt by the man's penis, the woman's orgasm, or the ejaculate.

ASK DR. RUTH

Q In the first twelve weeks of my pregnancy, the last thing in the world I wanted was to make love. Now, in my sixteenth week, I can't seem to get the thought of sex out of my mind. I jump on my partner as soon as he walks through the door. It's like being back on our honeymoon. Although the sex part is great, I am concerned that we might be hurting the baby. I know it is safe to have sex, but is that still true if you're doing it every day, sometimes several times a day?

A Once a day, twice a day, ten times a day, as often as you like, even though you are pregnant. As long as it makes you feel good and there are no contraindications, it's okay. Occasionally, some women may feel mild contractions during orgasm. The uterus is made out of smooth muscles, which, together with other muscles in your body, contract during orgasm. These contractions are short lived and no cause for concern. They are not the same as labor contractions, which grow more frequent and intense as labor progresses. However, if you experience contractions that seem to be lasting too long, contact your doctor.

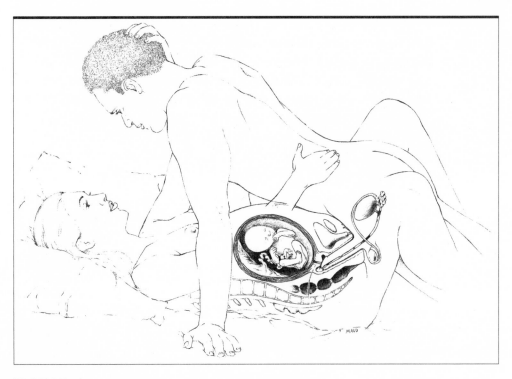

FIGURE 4
This couple is enjoying great sex in the second trimester of pregnancy.

We want to reassure you that more often than not these are unfounded fears. During sexual intercourse, the penis is thrust back and forth within the vagina. This is an activity usually enjoyed by both sexual partners, but is very rarely so rough that the woman is hurt. The fetus will be unaffected because it is ensconced behind the cervix and cushioned in amniotic fluid inside your uterus (Figure 4).

Although we have emphatically stated that sex is safe during pregnancy, there are some exceptions to this rule. In a very few, specific circumstances, sexual intercourse during the second trimester is prohibited. Conditions that would make sex unsafe during pregnancy include placenta previa, a condition in which the placenta blocks the cervix; premature dilatation of the cervix; an incompetent cervix; and you are at risk for premature delivery, for example, if you have a previous history of premature labor and delivery or a history of previous premature rupture of membranes.

In addition, while it's true that you can have as much sex as you want, the physical mechanics of getting close enough to have sex may start to become complicated as you come to the end of this trimester. Certain common positions may be less comfortable. For example, lying on your back and bearing the weight of your partner on top of you, along with the weight of your pregnant belly, may cause discomfort. You needn't worry that the baby will be crushed. Your child is well protected in the uterus by amniotic fluid, which acts much like bubble wrap around a fragile package. You're the one under pressure, and the extra weight could press down on important blood vessels and potentially interfere with blood circulation. So now is a good time to try new positions that take his weight off you.

Have him kneel on one knee to keep his weight off your abdomen (Figures 5 and 6). Another variation would be for him to kneel and for you to raise both legs. And for those who are adventurous enough, we have developed a new position for pregnant couples, called the "Dr. Ruth and Dr. Amos" position.

FIGURE 5

During the second trimester, you may need to find new and inventive ways to have sex comfortably. In this position, the man is kneeling to keep his weight off the woman's abdomen.

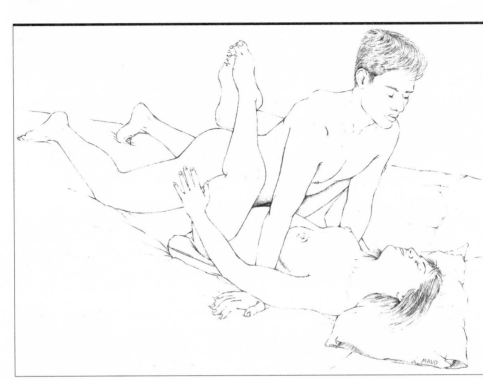

FIGURE 6

In this variation on Figure 4, the man keeps his weight off of the woman's abdomen, while she crosses her ankles behind his back.

DR. RUTH AND DR. AMOS POSITION

This position facilitates greater comfort and enjoyment during sex for the pregnant couple, while at the same time removing his weight from her abdomen (Figure 7). To assume the Dr. Ruth and Dr. Amos position, the pregnant woman lies on her back, placing one or both of her feet on a chair. This allows her the freedom to move around and to slightly tilt her body from one side to the other to assure greater comfort. The man kneels or stands between her legs, which enables him to easily caress her clitoris with his fingers, hand, and other body parts or by cunnilingus. When he penetrates her, there is no pressure on her pregnant abdomen and both can move without unnecessary restrictions. You should try and modify the position to make it even more enjoyable and comfortable for you.

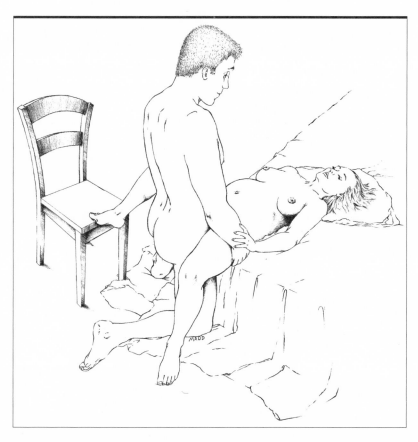

FIGURE 7

The Dr. Ruth and Dr. Amos position is a new position designed to maximize comfort and sexual pleasure.

CHANGES DURING SEX

Some changes can occur during sex at this time that may cause some concern. For example, the increased amount of blood and blood vessels that develop during pregnancy may make the cervix more sensitive to touch. During intercourse, your partner's penis may press against your cervix. Therefore, after intercourse, you may see some small drops of blood in the vaginal discharge. This is called *spotting*. In addition, some women experience slight cramping during sex or orgasm. Although this is something you don't usually have to worry about, if you are concerned, especially if you are spotting frequently, call your doctor for advice. You can take some precautions that will lessen the chances of

FIGURE 8

Sex during pregnancy requires some adjustments. With the woman on top, she can control how deeply his penis penetrates her vagina, thereby reducing irritation of the cervix.

spotting. Your partner, for instance, can avoid thrusting his penis as deeply as normal. Or you also can try to take more control by changing positions in such a way that you can control how deeply his penis penetrates your vagina, such as in the female superior position (Figure 8).

Finally, although many women have a greater desire for sex during the second trimester, not every woman's libido skyrockets to new heights during this time. The changes in libido are caused by variations in the level of hormones during pregnancy. Because there are individual variations in the secretions of and responses to these hormones, each woman will react differently.

Enjoy the Best Sex of Your Life

For some women, sex during pregnancy will feel much as it did before they were pregnant, although the new spontaneity they have with the burden of birth control lifted will certainly be a plus. You may discover that the greater blood supply to your genitals during pregnancy will significantly change your sexual experience. Some women who have never had an orgasm may have orgasms. And because the labia are engorged with blood during pregnancy, you may feel aroused virtually all the time.

While your hormones are on this roller coaster ride, your partner's sex drive may be outpaced by yours. He may respond positively to your increased libido, or he may find your sudden voracious sexual appetite somewhat overwhelming. Some men lose interest in sex with their partners once they become obviously pregnant. There will be times when you may want to relieve your sexual tension when he is not available. The obvious solution at moments like this is to masturbate. Masturbation will not hurt your baby. You can even use a vibrator, although we suggest using it near your clitoris, rather than using it inside your vagina. A vibrator is much harder than a penis and may cause harm when inserted deep into the vagina.

During pregnancy, some men may seem to have less interest in sex. This problem is usually more complex than losing interest in their partners. Many other reasons may explain why a man loses interest in sex. Fear of hurting the baby and worrying about the responsibilities of having a child are some of them. For some men, a pregnant wife reminds them of their mothers, resulting in a reluctance to have sex.

Whatever the reason, some men are unable to perform sexually when their wives are obviously pregnant. To say to yourself, "I'll just ignore this, and everything will go back to normal after the baby is born," would be a mistake. Your life is going to continue to change quite dramatically after the baby is born and for years to come. Talk it over. It may be true that your partner's libido may be revitalized once you are no longer pregnant, but nine months is a long time. There will also be a couple of months of abstinence after the baby is born while you are recovering from childbirth. That's close to a year, and during that time, two people can become estranged on a sexual level. That's bound to have a chilling effect on the rest of your relationship. As time goes on, you'll feel more and more awkward discussing your sexual problems. You may find yourselves in a sexless marriage, with each of you suffering silently, too embarrassed to talk to one another. The earlier you nip issues like these in the bud, the easier they are to resolve. Allowing them to drag on for months will only intensify and magnify the problem.

As with any problem, you need to communicate about your concerns and, if necessary, seek counseling. Start by having a discussion away from the bedroom—in fact, away from your home. Try to avoid having this discussion at night, when you're both in bed and may feel pressured. If you feel awkward discussing such an intimate subject in a public place like a coffee bar or a restaurant, go for a long walk, a drive in the country, or a picnic in the park where you'll both feel at ease.

Remember, part of the cure is taking a step back from your goal. In many marriages, when pregnancy or any source of stress exists, the bond between the two partners can become tangled up in other issues, and the marriage, which was uppermost in their minds when they started out, fades into the background. A whole string of possible distractions, such as jobs, house renovations, professional organizations, or family obligations, grab bits and pieces of the time you need to spend together as a couple. Little by little, you start to take each other for granted and grow apart. The cure, therefore, is to woo each other back again. How? Pretty much the same way you wooed each other when you first formed your relationship. Here are some ideas:

- Work at adding some anticipation to seeing each other. The best way of doing that is via some form of communication, such as sending flowers; faxing or E-mailing a love note; writing something sexy on a steamy bathroom mirror; making a date for lunch at a romantic restaurant; or even making a special invitation to a romantic dinner at home over the phone. And before you do see each other, spend some time dressing up the way you used to when you were first dating.

- Put aside time for yourself ahead of everything else. If you planned a special dinner at home, but work got in the way of preparations and the house is a mess, leave it behind you and go out for dinner. Trying to scramble and clean up will make you exhausted by dinnertime.

- Take a walk together to buy some ice cream.

- Make time for intimacy in the evening before going to bed. Give each other foot rubs or back massages (Figure 9). Or just touch each other gently (Figure 10).

- If you're married, browse through your wedding album.

- Write a steamy love story together.

- Set the VCR to tape your usual shows or a game on television. Instead of watching, you can spend time with each other.

You get the picture. If you start paying attention to each other the way you did way back when, you'll probably realize that the romantic feelings that you thought were gone just needed rekindling.

FIGURE 9

To create a romantic mood, try giving each other back massages.

FIGURE 10

If sex is uncomfortable or you need to get back into that romantic mood, one alternative to sexual intercourse might be mutual masturbation.

Get Ready for the Third Trimester

With morning sickness a thing of the past, your sex life invigorated, and that pregnant glow making everyone you meet tell you how great you look, you may start to think that this pregnancy thing is a cinch. You may take on new projects at work, volunteer your services to various organizations, or decide to take up race walking. Before you go ahead with such ambitious plans, take a deep breath and think ahead.

Just as the second trimester brought some noticeable changes from the first, the third trimester is going to be very much different from the second. As the baby grows, it's going to take a lot more of your energy to lug it around. It's also going to get a lot more crowded in there, and that will slow you down physically. So, be realistic. Rather than take it for granted, treasure your energy and use it very carefully, doing things that otherwise you'd have to do in the third trimester. If you work, try to get ahead of yourself so that you can sneak in an occasional nap in the last few months. At home, if there's any cleaning, repairing, or shopping that needs to be done, organize and oversee those projects sooner rather than later. Trust us on this one, and you'll be glad you did.

THE THIRD TRIMESTER: READY AND WAITING

YOUR body has been going through some dramatic changes in the past six months, but many more are still to come. In fact, the stereotypical image of a woman in her third trimester waddling down the street, her large, rotund belly filling out her maternity dress may very well be you.

Keeping the Bond Strong

The Home Stretch

The third trimester is a time for growing excitement and looming anxiety. In the first and second trimesters, the birth seemed a long way off, with plenty of time to prepare for the baby's arrival. Now, however, you are counting the weeks and days; the arrival of the baby seems imminent and very real.

At the start of your pregnancy, bringing a child into the world was still abstract. Now, you can both feel the baby kicking inside of you. Sometimes, you can actually make out the shape of your baby's foot or rump pressing against the skin of your abdomen. The closer you get to your due date, the more nervous you will become. And your partner has his share of concerns as well. He is probably anxious about his participation in the birth process. Will he be able to fulfill your needs or will he disappoint you (and himself)? Will his wife and baby be okay?

All of these emotions are going to affect your relationship. Whatever the source of your apprehension—fear of the birth process, worries

Samantha and Fred's baby was due in May. Fred was an accountant, and he knew that during tax season in April, he'd have to work 12 to 15 hours each day. He was grateful, though, that the big rush would be over when the baby arrived so that he could devote himself to his family.

In April, Samantha had to quit her job in a department store because she could no longer spend the long hours standing on her feet. With so much extra time on her hands, Samantha found herself anxiously waiting for Fred to finish work and come home. When Fred started working late during tax season, Samantha grew resentful. While waiting for Fred, she began to prepare a long list of things for him to do, such as fixing up the baby's room. So, as soon as tax season was over, Fred began to spend all of his free time working on Samantha's list—scraping, painting, and wallpapering the nursery.

Fred grew increasingly tired. Even after he dragged himself to bed, Samantha kept him awake tossing and turning as the baby kicked. During the day, he had no time to nap. Samantha, in turn, became more uncomfortable. As each became more irritable and cranky, they started bickering and arguing. Each argument ended with, "I can't wait until this baby gets here and things get back to normal again."

But, of course, things didn't go back to normal after the baby was born. There were middle-of-the-night feedings, constant visits from their families, and, to top it all off—a full-blown case of postpartum blues for Samantha that only aggravated an already prickly situation. Rather than abating, their bickering intensified, and Fred ultimately took to sleeping on the couch. They were close to breaking up when they decided to seek professional help.

After determining that there was nothing physically wrong, their therapist spent time with each of them separately before bringing them together. She was firm in suggesting that they forget about the last few months and start fresh. They then discussed how best to regulate household responsibilities with the extra responsibilities of the baby and still have time for each other and themselves.

Based on these sessions, Fred and Samantha hired a daily babysitter for just a few hours to relieve some of the burden and give them time to spend with each other or a friend or just visit a mall for some window shopping. Fred began to visit a gym; the exercise helped use up his energy and helped him sleep at night. Samantha understood that pressuring Fred to complete the baby's room before the delivery was unnecessary; all the baby really needed at first was love, warmth, and attention. Their relationship should have come first.

about new responsibilities, finances—the added stress will take its toll on both of you. As with the first two trimesters, the key is communication and sensitivity to each other's emotional state. Let each kick from the baby bring you closer to each other. Try to enjoy this time. Pick out names, talk or sing to your baby, play music. You know that you're going to be proud and want to show off your baby, so begin now by showing off your baby in his or her current home—your bulging belly.

Making Time for Each Other

From the moment labor begins and you head for the hospital, your lives will change and not settle down again for a few months. Even after the dust settles, your family will have grown by one. Now is the time to prepare for that period of upheaval by centering yourselves around each other. If you permit yourselves to get caught up in a prelabor frenzy, you will create a wedge between you that can continue to grow after the baby is born.

Remember that during the third trimester, emotions can run high on both sides. If Fred and Samantha had gone for counseling sooner, they might have resolved the problem before they stopped sleeping together. Both partners should be sensitive about taking out their discomforts and concerns on each other; it won't make either of you feel any better.

Make plans for spending time cuddling, hugging, and just talking together. Don't just say you're going to do it. Actually make a plan and put it into effect. The plan could be as simple as turning off the television, radio, or stereo an hour earlier than usual and spending that time concentrating on each other. You may want to dim the lights and sit by candlelight; you will certainly want to take the phone off the hook or put on the answering machine so you aren't interrupted by callers. Such quiet moments alone will be harder to come by soon, and you need to charge up your love batteries before three makes a crowd.

Maintaining a Healthy Pregnancy

Although you are pleased to know that the baby will soon be here, these final three months are physically less comfortable for you. The baby grows rapidly and becomes much heavier. As your uterus enlarges, it pushes aside other internal organs. Thus, in addition to changes you have already experienced, a few new ones will come into play.

Continuing
Changes

SWELLING HANDS, ANKLES, AND FEET

As your pregnancy progresses, you will become increasingly thirsty as your body demands more fluids to maintain an increased blood volume and wash away waste. Thus, the swelling you experienced earlier may become more pronounced. Aside from having to buy larger shoes, you may consider removing your rings before your hands swell to the point where you cannot remove them.

At this stage, you may also benefit from support pantyhose or elevation of your feet for about an hour each day. In addition, avoid sitting for prolonged periods of time. Every so often, get up and move around so that circulation increases.

INCONTINENCE

During the second trimester, you may have found yourself urinating more frequently than usual, but in the third trimester you may find yourself urinating involuntarily when you cough, sneeze, or laugh. This is called pregnancy incontinence, and it occurs when your uterus presses down on your bladder. To avoid leaking, keep your bladder as empty as possible by urinating frequently and wear a panty liner or a sanitary pad, which should be changed frequently. Here, too, your Kegel exercises will help by giving you better control over your PC muscles, which support your bladder and control urination.

TIP

Do not attempt to control occasional urine leakage by limiting your intake of fluid. Your body has a great demand for fluid, and you could dehydrate yourself and compromise your health if you try to reduce your fluid intake.

Continuing
Adjustments

SHORTNESS OF BREATH

To improve circulation through the uterus and the placenta, your heart needs to work harder as the pregnancy progresses. As a result, you may begin to feel short of breath. If this occurs, slow down or take a break if you are in the middle of an activity. If you are exercising, you should continue at a slower pace. Regular exercise improves the efficiency of your respiratory system and thus circulation and muscle tone.

You can also change your position to make you feel better. If you are sitting or standing in a slump, straighten up and push your shoulders back. This simple shift will help your body work better. If you find that it is harder to breathe when you are lying down, try sleeping in a semiprone position, propped up with pillows, or even in a reclining chair.

SLEEP AND PREGNANCY

Some women experience an increase in dreams during pregnancy. Others may find it difficult to get a good night's sleep. If sleeplessness becomes a problem, try taking catnaps during the day. Better yet, try to do appropriate exercises. At this stage, weight-bearing exercises, such as jogging, may be difficult, but you can ride a stationary bike or swim. Many pregnant women find swimming is a relaxing and effective form of exercise, particularly during the final months when the water helps support the extra weight you are carrying and minimizes stress on your joints.

> **TIP**
>
> *Swimming is a safe activity provided you observe a few precautions. Keep the water at a comfortable temperature, and try to swim in an outdoor pool to minimize the effects of the chlorine fumes. Don't dive, and exert care in entering and leaving the slippery areas around the pool. Be careful not to overexert in this comfortable environment. You should be able to carry on a conversation or hum a song at all times without experiencing shortness of breath.*

Finally, don't forget sex as a way of bringing on a delicious tiredness. Even if it doesn't put you to sleep, you won't regret the effort.

HEMORRHOIDS

Because of hormonal changes during pregnancy that slow the passage of stool through the large intestine, constipation is not unusual. When you add to this the increased blood volume that tends to pool in the lower body along with the pressure of the growing uterus on those veins, you have the perfect recipe for hemorrhoids. Hemorrhoids are essentially varicose or swollen rectal veins that are either internal or bulge out of the anus. They are especially common when a pregnant woman is constipated and strains to eliminate hard stool.

Although hemorrhoids are usually harmless, they may itch and become irritated, making sitting on a hard surface for long periods uncomfortable. They may also bleed (particularly after a bowel movement), which can be alarming, but is not a health hazard. You can try applying ice compresses or cotton balls soaked in witch hazel to alleviate the discomfort. Your health care provider can also recommend a medicated ointment or pad that will help soothe the area.

To minimize hemorrhoids, avoid sitting for prolonged times. Get up and move around. Practice your Kegel exercises which, in addition to strengthening your PC muscles, improves blood circulation in the rectal area. Moderate exercise will also help you have regular bowel movements. Finally, drink lots of fluids and increase the fiber content of your diet. If constipation is still a problem, ask your health care provider for a stool softener and, perhaps, a fiber supplement.

BREAST SECRETIONS

You may notice a yellow liquid leaking from your nipples during this last trimester. This is colostrum, the first milk produced for your baby and secreted by your breasts before they start to produce regular milk.

CLUMSINESS

With your center of gravity way out of whack and your ligaments loosened, you are quite literally more accident prone. Leave extra time to negotiate stairs and watch your footing on uneven terrain, such as gravel or broken sidewalks.

BRAXTON-HICKS CONTRACTIONS

During these final three months, you will begin experiencing very gentle contractions, called Braxton-Hicks contractions. These are usually short (less than a minute) and painless. You will feel as if your uterus is gradually becoming tight and then relaxing. Braxton-Hicks contractions are thought to be practice contractions that help the uterus prepare for the actual delivery.

The Growth of Your Baby

It should come as no surprise that you are looking more and more like a mother-to-be. During the third trimester, which begins in the twenty-eighth week, your baby will be gaining one fourth to one half pound every two weeks and will triple in size by the time you give birth! With

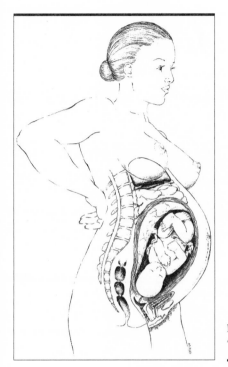

FIGURE 1
The pregnant you in the last month of pregnancy.

each day, the baby grows stronger and its movements more vigorous. Its proportions are those you would expect at birth. By the beginning of the ninth month, your baby will have long nails on its toes and fingers, the hair on its head can be up to two inches long, and, if its a boy, the testes will descend.

As your delivery time draws closer, the baby will also change its position. Its head will first move toward your pelvis and, by the thirty-sixth week, will usually descend into the pelvis (Figure 1).

Your Physical Exams

During this trimester, you're going to become a lot closer to your doctor. Visits will be scheduled every other week and then, in the last month, each week until you give birth.

Routine Procedures

As in your second trimester, each visit will include a check of your weight, blood pressure, and urine. In addition, your health care practitioner will measure the size of your uterus, listen to the fetal heartbeat, and check the position and size of the fetus.

*Special
Procedures*

In addition to the routine procedures that you have been under-going in the last months, health care practitioners have many more tests that reveal information about the health of the fetus in your uterus. Thus, the last months of your pregnancy may be character-ized by additional tests, particularly if there is some concern about the pregnancy.

FETAL KICK COUNT

Some babies are much more active and regular in their motions than others. Although such differences among babies are acceptable, each baby should remain true to its own pattern of activity. Thus, it is a good idea to determine your baby's level of movement so that you can re-port any significant changes to your doctor.

Although the fetal kick test has variations, the basic method is fairly simple and enables you to play a role in checking on the health of your baby. This test measures how active the baby is over a certain period of time during a specific time of the day. Your health care practitioner will tell you how often and at what time of day to perform the test. Look at a clock or watch with a second hand and note the time. If you have a stopwatch, all the better. Pay close attention to the baby's move-ments and count each kick until you get to ten. Look at the watch and note how much time has passed. Make sure to do the test when you won't be distracted so that you can get an accurate count. Record the results and review them with your doctor.

If at any time you notice a sudden decrease in the baby's move-ment or if the baby doesn't move at all, call your doctor or provider immediately. If your caregiver feels that this is significant, additional tests, such as a fetal nonstress test or a biophysical profile score, may be indicated.

NONSTRESS TEST

During this test, the mother is attached to a fetal monitor to measure the response of the fetal heart to fetal movement. If the heart rate in-creases (accelerates) with the fetal movement, it is called a reactive nonstress test and usually means that the baby is fine. If such accelera-tions do not occur, it is called a nonreactive test. A nonreactive test doesn't necessarily signify problems and further tests will be taken to check the fetus.

CONTRACTION STRESS TEST

This is a somewhat complicated test used to determine the fetus' response to contractions of the uterus. As with the nonstress test, the mother is attached to a fetal monitor. Your doctor will then induce contractions, usually with a drug called oxytocin, which mimics the hormone that naturally induces contractions in the body. During the contractions, the fetal heart rate and the contraction itself are measured by the fetal monitor. The response of the fetal heart to the contractions gives an indication of the baby's well-being.

A variation on this test is based on the fact that breast stimulation can cause contractions. Thus, instead of giving you intravenous oxytocin, the breasts are stimulated by hot towels or manually by the mother. This is called the breast stimulation test, and it is similar to the contraction stress test.

BIOPHYSICAL PROFILE

The biophysical profile is based on the results of several ultrasound tests that evaluate the status of the fetus. The tests measure the amount of amniotic fluid, fetal movements, fetal tone, and fetal breathing movements. When combined with the nonstress test, your health care provider can obtain a fairly accurate assessment of your baby's well-being.

This score can be calculated from a four- or five-test series, with each test scored between 0 and 2. A cumulative score between 8 and 10 on the five-test series is considered satisfactory. A lower score indicates that further evaluation of the baby may be required, and sometimes delivery may be indicated.

The Pregnant You

Don't worry about your appearance or growing awkwardness. Take advantage of a few new perks—people offering you seats on buses, help carrying packages, or letting you go to the head of the line in the ladies room. Continue to wear loose or comfortable clothing. If you are comfortable working and experience no difficulties, continue to do so. Perhaps you want to cut back on your hours or work part of the time at home, but keep your mind and body active.

Work through any anxieties by talking about them with your partner, your health care provider, and, if you feel comfortable, your mother or a friend who has been through it all.

Q I'm in my ninth month, and I've been having the same dream now for a week and a half. In my dream, I go to my midwife's office for a routine checkup. However, this time, the midwife takes out the baby, shows it to me and says, "See everything is going fine." Then she puts the baby back inside me, and I wake up. Does this dream mean anything?

A Women often have strange dreams toward the end of their pregnancies. Although no one knows why we dream or what our dreams really mean, we feel that they are one way in which the subconscious sorts through problems and handles anxiety. In your case, your dream would seem to be your subconscious's way of handling your anxieties about childbirth and motherhood.

Making Love

Although for some women, sex is a wonderful way to forget many of the physical discomforts brought on during the third trimester, for others, the very idea of sex makes them cringe. Whether a woman's libido is turned on or off during pregnancy is determined partly by the physical and partly by the psychological changes she's undergoing. Some women feel voluptuous, ripe, and desirable, and sail through pregnancy with only a few days of nausea at the beginning. Others feel clumsy, fat, and unattractive, and suffer from a rotating litany of physical ailments—from nausea to exhaustion to joint pain and backache—from the day they get pregnant to the day they give birth. For women in the latter group, the last thing they want, especially in the last couple of months, is to engage in sex.

For a moment, let's separate love and sex. You absolutely must have some peaceful time for the two of you to exchange signs of your love. In the past, more often than not, this may have led to sex. But now, one of you—the one, who, toward the end of her pregnancy, may feel too overwhelmed to be turned on—may not want to have sex. If sex is made a quid pro quo of each of these cuddling sessions, then these may be scheduled less frequently than they need to be.

On the other hand, the last trimester does not have to be a sexless one. Keep in mind that your sex drive may go down a notch every time your belt size goes up one, but your partner's sex drive may not be similarly dampened. Some men may not be turned on by the sight of a pregnant woman, but many more find the increased voluptuousness

Q I am 35 weeks pregnant, and I have been intimate with my husband only a handful of times throughout my entire pregnancy. At this stage I'm feeling very unattractive. When I am in the mood to be intimate, my husband always seems to be engrossed in doing something else. What can I do to make these last weeks of my pregnancy exciting? I will have six long weeks of waiting after my child is born. What can I do to make my partner interested in having sex with me again? Your comments will be greatly appreciated.

A Ask yourself this question: Have I been turning my husband away most of the time when he wants to have sex? If you have, then his reaction is understandable. Being rejected at one moment and being given an invitation the next may make him feel like a ping pong ball. Since you feel like a beach ball, the combination is just not working out. What the two of you have to do is find the time to talk this out. Tell him how you're feeling, and let him tell you how he's feeling. You also need to make specific plans for intimacy. I know that you can't turn yourself on and off like a switch, but if the two of you have made a date, and you know that you'll plan to make love to your husband in the evening, try to do everything possible to make yourself feel attractive and get in the mood. When you get dressed in the morning, put on your sexiest underwear. And if you don't have any sexy maternity-sized lingerie, go buy some. (They're available at many maternity stores.) Take some breaks during the day to daydream about what it's going to be like. If going to the beauty salon helps you to feel more attractive, then make an appointment and treat yourself.

exciting. If you reject your partner every time he makes an advance, eventually he may stop approaching you altogether.

Your partner can also get into the act by dressing nicely instead of wearing the same old tee shirt and jeans. Sending you a bouquet of flowers before your rendezvous also can help set the right mood. He might also stop at the barbershop for a trim and a close shave, as well as splash on his good cologne. You may not have sex as often when you're pregnant, but when you do, make the most of it so that the effect lasts as long as possible.

Finding the right mix may be a bit tricky, but it will be less so if each of you knows ahead of time what to expect. So if the two of you are scheduled to cuddle at 10 PM and the thought of sex that night is the last thing on your mind, let him know that at 8 PM. That way, he won't feel disappointed when he discovers that it's not on your agenda. Instead, you'll have a close, tender hour together.

T I P

One way to avoid rejecting your partner is to set up a system of communication so that he can know ahead of time when you're feeling up to being intimate. I once told a listener who had a similar problem and who liked to crochet that she should make a pillow with YES crocheted on one side and NO crocheted on the other. Depending on which side she left the pillow on, her partner would know whether she was feeling up to being intimate.

*It Won't Be
the Same*

During the first and second trimesters, you will have to make some adaptations in the way you make love. This is especially true during the last trimester, when some of the effects of late pregnancy may decrease your libido. But in this case, some is definitely better than none at all.

*Finding the
Best Positions*

During the third trimester, some positions will be uncomfortable, if not impossible, such as the missionary position in which the man is on top of the women. At this stage, if your partner is on top of you, he will look like a seesaw and you will feel like a pancake. But that's really the only common position that's out of your sexual repertoire.

All of the other positions—side-by-side, spoon, rear-entry, and female superior—are still possible (see Figures 2 through 6). For many couples, in fact, late pregnancy is a perfect time to experiment. For the new position developed by Dr. Ruth and Dr. Amos, see Chapter 5. If you communicate your feelings as you try these new positions, you might even discover some positions that you truly enjoy and will want to continue using after childbirth.

Even in these final months—even during labor, the penis itself cannot hurt the baby. In the first place, although an erection is called a hard-on, an erect penis is not that hard. It's only flesh and blood and cannot cause injury either to you or the baby under normal circumstances. Although we do not recommend vigorous thrusting for an extended period, intercourse is safe, as long as a modicum of care is exercised. If you have a problem pregnancy, consult your caregiver before engaging in intercourse.

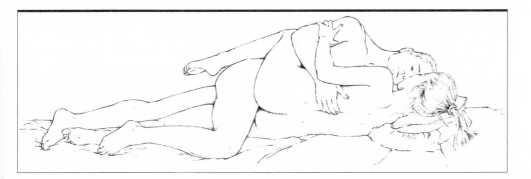

FIGURE 2

In this face-to-face position, there is no pressure on the woman's abdomen.

FIGURE 3

The "spoon" position is particularly comfortable for the pregnant woman. It allows her to stroke her partner's penis, while he can fondle her breasts and use his hand to stimulate her clitoris.

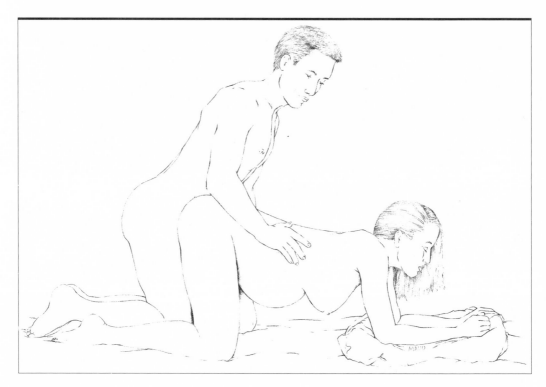

FIGURE 4

In this rear-entry position, there is no pressure on the woman's abdomen. She supports her weight on her arms, which rest on pillows.

Contractions from Orgasms

When a woman has an orgasm, whether she is pregnant or not, muscle contractions are triggered in various parts of her body, including her uterus. While she may not be conscious of uterine contractions under normal conditions, in pregnancy, she may notice them. The contractions that accompany orgasm are short lived, don't usually last beyond 5 to 10 minutes, and don't trigger premature labor in a healthy pregnancy. But if you continue to feel regular contractions for longer than 20 minutes after orgasms, we suggest you inform your health care provider. Releasing oxytocin—a hormone that causes uterine contractions—during orgasm in women may induce labor when a woman is close to her delivery date. In fact, women who are ready to deliver and just waiting for labor to begin sometimes have sex in the hope of going into labor. But if you are not at that point in your pregnancy and you have strong contractions following sex, don't hesitate to talk this over with your health care provider. He or she will let you know whether there is any risk from engaging in sexual activity.

FIGURE 5

This second rear-entry position may be more comfortable for both partners during the later stages of pregnancy. The woman supports her weight on her arms, but her arms and breasts rest on the edge of the bed and her knees are supported by pillows. Her partner kneels on the floor, which enables him to better control how deeply he penetrates.

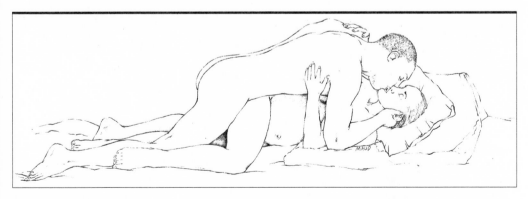

FIGURE 6

In this variation on the missionary position, the woman is on her side so that her partner does not seesaw on top of her enlarged abdomen.

*The Effect
of Semen*

Semen consists mostly of sperm and a fluid that is produced by the prostate and Cowper's gland. Another component of semen is prostaglandin—a hormone that some researchers believed might play a role in triggering early labor because it causes the woman to experience strong contractions. However, recent evidence has shown that the amount of prostaglandin in semen is not sufficient to have this effect.

Some women, however, do react to prostaglandin. Although there is no higher risk of premature labor, the contractions may provoke anxiety. Because sex should not become a cause for concern, women who experience such a strong reaction to semen might request that their partners wear a condom to determine if its use will prevent the contractions.

*Declining
Interest*

If you're one of those women who cringes at the thought of sex during this stage, you can take one of three paths. The first is to totally abstain from sexual relations of any sort. However, we believe that this is a mistake because of the damage such a long period of abstinence may do to your relationship. The second option is to engage in sex even though you don't feel like it. This may not turn out as bad as it initially sounds. Even though you don't feel like having sex when you climb into bed, you may find yourself enjoying it once you begin. Sex is like food—you may not crave it, but once it's in front of you, you may enjoy it. You may get into bed with your libido at a low ebb, but once you're naked beside your partner, your mood may change, and what seemed like a chore may turn out to be a pleasure.

The third variation is to give your partner an orgasm without having intercourse. You could masturbate him with your hands, apply your techniques at oral sex, or just stroke his brow as he masturbates himself. If you think that he'd like to watch an erotic video, encourage him rather than dissuade him. You could even rent one for him during the day and surprise him with it later on. Or, you could read to him some passage of your (or his) favorite erotic novel. At the very, very least, let him know that you give him your permission to masturbate in private. The one thing that you don't want to do is to make him feel guilty for satisfying a need.

Getting Ready for the Big Day

At one time, there was not much that a pregnant woman could do while waiting for the onset of labor other than to stay close to home. Today, the very advances that have increased the survival rates of both mother and child have also resulted in excessively elaborate planning by some couples. The best course, and hopefully the one that you'll follow, is somewhere in the middle. Yes, you need to prepare, but babies bring chaos with them from the minute they draw their first breath, so there's no point in getting set on one scheme. Your plans can only take you so far.

The Birth Plan   In the stone age of the birthing process—about twenty years ago— before there was such as thing as a birth plan, doctors—and only doctors—ruled the delivery room. No one thought to question what procedures would be used—that was why the doctor had gone so many years to medical school to learn. Although in some cases, doctors still maintain total control over their delivery rooms, more and more couples are demanding that their needs and desires be considered in the process. They will express their preferences on such topics as routine episiotomies (a cut made to enlarge the opening of the vagina), shaving the pubic hair, IVs, enemas before birth, walking during labor, electronic fetal monitoring, and holding the baby after the delivery. These are often the major points in birth plans, which are basically an outline of the couple's preferences about certain procedures during the birth.

The advent of birth plans has made the couple a partner with the health care provider. Each side is sharing some of the power over what takes place in the labor and delivery rooms. But that means that they are also sharing the responsibility for what happens. Every doctor has had to deal with complications, and in those instances, seconds do count. A delay caused by the need to insert an intravenous needle into an arm, for instance, might mean that the mother's blood pressure may remain too low for too long, just long enough to cause injury. Health care practitioners, who have seen these problems many times, would prefer to err on the side of caution. If you insist on having it your way, you have to weigh your freedom to choose over the possible consequences should an emergency arise. Make sure that you understand all of the implications of your choices before insisting on having things your way.

This is not to say that we need to consider returning to the dark ages, when practitioners put mothers to sleep and delivered their babies for them. Parents should know as much as possible about everything that has to do with the birth of their child. Thus, practitioners have to give up some of their authority, and parents have to take on a greater part of the responsibility.

For this team work to be most effective, your health care provider has to be a team player. You're probably confident in the provider you chose, but keep in mind that your provider may not be the one who delivers your baby. If, for some reason, he or she isn't available when you deliver your baby and you are attended by a practitioner who is not as open minded as your own, be frank about your wishes. In the final analysis, however, you'll have to trust the expert's instincts. If your own provider entrusted your care to an associate, you can usually rest assured that the practitioner is making decisions that are in your best interest.

Childbirth Classes

It was probably easier for health care providers in the days when fathers paced in waiting rooms instead of playing director/producer with their videocameras in delivery rooms. But, overall, the trade-off is a positive one. Making the birth of your baby a shared experience is a wonderful way to start your life as parents together, and most providers today encourage this.

From Our Files

Leslie was one of the last of her group of friends to become pregnant, but she had been too busy climbing the ladder of success to pay much attention to what childbirth might be like. When she did start asking questions, it seemed that all she heard were horror stories about how painful it was going to be. Her husband, Andy, tried to calm her down, but without much success. Soon Leslie started telling everyone that she was going to insist on delivering her baby by cesarean section so that she wouldn't have to be awake. Despite her attitude, Andy was able to convince Leslie to attend childbirth classes. Their instructor had been teaching prospective parents for twenty years and as she calmly described what happened during labor and delivery, Leslie felt all her panic subsiding. Leslie asked the most questions in class, and the instructor agreed to stay after class to answer those that Leslie hadn't managed to squeeze in. As a businesswoman, Leslie always dug for information about a subject before reacting to it. Now, she was using the same technique for childbirth. After getting the information she needed from her instructor, she was able to go into the labor room calmly. Although she was braced for the worst, she now knew that childbirth wasn't as awful as she had been told.

In addition to purchasing enough video equipment to outfit a major motion picture studio, most couples also prepare for the birth of their child by attending childbirth classes. These classes are wonderful—they give the father some concrete ways to support the mother and offer the mother practical tools to stay calm during labor contractions and delivery through breathing, relaxation, and focus techniques.

The classes also demystify labor and childbirth and debunk the often horrifying stories about four-day labors and excruciating pain that expectant moms—especially very expectant moms—are often regaled with at work, among friends, and even on the bus from strangers.

In childbirth classes, you will have an expert with whom you can put these horror stories into perspective. In birth, as in anything else in life, horrible as well as wonderful events occur, but the vast majority of births are fairly routine and come off as expected without any sudden crises, as your childbirth instructor will tell you.

Every couple can benefit from the confidence and reassurance they will gain from these classes. However, wonderful breathing, relaxation, and focusing techniques will not necessarily make every childbirth experience easier. Labor is an apt word. Delivering a baby is a rigorous experience, but it is as rewarding as it is arduous. Childbirth classes, however, can make the difference between feeling panicked and overwhelmed and being able to actually enjoy the rare and miraculous moment when you bring the life you've created into the world.

Most couples start attending classes during the seventh month. If you wait until the eighth or ninth month to sign up, you may not get to complete the class. Thus, sign up earlier during the pregnancy and take a refresher session, if necessary.

If you live in a large city, you'll have many choices for childbirth classes. This may not be true in smaller communities. Ask your health care provider for guidance on finding the right class for you. You may also find information on the Internet, in the phone book, and at community centers and houses of worship. If you have a choice of classes, ask the following questions to help you select which to attend:

1. At what point in my pregnancy should we sign up for the classes?
2. How many couples are usually in a class?
3. How much do the classes cost?
4. Where are the classes held?
5. How many hours of classes are given?

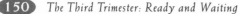

6. Who is the teacher and what are his or her qualifications?
7. Is a specific birthing method taught or is the education general?
8. What is the philosophy of the class?
9. How is the father's role perceived during the classes and at the delivery itself?

There are several different philosophies or styles of childbirth classes. The Lamaze Method is the most common, with thousands of couples attending such classes annually. Lamaze focuses on natural forms of pain control, such as breathing and relaxation exercises, as well as focus points, and approaches the couple as a team with the partner as a coach who is an integral and active part of the birth process.

Another popular method, the Bradley method, is similar to Lamaze, but does not rely on the familiar breathing techniques. Instead, it uses 12 relaxation techniques, many of which are based on the assumption that moving around, as opposed to lying still, will help alleviate pain.

In all the classes, your instructor will give you lessons on what to do during labor and delivery, as well as show you some exercises to do before giving birth. Most classes will also provide basic information about caring for your newborn and breastfeeding.

You will gain insight from childbirth classes by having your questions answered and listening to the answers given to questions of others. Not only might you say to yourself, "Why didn't I think of that?" but, more importantly, you'll be comforted when you hear that other couples are going through the same emotional and physical changes that you two are.

The Father-to-Be

Childbirth classes are very important for the father-to-be. They are the first formal occasion in which he will be asked to play the role of dad (well, aside from conception or those midnight trips to the supermarket for crackers). To participate in the classes, your partner may have to leave work a few minutes early, eat dinner later than usual, or miss the start of a ball game or two. In other words, he will have to adapt his routine to fatherhood responsibilities. That's an important psychological step. By sharing in this responsibility before the birth, today's fathers are better prepared to be parents after the baby is born.

He should also gain confidence in the role he is planning to play in the delivery room, as he familiarizes himself with the proper procedures for coaching you through the big event. By sharing his concerns and the learning experience with other expectant fathers, he will realize that he is not alone in his apprehension or excitement.

The Big Event

You must be familiar with the classic comedic situation of couples panicking as they frantically rush to the hospital when the mother realizes that the baby is about to make its appearance. But don't overreact; most babies take hours and hours of labor before being born. While there may be babies born in cars on the way to the hospital, it's doubtful that you want to have your baby that way. Therefore, being prepared for that big day as much as you possibly can is a good idea. Of course, you can never be fully prepared for the big day—unless you're scheduled for a cesarean delivery or an induction. But here are a few things you can do to prepare for the situation.

- Find the best route to the hospital. Take one or more dry runs. Both of you should go on these because two heads are better than one, and although you both plan on being there, each of you should know the way in case you have to go solo.

- Find one or two alternative routes. In case there's a garbage truck backing up traffic or a tree in your path, you'd be wise to have an alternative route or two.

- Keep the car ready to go. Make sure that you always keep enough gas in the tank to get you to the hospital. Check the tires. If you don't use the car for a few days, start it up anyway to prevent the battery from going dead (especially in cold weather).

- Make an extra set of car keys. Hang them in an accessible place that you'll be able to find even if you're in a panic.

- Make a list of taxi services. Whether you have a car or not, make sure that you have a list of taxi services available in case you need one. If you don't have an account with a certain company, call those on your list and find out how long they would take to arrive and what type of payment they require.

- Contact a baby or pet sitter and a backup. If you have children, make plans with a friend, relative, or caregiver who can be available

List of Things to Pack for the Big Day

Hers

Comfortable tee shirt or cotton pajama top

Slippers, sneakers, or heavy socks for walking

Lollipops, chewing gum, sucking candies to keep your mouth from getting dry

Moisturizer

Lip balm

Massage oil (stay away from fragrances that may offend you when you're in labor)

Your own washcloth and towel

Pillow for your back

Eyeglasses (you can't wear contacts)

Visual focus (pictures, religious objects)

Music player (CD, cassette player) and music

Address book with important phone numbers

Maternity or loose outfit for going home

His

Swim trunks, for your partner to shower with you

Tee shirt, comfortable top

Sneakers

Clean underwear

Change for the phone or vending machines

Photo/video equipment

Cellular phone and charged spare battery (ask if you can use a cellular phone in your hospital)

Ours

Drinks/snacks

Books/magazines/board or electronic games/playing cards (yes, there may be lulls to fill)

Watch with second hand or stopwatch

Dr. Ruth's Pregnancy Guide for Couples

Items for after the Delivery

Deodorant

Hairbrush

Make-up

Sanitary pads

Comfortable (loose) clothes for going home

Shampoo

Favorite soap

Cologne

Nightgown

Robe

Socks

Baby clothes, diapers

Child safety seat for car

Sandwiches

Champagne on ice!

on the spur of the moment. Have a back-up caregiver, just in case.

- Buy or lease a cellular phone or beeper. Either of these will allow you to stay in touch at all times.
- Have your camera ready. If you intend to record the birth in some way, make sure to load the film and have a spare battery. It would be a pity if you ran out of film or batteries just as the baby is about to make the grand entrance.
- Pack your bags. See the "List of Things to Pack for the Big Day" for items you will be needing during your stay at the hospital or facility of your choice.

$\mathscr{C}$OMPLICATIONS OF PREGNANCY

IF you think about it, the development of the fetus from a mass of cells into a fully formed baby is truly a miracle. And the fact that throughout history, even when medical knowledge was unsophisticated and often inaccurate, so many babies survived makes the miracle even more powerful.

With the advent of modern medicine, giving birth has become much safer—both for mothers and babies. During the twentieth century, amazing progress has been made in dealing with the complications that arise during pregnancy. Although problems still occur, your medical provider can remedy most of them so that you and your baby come through the birth with flying colors. The most striking advances have been technological developments that enable doctors to detect—and sometimes correct—problems while the baby is still in the uterus. And as new developments emerge, the future looks only brighter.

Still, encountering a problem during pregnancy or childbirth is always emotionally difficult. In addition to the understandable stress both parents feel, a signficant amount of guilt can enter into the picture. As with any problem, it is best to discuss your feelings with your partner, because complications during pregnancy can seriously affect your relationship physically and emotionally. Although relationships in which the partners draw strength from each other may grow stronger no matter the outcome, others may fall apart.

Although this chapter discusses most of the complications of pregnancy, it begins with those in which a ban on sexual intercourse may be necessary for a successful delivery.

Complications That May Preclude Sexual Intercourse

From Our Files

This was Penny's third pregnancy. The first two had ended in miscarriages at 18 and 16 weeks. The doctor had diagnosed that Penny had an incompetent cervix, which meant that her cervix was not strong enough to hold the baby inside of the womb. The doctor performed the standard technique, stitching the cervix closed with a McDonald cerclage when Penny was 12 weeks pregnant. He also instructed her to stay off her feet as much as possible and told Penny not to have sex, but did not explain specifically what that meant.

Penny and her husband interpreted the doctor's decree to mean that they should not have any sexual relations at all for the duration of the pregnancy. After three months of celibate life, and with four or more months staring him in the face, Eric became frustrated.

Sensing his frustration, they overcame their shyness and asked their doctor for advice. Their doctor sent them to a therapist, who encouraged Eric to find ways to give Penny lots of tender loving care—giving back massages without arousing her, touching her, and whispering words of reassurance. Penny was reminded to continue to satisfy Eric by using her hands, engaging in fellatio, and placing his penis between her buttocks or under her armpit. She discovered new ways to bring Eric to orgasm. Above all, they reminded each other that it was all just temporary.

Keeping Your Relationship Strong

If you develop certain conditions, your medical provider may determine that it is necessary to impose a ban on sexual intercourse. Unfortunately, a doctor rarely goes on to explain that a ban on intercourse may not mean a ban on all sexual activity—and no ban should stop your partner from having orgasms.

Thus, you should not feel shy asking your doctor about other options, so that you can learn the limits of what you can and cannot do. If your health care provider tells you to abstain from intercourse completely, but does not explain why or give you alternatives, we suggest you get a second opinion before turning away from each other for the duration of the pregnancy. If you don't, celibacy may become the path of least resistance, even if it is not required for a safe pregnancy. One possible alternative might be oral sex.

Although placing the penis in the vagina is certainly among the more common methods of stimulation, it is not the only one. In fact, many women cannot have an orgasm from intercourse alone because it does not sufficiently stimulate the clitoris. They require direct stimulation of their clitoris, either manually or with a tongue or a vibrator, to have an orgasm. And many men greatly enjoy having oral sex performed on them. Oral sex can lead to orgasm in one or both partners without intercourse. This is an advantage if your health care provider has imposed a restriction on intercourse for the woman.

Certainly, sex is often the focal point of intimacy in a relationship. No matter how busy your life is outside the bedroom, once you're in bed together, you become totally immersed in each other and in discovering anew the pleasure of each other's touch and tenderness. It is the one place where saying "I love you" comes naturally, even for the most laconic or reserved of partners. During those precious moments, all of life's other pressures slip away, and you can reaffirm and deepen the emotional bond between you. Without this emotional oasis, almost without knowing it, you may start to drift apart.

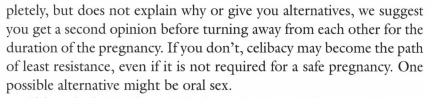

Specific Conditions

Any of the conditions described below may cause your health care provider to prohibit intercourse. In the vast majority of cases, if you follow your provider's advice, these conditions may be no more than a passing cloud on your pregnancy. The real cause for anxiety would be not knowing that you have a problem, because the lack of knowledge greatly magnifies the risk by preventing understanding and treatment of the condition.

PLACENTA PREVIA

The placenta should attach itself to the upper wall of the uterus. In placenta previa, which occurs in about one out of every 200 live births, the placenta attaches itself to the lower portion of the uterus and may completely or partially cover the edge of the cervix. It is often diagnosed early in pregnancy—usually between the eighteenth and twentieth weeks—when the first sonogram is performed. Under these circumstances, a repeat sonogram is performed several months later to check if the placenta has moved away from the cervix, which happens in most cases. If it has not, precautions need to be taken. Why? Because as the pregnancy progresses and the uterus stretches, placenta previa may cause severe bleeding that requires treatment at a hospital.

Pregnant women with placenta previa are often told to limit physical activity and should not have sexual intercourse. Either of these can disrupt the placenta and potentially lead to bleeding, labor, and premature delivery. If the placenta remains in this position through the third trimester, a cesarean section delivery is necessary to deliver the baby.

EARLY EFFACEMENT AND DILATION OF THE CERVIX

Recent studies have shown that a woman whose cervix is effaced (thinned out) or dilated (opened) early in pregnancy is at an increased risk for a premature delivery. Although most studies are inconclusive, vaginal penetration could theoretically lead to infection, rupture of the amniotic sac, or even labor. If you have had one or more babies before this pregnancy, however, it is not unusual for your cervix to be slightly open during the pregnancy. So, if your doctor tells you not to have intercourse under these circumstances, discuss all these factors and ask whether it would be okay to have sex with a condom.

HISTORY OF PREMATURE LABOR OR MISCARRIAGES

If you previously had either premature labor or a premature delivery or if you had a miscarriage in the second trimester, your doctor will want to take every precaution to prevent you from losing another pregnancy. One such precaution is likely to be a ban on sexual intercourse.

INCOMPETENT CERVIX

The term incompetent cervix means that the cervix is not strong enough to hold the pregnancy to full term, or at least to a point at which the baby can survive on its own. A woman with an incompetent cervix may have painless cervical dilatation, usually in the early part of the second trimester. The diagnosis is most often made after a woman has already lost at least one pregnancy because of symptoms typical of this condition.

A woman who has been diagnosed with an incompetent cervix requires a surgical procedure, called a stitch or cerclage, to close the cervix tight and give it the needed strength to support the fetus for the duration of the pregnancy. This is usually done at about the twelfth to sixteenth week of pregnancy. Although there is no scientific evidence that sexual intercourse will do any harm, most providers agree that it is best to restrict intercourse if you have a stitch in the cervix.

MULTIPLE FETUSES

Having multiple fetuses—that is, twins, triplets, or more fetuses—increases a woman's risk of premature labor and delivery. The incidence of twins, which is usually one out of every 80 live births, has now increased because of fertility drugs. On average, twins are delivered three weeks early and triplets six or more weeks early. It is generally advantageous for babies if the pregnancy lasts as long as possible. A ban on intercourse may be imposed between the twentieth and the thirty-seventh week, when the babies are at greatest risk of being born.

VAGINAL BLEEDING IN PREGNANCY

Vaginal bleeding during pregnancy is always of concern. It can be classified according to whether it occurs early or late in your pregnancy. Many women, maybe one out of five, who eventually deliver a healthy baby report some vaginal bleeding or spotting during the first several months of the pregnancy, usually around the time of the next expected menstrual period. It usually lasts only for a day or so, is less heavy than the usual menstrual flow, is not associated with pain, and usually stops

From Our Files

Susan, a law school student, was about two months pregnant with her second child. She was studying for her final exams when she noticed some vaginal bleeding. She called her doctor right away, and he told her to use a sanitary napkin rather than a tampon to absorb the flow, but that there was nothing she could do but let nature take its course and go on with her life.

Later that day, she realized that she was passing some blood. The flow was less than her usual menstrual period, but enough to make her concerned. She called her doctor who then asked her to come in for an ultrasound examination, which showed a good fetal heartbeat. Not only did Susan not miscarry, but she ended up going 10 days beyond her due date and delivered a healthy nine-pound baby.

on its own. If the bleeding is heavier and/or lasts longer, it could be the first sign of a miscarriage. There is little you can do to prevent a miscarriage, because it's usually a sign that the fetus is not developing properly. If bleeding or spotting in the first months of pregnancy is associated with pain, you should let your doctor know right away because it could be an ectopic pregnancy. Vaginal bleeding later in a pregnancy is of more concern, because it could be the result of serious complications such as premature labor and cervical dilatation, placenta previa (placenta covering the internal cervix), abruptio placentae (detachment of the placenta), and other less common reasons, such as injury to the vagina and cervix.

If you experience vaginal bleeding during your pregnancy, whether or not it is after intercourse, it is of utmost importance that you report this to your health care provider. He or she may be able to determine the cause through a sonogram or speculum examination. More often than not, no specific cause will be discovered. In that case, especially if you have not yet entered your thirty-seventh week of pregnancy, your health care provider may advise you to abstain from intercourse until the bleeding has subsided. If bleeding is observed again and if it is specifically associated with intercourse, most doctors will suggest that you stop having intercourse altogether.

LEAKING AMNIOTIC FLUID OR RUPTURED MEMBRANES

The membranes surrounding the fetus serve as a protective skin that separates the sterile amniotic fluid from the vaginal environment. Once the membranes are broken, bacteria can invade the fetus and placenta. When the membranes are ruptured early in pregnancy, premature delivery, or a miscarriage, may occur, and when it occurs in the latter part of the pregnancy, there is the danger of infecting the baby if it is not delivered soon.

Rupture of the amniotic membranes before labor is called premature rupture of membranes, or PROM. When it occurs before the thirty-seventh week (usually from the twenty-fourth to the thirty-fourth week), it is called preterm PROM. When it occurs after the thirty-seventh week, it is called term PROM. When PROM occurs before the 34th pregnancy week, doctors try to prolong the pregnancy to improve the baby's maturity. Intercourse at this time increases the risk of infection. In fact, just one vaginal examination by a doctor, even with a sterile glove, increases the risk of infection.

SEXUALLY TRANSMITTED DISEASE

If you or your partner has a sexually transmitted disease (STD), unprotected intercourse can transmit the organism to the other partner and the baby. Ask your health care provider if using condoms will prevent the infection from spreading.

Alternatives to Intercourse

What do you do when your health care provider tells you not to have intercourse until several weeks after your baby is born? Does this mean you have to take cold showers all day? Definitely not.

There are many ways in which you can safely have an orgasm without endangering the pregnancy. Oral sex is one of them. Mutual masturbation is another. Or, you can use a vibrator, but only on the clitoris. And with the plethora of erotic materials that are available, you can also take care of you own needs.

Could an orgasm ever be damaging to a pregnancy? First, ask yourself, "Have you ever had an orgasm in your sleep?" Some women do, and it is not something that can easily be prevented. As far as we're concerned, it is impossible to try and prevent it.

If you have a history of miscarriages due to an incompetent cervix, your doctor may try to avoid any and all possible dangers. Thus, he or she may suggest that you avoid orgasms because they can sometimes trigger uterine contractions. But, there is no scientific evidence that

ASK DR. RUTH

Q I've had two miscarriages as a result of an incompetent cervix. To carry this pregnancy to term, my doctor put a stitch in my cervix, gave me medication to reduce contractions, and told me to keep off my feet as much as possible. As a result, I am forced to sit around the house all day without much to do. I start daydreaming or fantasizing, and the next thing you know, I'm all excited. But, I'm afraid to masturbate for fear that an orgasm might cause me to miscarry. I'm so frustrated. What do I do?

A If you're staying off of your feet, your cervix is stitched up and you're on medication, it's very, very doubtful that an orgasm could trigger a miscarriage. If you masturbate and do have strong contractions as a result, then you obviously should stop. But if your orgasm does not cause contractions, then you can continue to masturbate.

an orgasm will trigger labor. We're not going so far as to say that it's a myth, but it is unlikely that an orgasm will start labor if your uterus is not ready for delivery. Nonetheless, if your provider tells you not to have an orgasm, we are not in a position to tell you to disobey doctor's orders. However, it does not hurt to ask for a second opinion.

A ban on sexual intercourse and orgasm need not cover the duration of the entire pregnancy. In some cases, intercourse is fine in the early months, but not recommended in the later stages. In other situations, the reverse might be true. For example, once the fetus has reached 37 weeks, it has reached term, so a ban on intercourse might be lifted once the doctor is certain that the baby (or babies) is developed enough. On the other hand, you may have some spotting early on in your pregnancy that would cause your provider to ban intercourse. Once your pregnancy has advanced and the spotting has ceased, you may be allowed to resume intercourse.

The same is true for orgasms. If you have had miscarriages early in pregnancy, once you are well past the point at which you previously miscarried and there are no signs of trouble, you may be able to begin having orgasms again. If you are told to abstain from sex and orgasms, make sure to ask for how long, and then inquire again when the current problem is resolved.

Additional Complications of Pregnancy

In addition to problems in which intercourse is contraindicated for a successful pregnancy, you should be aware of some of the other complications that can occur during pregnancy.

Ectopic Pregnancy

The fertilized egg is supposed to implant itself in the wall of the uterus, but sometimes it fails to do so, and implants in some other part of the body, like a fallopian tube, the abdominal cavity, or even the cervix. This is called an ectopic pregnancy.

An ectopic pregnancy that grows in a narrow area, such as a fallopian tube, may rupture the tube and result in a serious loss of blood. In such a case, surgery may be needed to repair the rupture. Ectopic pregnancies that develop in this way are one of the leading causes of death in pregnant women. Other ectopic pregnancies, however, merely wither away, and the woman may not even be aware that it has even occurred.

Q My sister had an ectopic pregnancy in a fallopian tube. She didn't know it until the tube had ruptured, and she almost died from the internal bleeding it caused. In fact, I had to give her blood. I'm about to get married, and I'm worried that if I become pregnant, the same thing might happen to me.

A There's no evidence that ectopic pregnancies are hereditary. In your sister's case, something, possibly some fibrous tissue, obstructed the fertilized egg from passing through the fallopian tube into the uterus where it should have implanted. Unless you have a medical history, which may have increased the risk of blockage in your fallopian tubes, you have little to worry about. Ask your health care provider if you have any reason to be concerned. And if you are still terribly anxious, you could find out early in pregnancy if the embryo is in the right place.

The symptoms of ectopic pregnancy are vaginal spotting or bleeding and pain in the pelvic area. Ectopic pregnancies are usually identified early in pregnancy. In very rare circumstances, an ectopic pregnancy will occur not in any part of the reproductive system, but in the abdomen. An abdominal pregnancy rarely goes to term, but when it does, delivery must be surgical.

Abruptio Placentae

Abruptio placentae is a rare condition in which the placenta separates, or abrupts, from the wall of the uterus prematurely, thereby depriving the fetus of oxygen and nutrition from the mother. If severe, this may result in death of the fetus.

Abruptio placentae is sometimes associated with hypertension and preeclampsia and occasionally with cocaine use by the mother. However, often doctors cannot find a specific cause. The symptoms are vaginal bleeding with severe and continuous abdominal pain. A woman suffering from these symptoms should contact her doctor immediately or go to the nearest emergency room.

Preeclampsia and Eclampsia

Preeclampsia, also known as toxemia, is a condition associated with an increase in blood pressure, usually accompanied by added fluid retention, or edema, and the presence of protein in the urine. It occurs in one out of ten women who have their first babies and one out of eighteen in subsequent births. When the symptoms of preeclampsia are accompanied by convulsions, it is known as eclampsia. Preeclampsia/eclampsia is a dangerous condition. In fact, prenatal care was begun early in this century for the sole purpose of preventing women from dying of preeclampsia/eclampsia.

Women who are at increased risk of preeclampsia/eclampsia are those having their first baby or those who are carrying twins; those whose mothers or sisters had eclampsia; and women with certain conditions such as chronic hypertension, diabetes, polyhydramnios (too much fluid), and lupus or lupus-like disorders.

Preeclampsia usually does not occur until well after the twentieth week of pregnancy. If mild preeclampsia is diagnosed in your pregnancy before the baby is mature, admission to the hospital and close observation are necessary in an attempt to prolong the pregnancy until the baby is more mature. If the symptoms are severe, then the baby has to be delivered early. If preeclampsia is diagnosed close to the due date, delivery is usually the preferred method of treatment. Your doctor will also prescribe medication to prevent seizures.

Diabetes

Pregnancy increases a woman's risk of developing diabetes, and it is now common practice to test pregnant woman routinely for diabetes. Diabetes occurs in women in one out of forty births. Screening procedures are a must for women who have had diabetes in a previous pregnancy, who have a family history of diabetes, who have given birth to a large baby or a stillborn child, and who are overweight. For these high-risk patients, testing is usually done early in their pregnancy, but even most patients without any risk factors will be tested by the twenty-sixth to twenty-eighth week.

A routine screening test for diabetes, called the glucose challenge test, is administered, and if glucose levels are elevated, a glucose tolerance test is performed. A pregnant woman found to have diabetes will be placed on a low-sugar diet and will be tested regularly for blood sugar level. If the blood sugar level cannot be controlled by dietary means alone, she may have to take insulin. The pregnancy should be closely monitored, especially as the due date approaches. Delivery will not be delayed very much past the due date because the placenta starts to deteriorate earlier than usual in women with diabetes.

Miscarriages, Fetal Death, and Stillbirth

Miscarriages

A miscarriage is a loss of pregnancy that takes place before twenty weeks of gestation. In the past, it was believed that approximately 10 to 15 percent of pregnancies ended in a miscarriage. With modern technology and early diagnosis of pregnancy, however, we now know that more than 40 percent of pregnancies end in a miscarriage, and more than 80 percent of these occur in the first trimester. The risk of a miscarriage increases with the age of the parents.

More than half of early miscarriages are the result of chromosomal abnormalities, such as trisomies or monosomies, in which there are too many or too few chromosomes. Other causes of miscarriages are infections, such as those from listeria; toxoplasma; and mycoplasma; external or environmental factors (such as smoking, alcohol, and caffeine); endocrine abnormalities (such as low levels of the hormone progesterone); and abnormalities of the uterus (such as leiomyoma or an abnormally shaped uterus).

How do you know that you have had a miscarriage? As we noted earlier, it's not uncommon for a woman to bleed early in pregnancy at the time when she would normally get her period. If you are bleeding severely, if the bleeding is accompanied by cramps, or if you pass a large clot, you may have had a miscarriage and should see your doctor for an examination.

SIGNS OF A MISCARRIAGE

A miscarriage does not always start with vaginal bleeding. Some women may first notice the disappearance of pregnancy symptoms—their breasts are no longer sore and morning sickness goes away literally overnight. If an examination, usually a sonogram, shows no signs of fetal life, and there is no vaginal bleeding, it is called a "missed abortion."

In other women, the first sign of a miscarriage may be heavy vaginal bleeding, usually with cramps. They will also pass clots and tissue. If the fetus and placenta are expelled completely, this is called a "complete abortion" or miscarriage, and the heavy bleeding will eventually diminish to a trickle. If you pass tissue at home, try to collect it in a clean jar and bring it to your health care provider for further examination. Sometimes, it may provide a clue to the reason for the miscarriage.

If some parts of the placenta and fetus are expelled, but there is still more inside the uterus, it's called an "incomplete abortion." Your doctor will usually perform minor surgery, called a D&C (dilatation and curettage), to remove the remaining tissue. This is a safe and short procedure and will usually not necessitate an overnight hospital stay.

Stillbirth

In rare circumstances, the baby dies inside the uterus and is born dead after the twentieth week of the pregnancy. This is called a stillbirth and happens in fewer than one in one hundred births. The death of a fetus is often first detected when the mother notices that the fetus hasn't moved for some time and when, on further examination, the health care provider cannot detect a heartbeat. Sometimes the cause of death may be obvious, for instance, when the umbilical cord is wrapped too tightly around the neck of the fetus, strangling the fetus, or if there are fetal anomalies. Often, however, the cause of death is not obvious.

The Psycho-logical Impact of Losing a Pregnancy

Many people assume that the later in the pregnancy that a woman loses her baby, the deeper the psychological impact. But recent research has shown that losing a fetus early in pregnancy—a fetus that may not yet be visible to the naked eye—can be a potentially painful experience.

At one time, a woman who miscarried was encouraged to forget that she was ever pregnant. But we've since learned that both parents need time to mourn the loss, and the more formal the process is, the better it will be for both of them. If the baby is big enough, the mother is allowed, if she chooses, to hold it for a time. A picture of the baby is usually taken for the parents to keep. If parents don't want the picture at the time, they can come back later and ask for it. The reason for such a formal approach is that, over time, the parent's feelings may change, and they may want to see the child. The picture is an important source of reassurance. Many parents name the child, have a funeral, and regularly go and visit the grave. All of these aspects of mourning are very healthy and, in the long run, will help them much more psychologically than trying to forget that the pregnancy ever occurred.

For these couples, approaching another pregnancy can be difficult. They may fear that the same heartbreaking experience will occur again. However, they should be comforted by the knowledge that although there is an increased risk, the vast majority of parents will have a healthy baby in a subsequent pregnancy. If you or someone you know has experienced a pregnancy loss, it might be helpful to read *A Silent Sorrow* by Ingrid Kohn and Perry-Lynn Moffitt.

TIP

Many hospitals have bereavement counselors who are trained to provide support to couples who have lost a pregnancy. Although you might not feel ready for such counseling immediately after the loss, we strongly encourage you to consult the bereavement counselor as much as possible. If you just want to be alone at first, take down his or her telephone number for later use in case you change your mind and decide to seek professional counseling.

Keep Yourself Informed

We listed these potential problems not to scare you, but to inform you. Some health care providers give their patients only cursory information, based on the theory that the less a patient knows, the less the patient will worry. However, medical complications have few definite answers, and there is not always a consensus on how to treat a particular condition. You need to understand as much as you can about what is happening to you during your pregnancy. Only then, if a condition does arise, can you make an informed decision on whether to agree to your health care provider's suggested course of treatment or seek other opinions.

CHAPTER

8

$\mathcal{L}$ABOR: THE TIME HAS COME

EVEN with the recent emphasis on health in our society, most people know comparatively little about how the body actually works on a day-to-day basis. We take such important functions as breathing, seeing, and smelling for granted and pay attention only if something goes wrong. During your pregnancy, you have become more conscious of your body because of the changes it has experienced. You have not, however, really been aware of how your body is creating your baby, cell by cell, limb by limb, organ by organ, and when your baby is ready to come into the world, you won't be able to think of anything else. Delivering a baby demands your full physical concentration.

In many cultures, giving birth is a family affair that is part of life's normal routine. At the time of delivery, the mother is at home surrounded by family and close friends. Most Western women, however, deliver their babies in a medical facility with only their partner and a medical team present. Despite these medical trappings, remember that giving birth is as natural as breathing or seeing. Keeping that in mind can be very comforting, especially when you are in unfamiliar surroundings, attended by an entourage of medical professionals.

It is only in modern times that giving birth almost automatically means going to a hospital. Women have always had help, but that assistance was often provided by relatives, neighbors, and the community midwife, who usually had only a fraction of the training of modern,

169

accredited midwives. Of course, when modern medical facilities weren't available, the mortality rate for women and their babies was much higher than it is now. Remarkably, though, even under the most rustic settings, such as a field or a hut far away from modern technology, labor usually results in a healthy mother and child.

As routine as childbirth may be, it still is often a long and arduous process. Although occasionally the baby practically delivers itself, in most cases, it takes many hours and women have to use all their strength and fortitude to push the baby out into the world. As most mothers will tell you, psychological factors come into play during the latter part of your pregnancy that help you rise to the occasion. As you approach your due date, your baby will be taking up so much space in your body that you'll be willing to do anything to get back to yourself. Rather than fearing childbirth, you'll be anxiously and eagerly looking forward to it.

It's also true that the pain of childbirth is different from other types of pain. Rather than signaling a problem, pain from childbirth is a sign of progress. Usually, the more intense your labor becomes, the closer you are to delivering and holding your baby.

The Waiting Game

As the due date for the baby's birth approaches, the number one question on every couple's minds is: How will we know when it's time? Perhaps one day science will devise a way of accurately predicting exactly when labor will begin, but we don't have that knowledge yet. Only mothers who are scheduled for a cesarean section or induction of labor may know exactly when they're going to give birth.

In the final weeks of your pregnancy, you and your partner will begin each day wondering if this is the big day; it's even more difficult when relatives and friends become preoccupied with your delivery. It is important to put things in perspective so that the waiting becomes more bearable. Our suggestions are:

- Relax and enjoy each other. Remember that you can't make yourself go into labor. It's out of your control. The best thing you can do is relax; practice your breathing, relaxation, and focus exercises; and enjoy your time together alone (Figure 1).

- If you don't feel like going out, spend a romantic evening at home either with videos and popcorn or candlelight dinners. Look at your wedding photos and old family photos of yourselves when you were babies. Have fun speculating who the baby

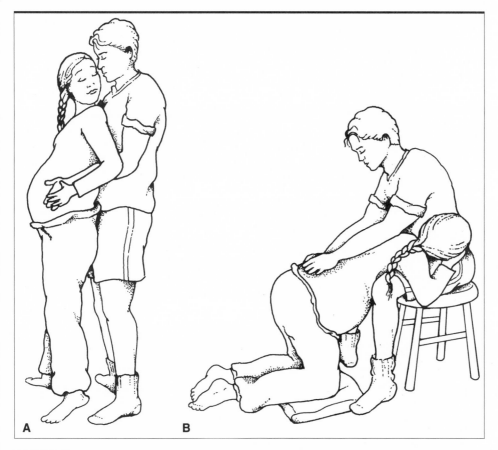

FIGURE 1

The following exercises will help you to more effectively and efficiently push the baby out during labor. In these exercises, your partner applies pressure to your lower back in a standing (A) or kneeling (B) position.

will look like. Invite friends over for a game of cards, a board game, or any other game you enjoy.

- Make love.

- Keep the anxiety level down, so that the rising tensions that come from waiting for labor to begin won't eat away at your relationship. This is particularly true if your due date comes and goes without any signs of labor. Without realizing it, both of you can start to become irritable. The key to controlling this behavior is to be conscious of the problem. Any time you feel like biting off your partner's head, bite your tongue instead and take a deep breath. Yes, you're feeling nervous. But remember, you're nervous about something good, not something bad. Don't allow your anxieties to sour this final part of your pregnancy experience.

- Expectant mothers should try to avoid blaming the father for their constant feelings of discomfort, while the father should try to understand what his partner is going through. The last few weeks are particularly difficult. She will find it hard to sleep. She will either be short of breath or will run to the bathroom every few minutes, depending on whether the baby is pushing up or down. Time will seem to move very slowly, particularly as she grows more impatient to deliver. But if you direct your frustrations at each other, the relationship is going to suffer. Fighting isn't going to calm anyone's nerves; it's only going to add additional stress.

So what can you—the soon-to-be mom—do to alleviate tension? If you can still walk comfortably, go out of the house for a walk. Go window shopping. Exercise is a great way to let off steam, and walking is one of the few exercises that most women can still enjoy as they near their due date. If you can't walk easily, try making bread and use the dough as a punching bag, pounding and kneading it between risings. If the thought of making bread is overwhelming, work with clay instead. Engross yourself in some activity, such as putting pictures in photo albums, working on a jigsaw puzzle with your partner, or catching up on the list of books you've been meaning to read. Instead of complaining to your partner, call a friend or relative who you don't see very often and complain to him or her. Remember, your partner is probably as keyed up as you are. Other friends or relatives can probably lend a sympathetic ear as you vent your feelings.

- Make yourself more comfortable physically. If your back is aching, ask your partner for a rubdown (Figure 2). Sinking into the sensations of a good rubdown can be very soothing to your nerves. If he's not around to get the knots out of your back and

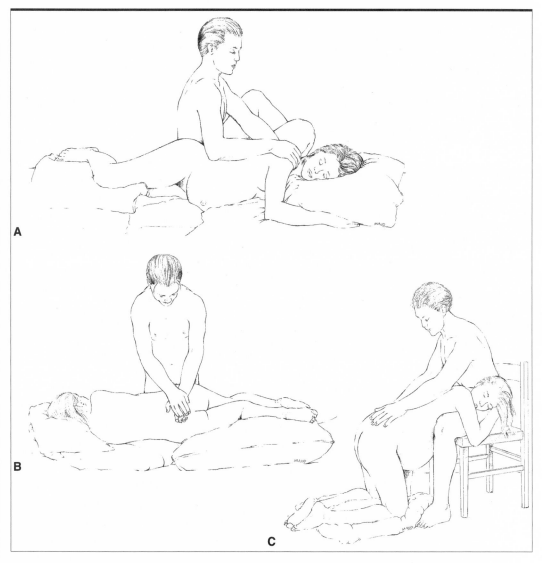

FIGURE 2

Late in the pregnancy and in the early stages of labor, your partner can help you relax by massaging your neck/shoulder area (A) or your lower back (B, C).

Q I was an only child without a lot of other relatives around, so I haven't spent much time with babies. As my due date approaches, I'm feeling more and more nervous about how I'm going to cope. What if I'm just not cut out for motherhood?

A You sound like someone who's getting ready to take a big test. It's so big that you can't really prepare for it, as you could for a test on a particular subject at school. It seems so out of your control that you have become very apprehensive. The difference is that in motherhood, grades aren't important. All that is needed for you to "pass" this test is a lot of love and patience. You'll find that there are many right ways to take care of a baby because each one is an individual—an individual who changes from day to day, at that. One day, you'll find that rocking will calm your baby; the next day, the same thing will make your baby howl, and tummy-rubbing will do the trick. It's great to be prepared, but there are some events in life where you just have to trust your intuition, and this is one of them.

---

shoulders, use a cold pack on those muscles for 15 or 20 minutes. Turn the shower on as hard as you can and let the warm water massage your sore muscles.

• Recognize that it is natural to have anxieties about becoming a new mother.

Your Due Date

During the first trimester of your pregnancy, the actual birth of your child was an abstract reality and knowing the exact date of arrival of your baby was probably inconsequential. As the day gets closer, it will be natural for you to want a more specific answer to the question "When?" The problem is, your due date really is not one single day, but a range of days—usually a time period of about five weeks. The odds of labor beginning on your due date itself are rather small. In fact, there is only a 1 in 20 chance that you will deliver on the anticipated due date.

Fortunately, nowadays early sonograms are helpful in more accurately identifying when the baby is likely to appear. Your health care provider can usually confirm your estimated date by reviewing your records—your sonograms, the record of your pregnancy test, the date when you first felt your baby move, your first examination, and other pertinent information.

> **T I P**
>
> *In the early stages of labor, you should conserve energy. Your delivery could take some time and as you near the end, you'll need as much energy as you can muster to push out your baby. If at any point you can sneak in a catnap, do so, and have your husband stand guard so that nobody wakes you unnecessarily.*

What Are the Signs?

As the arrival of the baby comes near, your body will often start to change in anticipation of the birth. There are several signs that your body may be getting ready to go into labor.

RIPENING OF THE CERVIX

Your cervix will soften in anticipation of effacing, or thinning, and dilating or opening. However, your cervix can be fully effaced and even a couple of centimeters dilated for a few days or even a couple of weeks before you go into labor, especially if this is not your first baby.

SPOTTING AND INCREASED VAGINAL DISCHARGE

As the cervix effaces, tiny blood capillaries are broken, resulting in a pinkish or blood-streaked vaginal discharge. Some women may also discharge the mucus plug, which usually seals the cervix and becomes loose when the cervix dilates. Sometimes, but not always, this may be an indication that delivery is close.

INCREASED BRAXTON-HICKS CONTRACTIONS

By now, you're probably used to these practice contractions that cause no discomfort but make your belly hard enough to bounce a coin. As you get closer to labor, these contractions will become more intense and may feel painful, not unlike menstrual cramps. These contractions play a part in getting your body ready to give birth by helping reposition the baby, efface the cervix, and begin dilation. In fact, many women become fully effaced and even one or two centimeters dilated a week or more before they actually begin labor. These contractions will subside, unlike labor contractions, which are persistent and become stronger and more frequent as time goes by. Labor contractions also are usually first felt in the lower back rather than in the abdomen, where Braxton-Hicks occur. You can take some measure of comfort from the realization that these practice contractions are definitely moving you closer to labor by gradually thinning your ordinarily thick, cone-shaped cervix, and causing it to dilate.

False Labor   The term false labor refers to these Braxton-Hicks contractions that intensify as you get closer to labor. These contractions are called false labor because they don't lead to childbirth, but sometimes appear to

About two days before her due date, Marilyn started to feel cramps low in her abdomen. They came and went 20 minutes before she went to bed and continued for about two hours. She was sure she was in labor, so she called her doctor's office and her husband, Tony, started the car. However, during the 40-minute drive to the hospital and the time in the hospital admitting room, she didn't have any contractions. By the time the doctor came to examine her, the contractions—or whatever they were—completely stopped. Marilyn went home feeling terribly embarrassed.

The next night—the night before her due date—the same thing happened all over again. This time Marilyn was again sure that she was really in labor, but decided to wait longer before calling her doctor. After about two or three hours, the cramps went away. A week then passed, and Marilyn was still waiting.

During her last checkup, her doctor explained that this was a classic case of false labor, which is characterized by contractions in the abdomen rather than in the lower back. These contractions don't increase in frequency or intensity and stop altogether once you get up and move around. Often, a woman has episodes of false labor days, or even a week or two, before she actually gives birth. Such prelabor contractions are your body's way of preparing for birth. During these contractions, your cervix is effacing and dilating.

Marilyn had no reason to be embarrassed about her early trip to the hospital. False labor can be very confusing, even for women who have already had children. Think of it as a dress rehearsal! Remember, when it comes to childbirth, it's far better to come a little too early than to come a little too late.

have enough of a pattern to convince anxious expectant mothers they are about to give birth. When you're hoping that every twinge is the beginning of labor, it's easy to mistake these prelabor sensations for the real thing. It does not hurt to err on the side of caution and contact your health care provider about your symptoms.

ENGAGEMENT

The term engagement, also called dropping or lightening, refers to the baby's descent into the pelvis. Engagement is another sign that you're getting closer to the beginning of labor. Engagement is measured during a vaginal or abdominal examination in which the position of the baby's head is determined in relation to the ischial spines, or zero station, two bony parts of the pelvis. Your doctor will measure how many centimeters above or below this line the head is positioned. A baby's head that is above this level is "floating" and not yet engaged. A baby's head that is below this level is "engaged."

As the baby descends into the pelvis, your body will go through another series of changes. Your stomach may look not only lower, but smaller. You will also find it easier to breathe, because the baby is no longer pressing against your diaphragm and lungs. But, because the baby is lower, you'll feel increased pressure on your bladder and bowel, causing constipation and frequent urination.

When the baby's head is engaged, it usually means that it will fit through the pelvis. The reverse, however, is not necesssary true. If the baby's head is not engaged when labor begins, it doesn't mean that the baby definitely will not fit through the pelvis. Studies have shown that mothers have a better than 80 percent chance of delivering vaginally even when the baby's head is not yet engaged before or in early labor. The majority of women who have already had a baby will go into labor while the baby's head is still floating. The baby's head usually will enter the pelvis late in labor or even when the mother starts to push.

Can you still have sex after the baby's head is engaged? Absolutely, if you feel like it, and there is no contraindication. Just remember that because the fetal head is now lower in the vagina and the total length of the vagina might be shorter, thrusting the penis too deeply in the vagina might feel uncomfortable for the man. The penis in itself can do no harm, but both of you might feel better doing more gentle movements. For example, he may insert his penis less deeply.

LOSS OF WEIGHT (OR NO WEIGHT GAIN)

In the ninth month of pregnancy, you may stop gaining weight or even lose weight. This may be a sign that you are getting closer to labor.

LOOSE BOWELS

Just before the onset of labor, many women experience loose bowels, which may be nature's way of emptying the lower bowel in anticipation of birth.

INCREASE IN ENERGY

A few weeks before going into labor, some previously cranky and fatigued women suddenly feel energetic and elated. Although not a scientifically studied indication of impending birth, such a change in mood or energy may be one way that your body revs up in anticipation of the rigors of childbirth.

Making Final Plans

Now is the time to make sure that you have everything ready to go for the big day. Check not only your route to the hospital, but also make sure you know which entrance is the preferred one for maternity patients (although the closest one is the best one for an emergency).

Now is also the time to find out if your hospital has a preadmission policy that allows you to fill out the admission paperwork before your due date. Taking this step will enable both of you to go right into the maternity ward without stopping to complete the paperwork when you're having contractions every two minutes.

Going into Labor

Labor is the process that starts with strong, regular contractions leading to dilation and effacement of the cervix and, ultimately, to the delivery of the baby. We don't yet know exactly how and why labor begins, although we do believe that certain hormones and signals from the fetus itself may play a role. When it begins, true labor is characterized by regular contractions that become progressively stronger and more frequent, regardless of whether you change position or move around.

Some women know right away that they are in labor because the contractions are regular, intense, and longlasting. Other women may begin labor with mild contractions that slowly build up over hours. And in other women, labor begins after the waterbag has broken. No matter how your labor begins, you'll wonder later on how you could have confused real labor with anything else.

The Stages
of Labor

Although labor is different for every woman, most labor processes go through three stages. The first stage begins when strong, painful contractions—usually 2 to 3 minutes apart and lasting 30 to 60 minutes—cause the cervix to efface and dilate. This first stage is further divided into three phases—latent, acceleration, and deceleration.

The latent phase is usually the longest, especially for women having their first baby. A woman in labor for 36 hours will probably experience the latent phase for 24 hours. During this phase, the contractions are comparatively mild and the cervix dilates slowly. It is the slowest, least intense, portion of the first stage of labor.

When the cervix is dilated to about 3 to 4 centimeters, the acceleration phase begins as the cervix dilates much more rapidly. When it has almost reached its maximum dilation of 8 to 9 centimeters, the deceleration phase begins, in which labor slows down a bit until the cervix is fully dilated. When the cervix is fully dilated to about 10 centimeters, you are ready to push and the first stage of labor is over.

The second stage begins when the dilation of the cervix reaches 10 centimeters and ends when the baby is born. The second stage is the part of labor when women do their most work. Often, by this time, there is an urge to bear down and push. This is the stage in which the woman works to push the baby out. It lasts about 30 to 45 minutes on average, but can take longer—up to 2 to 3 hours. The length of this stage depends on many factors. For example, if the baby is small or if the mother has had previous vaginal deliveries, this stage may be shorter, but it may last longer for a woman having her first baby.

The third stage lasts from the moment the baby is born until the placenta is separated from the wall of the uterus and expelled from the vagina. This process usually only takes a few minor pushes on the part of the mother and rarely lasts longer than half an hour.

When to
Contact Your
Health Care
Provider

How do you know when to call your doctor and go to the hospital? Several clues will help you identify the right time. Usually, your doctor will give you guidelines on when to call based on the timing and the length of your contractions. Both of these variables can be precisely measured. Intensity is also important, but intensity is something that can be evaluated differently by each woman.

TIMING OF CONTRACTIONS

In true labor, contractions come in a regular series. You first experience 30- or 60-second contractions that are about 15 to 20 minutes apart. After some time, the intervals between contractions will decrease—13 minutes, 10 minutes, 7 minutes, and so on. They will also last longer—up to 90 seconds—and become more intense as labor progresses. The whole process can take 12 to 24 hours or longer, so relax, rent a movie, and try to get some sleep for the real work ahead.

In the past, many husbands thought that when labor began, they were no longer needed. They felt there was nothing for them to do. Today we know that nothing is further from the truth. When labor begins, your wife really needs your support. You can help by supporting her emotionally, serving something to drink (and light food if it's allowed), giving her a massage, and monitoring the contractions. To monitor contractions, you need either a stopwatch or a watch with a second hand and a pen and paper (or a laptop or palmtop if you're more technically inclined). Make a note of when the contractions begin and end, and how long they last.

Some health care providers will instruct you to call when the contractions last for 45 to 60 seconds and are 3 to 4 minutes apart. Others might suggest waiting until the contractions are 2 to 3 minutes apart. Although this might sound like cutting it close, don't worry. There is usually still plenty of time to go before your baby is born.

INTENSITY OF CONTRACTIONS

Contractions usually intensify in strength as labor progresses. They often begin as twinges that won't interrupt what you're doing and eventually reach a point where you can no longer talk through them. Because women have different perceptions and thresholds of pain, the intensity of contractions is not as good an indicator of labor as the timing and length of contractions.

WHEN YOUR WATER BREAKS

When the membranes that surround the fetus break, amniotic fluid is released. This is called "when your water breaks." In the movies, expectant moms almost always exclaim that their water has broken before rushing to the hospital. In real life, most women are well into labor and already at the hospital before their water breaks. So don't wait for your water to break before calling your health care provider if your contractions are regular and intense.

Most women worry that the occasion of their water breaking will be cause for embarrassment. They imagine a sudden gush of water running down their legs. Even though this is what the phrase "water breaking" calls to mind, the flow when your water breaks is usually slow, depending on your position. When you are standing or sitting, your baby usually acts as a stopper when the surrounding membrane breaks, and the amniotic fluid leaks out in a trickle. Using a panty liner will often give you enough protection. You may feel better having a small towel and a change of panties handy, just in case.

The likelihood of the amniotic fluid coming out all at once is rare. Thus, if you wake up in the morning and your bedsheet is wet, check to see if it smells sweet rather than like urine. If it doesn't smell like urine, it's likely that your water has broken.

It is not necessarily an emergency if your water breaks, but most health care providers will want to be contacted, no matter what time of day (or night) it is. Make a note of the time and the color of the amniotic fluid. It should be clear or light yellow, similar to urine. Sometimes, it's very lightly tinged with blood. If it is greenish or brownish in color, or if there is a lot of blood in it, your health care provider should be informed. If this happens, the fetus needs to be monitored closely and this can be done only in the hospital.

Although there's usually no immediate danger to your baby after your water breaks, the membranes that kept out infection are no longer intact. Thus, the chance of infection increases the longer the baby remains in the uterus. If your water breaks close to your due date, your health care provider will prefer labor to begin within a specific amount of time. If labor doesn't begin naturally within that time, he or she will want to induce it.

How long your provider will wait to induce labor depends on several factors, such as level of risk for you and the baby. Many providers will induce labor as soon as your water breaks at term, while others may be willing to wait. Most will want to monitor you and the baby during that time to make sure that everything is okay. That is why it is important to let your caregiver know as soon as you think your water has broken; he or she needs to accurately gauge how much time has elapsed.

Sex After Your Water Has Broken

You might think that having sex isn't going to be the first thought in your mind after your water has broken and, if you're also experiencing contractions, it's a safe bet that it won't be. But you may remain pregnant for some time after your water breaks, and since intercourse won't be in the cards for about six weeks after your delivery, the thought might come to you to have sex one last time before taking a long, enforced abstinence. Should you automatically reject this idea?

Because patients sometimes ask this question, we want to tell you that although there is no definitive answer, most doctors suggest that you not put anything into your vagina after the membranes have ruptured. This is definitely true if the membranes break before the thirty-seventh week of pregnancy, because there is an increased risk of premature delivery and possible infection of the baby.

Going to the Hospital

You're timing your contractions. You've called your health care provider. You're on your way. Our first word of advice is to get there safely. Having an accident as you race toward the hospital is not a good way to start your baby's life. If the stress of hearing mom groaning next to him makes dad step harder on the gas, keep in mind that even a minor accident would only make the trip longer, so keep that speedometer down. As we have already said, the vast majority of babies are born after many hours of labor, so you have enough time to get to the hospital.

T I P

If you happen to see a police car, don't hesitate to roll down your window and ask for assistance. With the police siren and flashing lights leading the way, you'll get to the hospital quickly and safely.

$\mathcal{D}$ELIVERY: THE BIG DAY

SO, you've arrived at the hospital. If you are not preadmitted, your partner can bring you to the admitting office to fill out forms (if you are able) while he parks the car. Once you're admitted, you'll be led to an examination room, and you'll trade in your street clothes for a hospital gown.

Know What to Expect

Your Health Care Provider

If your health care provider is already at the hospital, he or she will examine you. If he or she is not yet at the hospital, the staff will take your vital signs, listen to the fetal heartbeat, and examine you to ascertain whether or not you are to be admitted. Some hospitals may have doctors and midwives available 24 hours a day, while others have experienced labor and delivery nurses who know how to handle obstetric patients.

Labor/Birthing Rooms

When you are admitted, you are usually taken to a labor room. This is not necessarily the place where you will give birth, although many hospitals now have labor-and-delivery rooms (LDRs), where you may go through labor as well as deliver your baby.

Monitoring the Expectant Mother

In the labor room, you may have an intravenous line started. This will give your health care provider immediate access to your system in case medication is needed. Throughout your labor, the dilation of your cervix will be checked regularly, as will your vital signs, such as blood pressure, pulse, and temperature.

Most hospitals have abandoned what used to be routine practices, such as shaving the pubic areas. You will also be given a choice as to whether or not you want an enema.

Monitoring the Fetus

The baby's heart rate is almost always monitored during labor. This can be done by auscultation or electronically by monitoring the fetus externally with a monitor that is attached to your abdomen or internally with a monitor attached directly to the baby. The electronic monitors record both the fetal heart rate and uterine contractions and record the results as a graph.

The baseline normal fetal heart rate is between 110 and 160 beats per minute. Monitoring the fetus allows the doctor to track your baby's health and take measures to help it in case of any problems.

ASK DR. RUTH

Q During the birth of my third child, I am certain I experienced an orgasm. Although I mentioned this to several friends, none of my friends have ever heard of this. Have you?

A There are many similar physical reactions between sexual intercourse with orgasm and childbirth. For example, there is an increase in heavy and more frequent breathing; vocalization; changes in facial expression; regular contractions of the uterus (albeit labor contractions are much stronger and painful); increased sweating; physical position, strong muscular activity, clitoral engorgement; increased vaginal lubrication; and an altered state of awareness. When you look at these similarities, it is understandable that you might feel similar sensations during labor as you do during an orgasm. It should not bother you. After all, if the baby was conceived with an orgasm, you may think it fitting to deliver that baby with one.

During this time, you and your husband will grow even closer. Rarely will you spend so much time together, focused intently and working together toward the same goal. And how many times will you be bringing a life into the world together? So, why not try to make the experience as loving as possible. And since your contractions will tend to come in cycles, there definitely will be time for you to focus on each other.

*If It's Not
Time Yet*

Many hours usually pass between the onset of labor and the actual birth of your baby. Meanwhile, you may find yourselves at the hospital or in the labor room with nothing much to do. Whatever commotion is going on around you, which will include the sounds and activities from other mothers in labor, you and your partner should find ways to make this occasion special for you together.

Find ways to share the waiting time together. It can be a simple activity like holding hands, playing music, and even dancing if you are still able to move comfortably. If you brought a book with you, you could use this time to read passages to each other. This could be from a work of fiction, something inspirational, including the Bible, or maybe some favorite poems. If you haven't decided on a name for your child yet, this is a perfect time to review the possibilities in one of those ever-growing books of baby names.

Your Partner's Role

From Our Files

Peter and Joanne were expecting their second child. During the delivery of their first child, he stood at his wife's side and coached her through her breathing exercises. At one point, while the medical team was busy easing their child into the world, he alone noticed that Joanne was hyperventilating, and he helped her breathe easier, just as he had been taught, until she felt better. Their health care provider allowed them to have what is known as a Leboyer birth, a childbirth method that includes soft lights and soft music. After the baby boy was delivered, Peter cut the cord and the baby was handed to Peter, who then gave his son his first bath in a tub of warm water.

Now, four years later, they were in the delivery room together again. All was going well, but this time the baby ended up being a breech. When the midwife announced that the baby's butt was visible, Peter grew faint and had to sit out the birth in a chair in the doorway to the delivery room. A labor nurse took over coaching Joanne through the delivery of their son.

When Joanne was recovering, Peter was concerned that she would be disappointed with him. But Joanne understood that Peter's concern for her and the baby had overwhelmed him and loved him all the more for recognizing the wisdom of stepping aside.

Unlike past generations when the mother went through delivery with a doctor and the hospital staff, she is now encouraged to have a partner—or coach—attend her during the delivery. Nowadays, that partner is often the baby's father, but neither parent should feel pressured into this arrangement and neither should feel guilty about choosing another approach. You need to do what is best for the mother. If she feels more comfortable with a professional coach (sometimes called a doula), with her mother or a friend, or wishes to have the baby alone with the help of a labor nurse, her preferences should be considered. If the father feels uncomfortable or queasy about attending, he should explain his feelings to his partner. It is better for him to wait outside than coach you nervously and inefficiently. Whomever you pick as your coach, you should both attend childbirth classes and have time to finish before your big moment.

Besides helping you maintain the proper breathing technique, your coach can also help in other ways, such as:

- Offering emotional support, which you will need if your labor lasts longer than expected. Let him know ahead of time that if you scream at him, it's only because you don't feel comfortable screaming at the doctor.

- Massaging various parts of your body, either to make you less tense or to distract you from the contractions (Figure 1). Light stroking, called effleurage, of the abdomen, with the fingertips is one recommended style of massage.

- Making sure you are as comfortable as possible by getting pillows, water, lollipops, or ice chips for you or by calling for a nurse or your health care provider if you need assistance.

- Holding you while you push so that you have a firm support to push against and coaching you so that you push in the most effective manner.

Pain Relief During Labor and Delivery

The birth of a baby has always been associated with a considerable amount of pain, but today, mothers can choose to practice natural pain relief techniques or accept medication that will safely and effectively reduce pain.

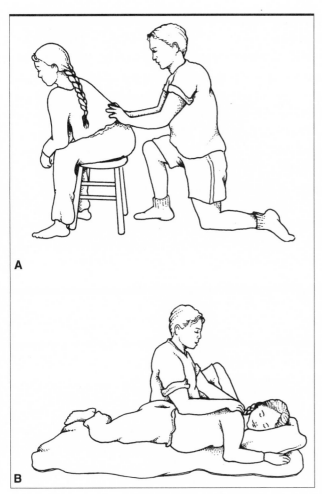

FIGURE 1

These exercises may help you cope with the back pain that usually comes with labor and delivery. In (A), your partner massages your buttocks, and in (B) he massages your neck/ shoulder area.

Pain Relief Without Medication

The behavioral techniques that you learn in childbirth classes—breathing, focus exercises, and massages—have been proven quite effective in reducing the pain of childbirth for many women. But, if you experience pain at an unacceptable level, our advice is not to grit your teeth and bear it. Whenever you cannot tolerate the pain during labor, let your nurses or doctor know and pain relief will soon be on its way.

Pain Relief with Medication

You should discuss your preferences for one type of anesthetic over another with your doctor long before you are admitted to the hospital. However, circumstances arising during your labor and birth will influence which type of anesthetic is available to you and which kind you would want to choose.

Your doctor or health care provider will often work in cooperation with an anesthesiologist. Together, with your informed consent, they will decide the best path for you to manage the pain of childbirth, always keeping in mind the possible effects that any medication might have on your fetus. These need to be weighed against the benefits they have for easing your pain.

Regional Anesthetics

Regional anesthesia involves administering anesthetic medication in the area surrounding the nerves in the spine. It decreases the feeling in the abdomen and sometimes part of the lower body. Several forms of regional anesthetics are available today. The most commonly used are epidurals, combined spinal-epidural, and spinal.

EPIDURALS

One of the most frequently used anesthetics in the United States during labor is the epidural. In this procedure, a small needle is inserted between two bones in the lower back (after the site is numbed with a local anesthetic) while the patient is either sitting up or lying on her side. An anesthetic drug, similar to the one used by dentists to numb your gums, is injected just outside the spinal canal, thereby numbing the abdomen. The epidural is usually administered during the active phase of labor, although it may be given earlier if needed. Epidural anesthesia takes between 10 and 20 minutes to become effective, and depending on the exact drug being used, may last from one hour to more than two hours. Because one dose of the anesthetic will often wear off before the baby is born, the anesthesiologist usually places a small catheter in the space where the epidural was initially injected so that additional medication can be administered either intermittently or by continuous infusion without further injections. The continuous infusion eliminates the need for repeated injections if labor lasts longer. Your anesthesiologist will know how to balance the epidural so that your pain is relieved while you remain able to push effectively. If you ultimately require delivery by cesarean section, pain relief for that procedure is provided through the same catheter, only with different drugs and in higher doses.

Most woman who have an epidural say that it is the perfect anesthetic for pain relief during labor, because it does not affect your consciousness in any way. You remain awake and alert and can move all your limbs, but you cannot feel the pain caused by the contractions.

Some researchers claim that epidurals increase the need for assistance during delivery through the use of forceps, a vacuum, or even surgery. Although these assertions have not been conclusively established, epidurals can sometimes make the lower part of your body feel heavier, thereby making it difficult to push as effectively and to move unassisted from one position to another. In addition, you may need a catheter to remove urine. Although epidurals have not been shown to have negative effects on the fetus, you will be hooked up to a fetal monitor just to be sure that the baby's heart rate is okay. Because a possible side effect is lowered blood pressure, you will have your blood pressure checked frequently. There are a few conditions for which it is not advisable to have an epidural anesthetic. If you have an increased tendency to bleed, a skin infection at the site of administration, or recent back surgery, an epidural anesthetic may not be ideal for you.

All of this information about epidural anesthetics does not mean that you should let anyone pressure you into having one. At the same time, you should also not let friends or family members pressure you into being brave and going the distance without relief. There is no heroism in pain, and suffering more isn't going to make you a better mother. If you need relief, don't be shy about asking for it.

COMBINED SPINAL-EPIDURAL ANESTHESIA

Recently, a new form of epidural analgesia, called the combined spinal-epidural anesthesia (CSE), was introduced. This is also known as the "walking epidural" because, contrary to the traditional epidural, the CSE often allows you to move freely and actually walk around during labor. In many hospitals, the CSE has largely replaced conventional epidural anesthesia.

The CSE is similar to the epidural. After numbing the entry site, a small needle is first placed into the epidural space in the lower back near the spine. Then a tiny second needle is placed through the epidural needle, beyond the epidural space into the spinal column. A small amount of anesthetic is then injected into the spinal canal. The small needle is then withdrawn and a catheter is placed in the epidural space through which additional anesthetic can be administered if needed.

The effect of CSE begins within one to two minutes and lasts for about one to two hours. When you start to feel the pain again, a local anesthetic can be infused through the catheter. With this combination, the amount of local anesthetic can be decreased while achieving excellent pain relieving effects.

SPINAL ANESTHESIA

This form of anesthesia is usually not used for women who deliver vaginally, but for women who require surgery, such as in cesarean deliveries. A very small amount of anesthetic is injected with a very tiny needle, slightly deeper than with an epidural, directly into the cerebrospinal canal. This type of drug is effective within seconds, making it the desirable drug when speed is important. Its effect may not last quite as long as the epidural. After one of these injections you may become completely numb below the area of the injection and unable to move your legs for several hours.

There are some risks associated with a spinal anesthetic. There is a small risk that you will develop a spinal headache. With newly developed spinal needles, however, this risk has decreased to less than one in a hundred. There is even the smaller possibility of a high spinal occurring, a condition in which the numbness also affects the upper body. Today, however, spinal anesthesia is considered best for cesarean sections and in forceps or vacuum deliveries, where speed is of the utmost importance and a solid block is necessary.

General Anesthesia

General anesthesia involves the use of an anesthetic to make you unconscious. General anesthesia is not used to manage the pain of labor, but may be used when operative procedures are necessary, such as emergency delivery by cesarean section. The reason why most hospitals today prefer regional anesthetics, such as epidurals or spinals, even for most surgical deliveries, is because of the increased risk of complications with general anesthetics, such as the possibility of a patient vomiting while unconscious and inhaling and choking on the vomit. That's also why it's a good idea to eat lightly once you realize you are in labor and why many hospitals will not allow you to eat once you are admitted.

Narcotic Pain Relief

Narcotics, or narcotic-like drugs, such as Demerol (meperidine hydrochloride), Nubain (nalbuphine), and Stadol (butorphanol), are sometimes used for pain relief in labor. These drugs are usually injected either intravenously (through your intravenous line) or intramuscularly (in the arm or hip). They are used to dull the pain of contractions, but are most effective in the first stage of labor. If given too close to delivery, they can have a negative effect on the baby's breathing, fetal heart rate, and ability to suck. Side effects for the mother include nausea, vomiting, and a drop in blood pressure. In most cases, though, the side effects are short lived.

Some women feel that the drowsiness caused by narcotics left them disoriented and less able to stay on top of their contractions, while others report that the relief from narcotics was just enough to allow them to continue with their breathing and push effectively.

Inducing or Stimulating Labor

While labor usually begins and progresses without any prompting, sometimes it takes a little too much time to get going. Your doctor will occasionally suggest inducing or stimulating labor artificially to give nature a helping hand.

Stripping the Fetal Membranes

If your cervix has already partially opened, your provider might suggest trying to strip the cervical membranes to induce labor. To do this, your cervix needs to be dilated so the doctor can place a finger in your cervix, gently stretching it in a circular fashion to cause the fetal membranes to separate from the cervix. Research has shown that this method can be effective in hastening the onset of labor. The procedure may be uncomfortable, so make sure to use your breathing exercises and have your partner beside you for support.

Amniotomy

Amniotomy is a procedure in which the fetal membranes are artificially ruptured to speed up labor. This might be done to induce labor, to insert an internal electrode of a fetal monitor to check the baby's heartbeat, or to check the amniotic fluid. Because the fetal membranes do not have nerve endings, the procedure is painless. Your health care provider will use a special device called an amniohook that is inserted and guided along inside by your provider to break the fetal membranes. This will cause your water to break and you're on your way!

Prostaglandins

Under normal circumstances, toward the end of your pregnancy and before active labor begins, the cervix becomes soft in preparation for effacing (thinning) and dilating (opening). If this has not happened and you need to deliver your baby soon, prostaglandins are sometimes used to cause these changes in the cervix. This substance is usually inserted into the vagina, close to the cervix, either as a gel or as a small suppository.

Oxytocin or Pitocin

Another method of inducing labor is to use a synthetic form of the natural hormone, oxytocin, also known as pitocin. Oxytocin is administered intravenously, most often by a controlled drip, at a very low dosage that is gradually increased until labor begins. Some women who have had natural labor feel that the contractions brought on by pitocin are more intense. However, pain relief measures can be used as soon as labor is established.

The Delivery

 *From Our Files*

Laura had been trying to push her baby out for about two hours, but she wasn't making any progress. Her doctor told her that he'd give her another hour, but if the baby hadn't come down any further in the birth canal by then, he was going to have to order a cesarean section. The thought of having to go through surgery after all these long hours of labor didn't appeal to Laura at all. Knowing that she only had an hour left, she gathered up her resolve and pushed with every ounce of strength in her being.

It was the hardest thing she had ever done. She felt as if she were about to break in two, but she kept on pushing. At one point, she was ready to give up. Once, she even started to get off the table, muttering that she wanted to go home. But her husband and her doctor helped her regain her focus by telling her that the head had crowned and that they could even see the color of her baby's hair—red—like that of her favorite great aunt. Laura gave one last almighty push, bearing down so hard that she broke many of the little blood vessels under the skin of her neck and face with the effort. Finally, she heard the lusty holler of her baby, and with one more mighty push, the baby was finally in the world.

Once your cervix is fully dilated, the second stage of labor begins and you are ready to start pushing in anticipation of delivery (Figure 2). If you've been administered an epidural, it may take more time for you to feel the urge to push, but when your health care provider tells you that it's time, you can start pushing.

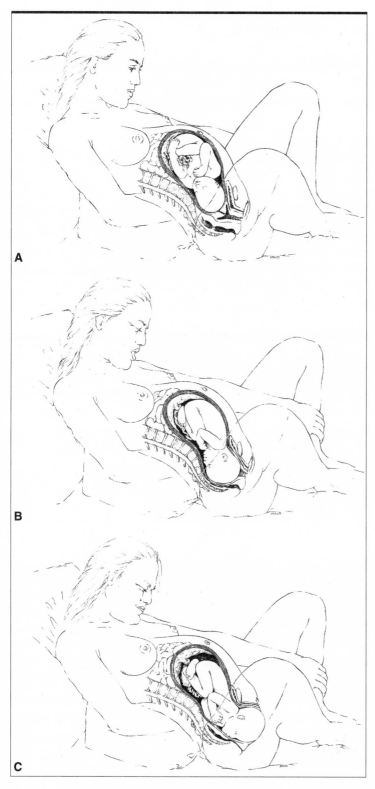

FIGURE 2

The process of delivery as the baby (A) engages, (B) passes through the birth canal, and (C) finally makes its appearance.

There is one secret to the art of pushing the baby out, and that is to know where you are pushing. You are not pushing out through your stomach, but bearing down and out, just as if you were pushing out a bowel movement.

Some women are inhibited at first because they worry that they will, in fact, push out some stool. However, you don't need to worry about this happening. For one thing, your bowels have, in most likelihood, been loose for the last couple of days before delivery. This is nature's way of clearing out the bowel in anticipation of birth. Even if stool comes out, the nurse will simply wipe it away with one of the disposable liners under you. Medical professionals are used to these sorts of things, so don't be nervous.

It can be frustrating and exasperating at first to push as hard as you can and make no progress. But as soon as you catch on to the concept of bearing down, you'll make up for lost time.

Positions for Pushing

There are many different positions for pushing. Try some to see which one is most comfortable for you. You can lie on your side or have your partner support you in a semireclining position. Squatting or standing can sometimes help you push with the force of gravity rather than against it. To do this, you'll need the support of your partner, either assisting you from behind or in front.

If you've had a baby before, or if this baby is small, the time needed for pushing may be very short. For some women, all that is required is one concentrated push to deliver the baby. If this is your first baby, however, or if this baby is bigger than your others, it will probably take longer.

In the past, the practice was to allow a woman to push only for a fixed time period. If you exceeded that magic number, which used to be two hours, the doctor would intervene, either by using forceps or a vacuum, or by performing a cesarean section. Today, the concept of a magic number has been cast aside, especially if you have been administered an epidural anesthesia. As long as the fetal heart rate remains within a safe range and the head continues to move through the birth canal, many practitioners and midwives will allow you to continue to push for a longer time, sometimes up to three hours or more. Beyond that time, however, exhaustion takes its toll. If by this point, your strength starts to falter, there is not much point in allowing you to continue.

You don't have to push continuously. In fact, it might be advisable to take a break once in a while, both for your sake and the baby's. Sometimes, prolonged pushing may cause a change in the baby's heart rate. When you stop pushing, the baby's heart rate returns to normal. Giving the baby's heart a break occasionally is no doubt a good thing and allows the baby to recover between contractions, when there is more blood flow through the placenta.

Once you have taken a break and regained some of your strength, you might consider trying a different position before starting to push again. Don't be afraid to try any position you can think of. Whether or not there is any physical advantage of one position over another, there might be a psychological lift in changing positions that will give you the courage to keep going.

BIRTHING BEDS

In many hospitals, old-fashioned delivery tables have been replaced by soft, comfortable birthing beds. The back can be raised to provide support for the mother and the foot removes easily to make room for your health care provider.

Back Labor

Back labor refers to the strong pain you experience in your back during labor, sometimes, but not always, as a result of the baby pushing against your back. Back labor is more severe during contractions, but may persist as you go through labor. To relieve back pain, try changing positions. Another often-cited remedy taught in most childbirth classes is applying counterpressure against the place where the labor is worst. Back massages also can be helpful as are hot or cold compresses, depending on which you prefer.

Crowning

The first sign of the actual birth is called crowning, the moment when the baby's head can be seen in the vaginal opening. (It is often at this time when dad will be called over to get his first glimpse of the baby.) Many hospitals now have a large mirror placed between your legs so that you can also see the baby's head as you push. This is often the point when your will and energy are at their lowest, and the first glimpse gives most mothers a final burst of strength to finish the job. The time lapse between crowning and actual delivery is usually very short.

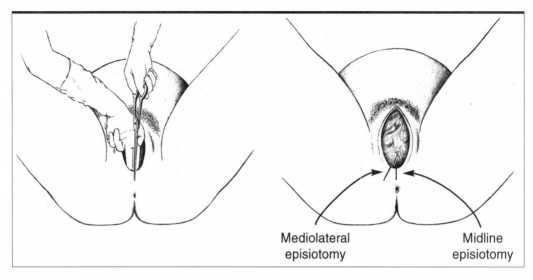

Mediolateral episiotomy

Midline episiotomy

FIGURE 3

In an episiotomy, the incision is made through the skin and sometimes through the muscles. Your doctor or midwife may decide to use a mediolateral or a midline incision.

Episiotomy

An episiotomy is a procedure in which a small straight-cut incision is made in the perineum (between the mother's vagina and anus) just before the baby's head crowns to make space for the baby to pass through. Now, routine episiotomies are performed less often, but there are often reasons to do one. Because this is not a minor procedure, you should be part of the decision-making process and should clarify your feelings with your health care provider before you go into labor.

The Birth of Your Baby

In most cases (actually 97 percent of the time), the baby's head comes out first. It is usually face down, but sometimes face up. Before delivering the rest of the body, your health care provider will do several things, including checking to see if the umbilical cord is wrapped around the baby's neck, suctioning the baby's nose and mouth, and wiping the baby's face.

The baby's head will then turn, either by itself or with the help of your provider, and the rest of the baby is delivered. A clamp will then be placed in each of two sections of the umbilical cord, and then the cord is cut between the two clamps. If you or your partner want to be a part of this last act of birth, tell your health care provider to let you know when it's time to cut the umbilical cord.

The question most often asked of obstetricians is, "How long will my labor last?" If you've spoken to other mothers who have gone through several labors, then you must already know the answer: Each labor is different. In general, labor lasts longer for first-time mothers than for women who have already given birth. In your case, though, statistics may not tell you much. You could take 24 hours or only 4 hours.

We know of one father who went for a sandwich after parking the car, figuring he should prepare himself for the long haul ahead, and ended up missing all of the action. On the other hand, another father put on five pounds in a 24-hour period as he kept going down to the hospital's cafeteria for a burger and fries. The only advice we can give you is that once labor starts, don't make any plans for at least 48 hours.

Premature Delivery

Approximately 5 to 10 percent of babies are born before the thirty-seventh week. These babies are called preterm babies, or preemies. A premature baby may be born with several problems, and the earlier the baby is born, the more severe the problems usually are. Among these problems are underdeveloped lungs; an immature immune system; immature blood vessels, which could lead to internal bleeding, possibly in the brain; and disorders of the intestines, specifically a condition called necrotizing enterocolitis, a condition that destroys the bowel. With recent improvements in neonatal intensive care units and the use of intensive drugs before and after delivery, more and more babies survive a premature delivery.

In the majority of cases, no one can predict a baby's early arrival. Some women, however, are more at risk for premature delivery,

TIP

If you are feeling any regular contractions or if you have watery vaginal discharge of any kind before your thirty-seventh week of pregnancy, let your health care provider know as soon as possible. Labor before the thirty-seventh week is considered premature and, if diagnosed early, may be stopped so that your baby can be born at full maturity.

particularly women with multiple gestations (i.e., those having twins, triplets, or more) or those with a history of previous preterm deliveries; women with abnormally shaped uteruses or cervixes or those who have too much amniotic fluid; women who ruptured their fetal membranes before their due date; women who have not had appropriate care during pregnancy; and women with certain medical conditions.

Postterm Delivery

At the other end of the spectrum are babies who are born too late. This may be cause for concern because as you go significantly past your due date, your placenta ages and provides less nutrition to the fetus. As a result, babies born after 42 weeks are at increased risk for complications.

Most doctors will begin fetal testing somewhere between the fortieth and forty-first week. These tests include the biophysical profile, the nonstress test, the fetal kick count, and the contraction stress test. Assessing the amniotic fluid when you go past your due date is, perhaps, the most specific test of your baby's health because it may indicate that the placenta is no longer providing proper nutrition to the baby anymore. If any of these tests is abnormal, delivery of the baby is usually indicated.

Cynthia is only five days beyond her due date, but her cervix has already dilated to about 1 to 2 centimeters and is thinning out. Although she wants to wait until labor begins naturally, her doctor is insisting that she induce labor if it does not begin naturally in 24 hours. Cynthia feels she is being rushed. After all, her best friend waited almost two-and-one-half weeks after her due date to go into labor naturally. Unfortunately, Cynthia is not taking into account the impact of the gestational diabetes she developed halfway through her pregnancy.

Cynthia's doctor explained that certain medical conditions, such as high blood pressure or diabetes, may cause the placenta to age earlier than in a normal pregnancy. Most doctors prefer that pregnant women with such conditions don't go too much beyond their due date, specifically if the cervix is ready for delivery.

When Nature Needs Help

Occasionally, mothers and babies can't seem to separate from each other without assistance from the outside world. In such cases, where the baby just doesn't seem to want to leave the womb, outside help becomes imperative. Some methods used to help the baby leave the uterus are the use of forceps and vacuum, or a cesarean section.

Forceps
Delivery

Forceps, long metal tongs that look similar to salad-servers, have been around for a long time (Figure 4). Doctors use them to get a grip on the baby's head so that the baby can be pulled out of the vaginal canal. Remember that at the turn of the twentieth century, women had, at most, a 50 percent chance of surviving a cesarean section. Thus, at that time, and even today, when it's difficult to do a cesarean section, forceps can be literally a lifesaver for both the mother and the baby.

Vacuum
Delivery

In many hospitals, especially in Europe, a vacuum is employed instead of forceps to facilitate a vaginal delivery (Figure 5). A vacuum is a round cup attached to a hollow tube that resembles a suction cup. The cup attaches itself to the baby's head by suction when a vacuum is created, usually by a hand pump. While you push, the doctor can then ease the baby out by gently pulling on the vacuum tube during a contraction. This usually takes no more than a few contractions.

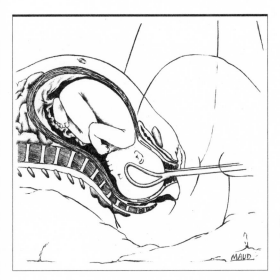

FIGURE 4
The use of forceps helps the doctor bring the baby's head out of the birth canal.

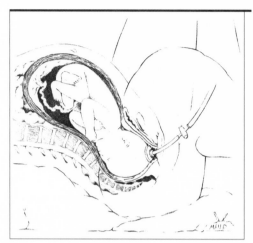

Forceps or a vacuum are commonly used when the baby's head is already in the vagina, and when the mother is exhausted from prolonged pushing, when there is a need to expedite the delivery of the baby, or when a cesarean section is not immediately available. Now that cesarean sections have become much safer and doctors are less familiar with these alternative procedures, forceps and a vacuum are used less often.

Cesarean Delivery

A cesarean section, or C-section, is the delivery of the baby surgically through the mother's abdomen (Figure 6). The most frequent reasons for performing a cesarean section are repeat C-sections; breech presentation, in which the baby's buttocks or feet come out first; presumed fetal jeopardy (also called fetal distress); when the fetus does not pass through the mother's pelvis; certain obstetric complications, such as abruptio placentae and placenta previa; and medical complications requiring expeditious delivery (that is, hypertension, diabetes). Presently, appproximately 20 to 25 percent of all babies born in the United States are delivered this way.

Approximately one third of C-sections are "repeats," in women who had previous C-sections, while the other two thirds are first-time C-sections. Your doctor sometimes knows ahead of time that a C-section will be necessary, but most C-sections are decided on during labor.

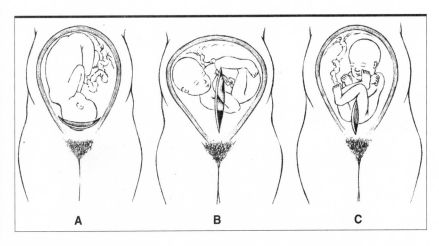

FIGURE 6

In a C-section, your doctor may use a (A) low transverse, (B) classical, or (C) low vertical incision in the uterus.

Your Baby Has Arrived

You've given the final push, looked into the mirror, and witnessed the miracle of birth. The traditional image of a newborn baby is one with its head hanging down, screaming, as the doctor holds its feet and gives it a whack on its tiny behind. Those days are gone. If the baby requires any assistance in breathing, an aspiration device, and not a slap on the rear, is used to clear out its lungs.

Once the baby emerges, one or both parents may cut the umbilical cord. The newborn is then handed over to a nurse or pediatrician or placed on the mother's abdomen or in a crib. Babies do not always have to scream loudly to be healthy. If your provider believes in the Leboyer method of delivery, in which the lights are lowered so the baby doesn't have to go from a dark womb directly into the bright lights of the delivery room, dad might get to give his baby a bath right after birth, assuming that the baby is in good health. Even if the nurse does give the baby its first bath, dad will certainly have a chance to hold it while mom is being cared for and cleaned up.

The baby's status is then checked and rated according to the Apgar score (Table 1), a test developed by a New York anesthesiologist, Virginia Apgar. Under this system, five vital signs are assessed, and each is

TABLE 1   Apgar Scoring System

Sign	0	1	2
Heart rate	Absent	Slow (< 100)	> 100
Respiratory effort	Absent	Slow, irregular	Good, crying
Muscle tone	Flaccid	Some flexion of extremities	Active motion
Reflex irritability	No response	Grimace	Vigorous cry
Color	Blue, pale	Body pink, extremities blue	Completely pink

given a score of 0, 1, or 2 for a total of 10 possible points. The vital signs are heart rate, muscle tone, respiration, reflexes, and color.

The vital signs are assessed twice—one minute after birth and five minutes after birth. The scores are added up each time for a maximum of 10. A high Apgar score usually means you have a vigorous baby, who does not need further assistance. Low scores, on the other hand, indicate that the baby needs some immediate attention. For example, a low Apgar score means that the baby might need extra breathing support, while a higher score usually means that the child can breathe on his or her own.

When you first see your baby, remember that nine months in the womb and the trip down the birth canal do not produce movie star looks. Babies are born with disproportionately large heads, sometimes with a point or lump as a result of the birth process and often with a covering of soft hair that will later be replaced. Your baby may also have puffy eyes, swollen genitalia, red blotches, and hair temporarily covering the shoulders, back, and forehead. It may take some time for that picture perfect baby to emerge, but just after delivery, you will probably notice only how beautiful and healthy the baby is and how happy you both are that your new child has finally arrived.

Nowadays, many mothers and fathers expect to hold their baby immediately after birth, which gives them a chance to bond with their baby. If your baby is in good health, you'll be given some time to spend with him or her right after birth. You might try to put the baby to your breast, and he or she may begin to suck. However, don't be surprised if your baby doesn't understand why you're shoving your breast in his or her face. Some babies take to the breast right away, while others learn about breastfeeding along with you.

Meanwhile, dad has one more task—to pick up the phone or a bag of quarters and start calling assorted grandparents, aunts, and uncles. There are no better messages you can give over Alexander Graham Bell's invention than the ones starting with "It's a boy!" or "It's a girl!" and "Both mother and baby are doing well!"

$\mathscr{L}$IFE AFTER CHILDBIRTH

SO, you're home from the hospital with the newest member of your family. You're both thrilled with the baby and happy that your pregnancy—with all its discomforts—is over. Now, you may be thinking, you can exercise and regain your figure, entertain family and friends who want to come see the new arrival, and possibly even resume your professional career on a part-time basis at home. If these are your plans, you're going to discover very quickly that the unbounded joy of the first few months of parenthood can also be a time of adjustment, turbulence, and just plain exhaustion. Thus, you should have realistic expectations about what you can and cannot do.

Pregnancy and delivery are rigorous experiences—both physically and emotionally. As such, they are good preludes to the rigors of early parenthood. Your body needs to recover physically, the baby will make constant demands on your time, and you will find yourself running the whole gamut of emotions—from elation to depression. During these months, patience, adjustment, and understanding are the key words. It will take time to balance your new responsibilities with the old. In addition, you and your partner need time together just for yourselves; time to strengthen your emotional bonds and to reinvigorate your sex life. We want you to be enthusiastic, but we also want you to make appropriate plans so that you don't crash and burn out in your first few months as parents. If you focus on yourselves and your baby, you'll be fine. But, if you try to take on the world at the same time, you'll be overwhelmed.

Recovery: A Time of Healing and Adjustment

rom Our Files

Judy had come to the hospital at 1 AM. Labor had proceeded normally, and she gave birth without problems at 6 AM to a healthy 6 pound 11 ounce baby girl. Judy was delighted about the easy delivery, but she was disturbed by the fact that because she had gone into labor two weeks before her due date, she had not had time to clean her house before she left for the hospital. Now she felt that her house was not clean enough for her in-laws and everyone else who was going to visit.

So, she insisted on leaving the hospital the same day she delivered. As soon as she arrived home she and her vacuum cleaner performed the housecleaning of the century. They were interrupted only every two hours by the one-day-old baby's cry and need to be fed. The next day, Judy felt totally exhausted, and it took her weeks to feel her usual self again.

It is important to remember to take it easy after birth. Pregnancy and labor do take a toll on your body. Be intelligent for the first weeks after delivery and manage your energy carefully. Don't try to do it all yourself. Ask for help!

There is no question that an adequate recovery period after delivery helps you feel better. How much time you will need depends on your experience during childbirth and how quickly your body heals. Some women feel well within a week or two after delivery; others take months to feel fully recovered.

Recovering at the Hospital

These days, new mothers are hurried home from the hospital as fast as possible after they have their babies, often, even sooner than they have to. If you had an episiotomy, a procedure in which a small incision is made in the perineum, it will take some time—a few weeks or even months—to heal completely. If you had a cesarean section, your abdominal incision will take quite some time to heal completely. Modern medical techniques undoubtedly save lives, but still cannot enable you to instantly recover from childbirth. We suggest that you stay at the hospital as long as you're allowed (two days after a normal delivery and three to four days after a Cesarean)—and take advantage of the room service, the baby care, and the opportunity to learn about breastfeeding and other child care essentials. If you are feeling sociable, chat with other new mothers about their experiences and hopes. You may find new friendships forming that will continue after you leave the hospital.

Remember that your first order of business is to rest. Once you get home, you will be on "24/7" call—24 hours a day, seven days a week. The hospital is probably the only place where you'll have a staff of people ready and waiting to whisk away your baby, change its diapers, bathe it, and send it back smelling sweet. So take a nap between the baby's feedings.

A father also has a crucial role to play at the hospital. He should keep phone callers and visitors at bay when the new mom is resting. If you doze off, he should take the phone off the hook and stand guard at the door, guiding visitors to see the baby or to the lounge to chat while you sleep. That way, your friends and relatives will have a chance to see your new baby, and not feel disappointed, and you can still get the rest you need.

If you delivered vaginally, you might be given a sitz bath, which allows you to sit in warm soothing water and soak your perineum. This encourages circulation to the area and hastens healing. Make sure to soak three or four times a day for about 15 minutes.

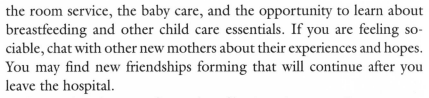

TIP

Buy a doughnut-shaped pillow that will allow you to sit without actually resting on either your episiotomy or your hemorrhoids.

Because a cesarean section is a major form of surgery, the potential for complications is greater than for a vaginal delivery. If you had a spinal or epidural anesthetic (and more than 90 percent of women do), the first thing you will experience is the return of feelings in your lower abdomen and legs. If you had a general anesthetic, you might feel nauseated for some time. If you were intubated, you may have a sore throat for several days. In addition, during the first days following the cesarean, you may be given pain medication that makes you dizzy and sleepy. As you recover, the medication will be changed to one less potent. When you begin to eat regular food, any time from the day of surgery to two to three days later, you'll experience some abdominal bloating and gas pain, which will disappear as soon as you start passing gas and have your first bowel movement. The skin in your abdomen is usually closed with dissolvable sutures or with staples, which are usually removed within three to five days. Call your doctor if the incision starts discharging blood, clear or cloudy fluid, or if it becomes very painful or turns red.

You may also experience difficulty in urinating, because the urethra gets bruised during birth. You will be given several hours to try to urinate on your own, but if you are uncomfortable or if your provider feels it is necessary, you'll have a catheter placed up your urethra to release the urine. Sometimes women also find it difficult to urinate at first after the catheter is taken out.

Before you are released, both you and your baby are checked to make sure you are okay. You will also receive instructions on how to care for the baby during its first weeks and when to arrange checkups for both of you.

Recovering at Home

As amazing as the changes in your body were during pregnancy, the changes that occur following pregnancy are more so. Immediately after birth, hormone levels in your body change to begin the recovery process. Within several weeks to months after delivery, your uterus will have shrunk to nearly the size it was before the baby was conceived, a process called uterine involution. During those weeks, you will have a bloody vaginal discharge, called *lochia*, which will gradually become lighter until it is yellow and faint at the end. It's normal if you pass a large blood clot. Your blood volume quickly will return to what it was before your pregnancy. Most of this decrease will result in increased urination, so get ready to use the bathroom more frequently during these weeks.

After approximately six weeks, you'll return to your health care provider for a checkup to make sure that your body's immediate recovery from childbirth is complete. Other changes will occur more gradually. For example, within months after delivery, the extra hair growth that occurred while you were pregnant will gradually fall out, and your hair will return to its normal thickness.

A question that almost every new mom asks is, "When will I be able to fit back into my old clothes?" Although some women slip back into their jeans in a few weeks, they are a small minority. For most women, the rule of thumb is, "Nine months to get there, and nine months to get back."

The more extra weight you gained during pregnancy, the longer it will take to fit into your regular clothes. However, all the experts agree that this is not the time to speed up your weight loss by going on a diet. You need a nutritious diet to recover from childbirth and to maintain the energy level needed to care for your newborn. Breastfeeding mothers need to add calories to their daily diet to maintain the breasts' ability to produce milk. The best way to get your figure back is to eat healthily, snack on fruits and vegetables, and exercise, and continue your prenatal vitamins and calcium supplementation.

You may ask, "How can I get to an exercise class when most days I can't even take a shower until four in the afternoon?" The solution is to exercise right in your own home. Your baby is a great exercise machine. Taking your baby on a brisk stroll every day is a great way to exercise. Take it easy at first, and try a fifteen-minute walk. Then, work your way up to 30 or 45 minutes daily, and you'll see results.

WHEN TO CALL YOUR DOCTOR

Women who have undergone childbirth will encounter various after-effects of the delivery. Most of these are normal, but some may require medical attention.

The discomfort and pain that accompany a vaginal birth can be soothed by a sitz bath. However, if your have severe pain in your perineum or reddening of the area, call your health care provider to determine if these are signs of an infection, which would require medical attention. If the normal vaginal discharge that occurs during the first few weeks after childbirth becomes bright red or is foul smelling, contact your health care provider immediately. You should also call if you experience severe and persistent abdominal pain, a persistent fever of more than 100.4 degrees Fahrenheit, and any other unusual problems.

At Home with the Baby

When you first come home, you will hopefully have a lot more hands to help out than you need. Often, the baby's grandmother or aunt comes to stay for the first few days. If possible, impose on another family member or hire a caregiver for the next week or so. You may chafe at having the extra body in the house and long for your privacy, but don't turn down the help. Take advantage of the luxury of having someone else run and fetch diapers, make formulas, do the laundry once or twice a day, and shop and cook, while the two of you take turns feeding, burping, and changing your new family member. When the day comes that you are first alone with your baby, you may find yourself overwhelmed with all the chores that need to be done.

The first few months of being new parents are difficult in themselves because of all the new instincts you need to develop and the anxiety about doing something wrong. These anxieties will be heightened by sleep deprivation. Your baby will probably wake up several times at night to be nursed. If you're breastfeeding (and we recommend that you try), then you will have the sole responsibility for feeding your baby.

T I P

Even if you're breastfeeding, your partner can still help out. Feeding the baby at night entails more than just giving a bottle or putting the baby to your breast. In addition, the baby usually needs to be changed, burped, and put back in the crib, a process that can take up to an hour. So, if your husband helps out with those chores, you might get an extra 30 minutes or so of sleep.

Sleeplessness

Not getting enough sleep might affect you in many ways during the day. For example, you might have less concentration and be less able to focus on important tasks, all of which could affect how you care for your baby. With less sleep, you and your partner also become more cranky and get in each other's way. When this happens, don't let your sleeplessness interfere with your relationship. Remember what your mother told you when you were little: Count to ten before saying anything when you're mad. During those ten seconds, remember that you're both tired and overwhelmed and that you're in this together. As a result, your rush of anger at some oversight will probably fizzle out before the argument begins.

The only solution to lack of sleep is sleep itself. To get more rest, you may have to adjust to your baby's behavior patterns. During the first few weeks, most newborns have their days and nights confused. They are asleep during the day when you want to show him or her off and are alert at 4 AM when you want to rest. If you have help, take advantage and nap. If you're on your own, adapt to your baby's rhythm as best you can by sleeping when the baby sleeps.

Although this may sound easy, many new parents still try to do too much. If the baby is napping, they try to rush around completing other tasks, such as straightening up the house, doing the laundry, or catching up on calling relatives. Of course, this simply leaves them more exhausted. Just as during childbirth, you need to let go of your preconceptions and do what is best under the present circumstances. Forget about the picture-perfect home. Put yourselves and your newborn first. Rest is the key to your health and your ability to be good parents, so make that your primary concern. And remember, before you know it, this stage will be over and your baby will be sleeping through the night. You will wistfully remember the wee hours of the night when you and your partner gazed in wonder at your marvelous creation when the rest of the world was sound asleep.

Breastfeeding

By the time you give birth to your child, you probably will have been taken aside by both advocates for and against breastfeeding, each equally as adamant that theirs is the best way. However, we feel that you should breastfeed your baby whenever possible. It is healthy and satisfying for both you and the baby. Even working women, given today's modern breastpumps and insulated bottles and bags for storage, are finding that work and breastfeeding can be combined successfully.

> **TIP**
>
> To support breastfeeding and encourage women to return to work, many companies have set up separate areas for breastpumping. If your employer does not provide you with this space, ask your boss to provide you with private space for this purpose.

Remember that breast milk is still the best nutrition for a newborn. It's free, it's always available, and it's always at the right temperature. Compared to cow's milk or even formula, breast milk contains many important ingredients unique to humans, such as antibodies that serve to nourish and protect the baby from infection. In addition, breast-fed babies contract fewer illnesses in the first year of life than bottle-fed babies and are less colicky if fed directly from the breast. Breast milk is also better tolerated by the infant's digestive system. Breastfeeding also triggers contractions that will help shrink your uterus to its normal size. Although these uterine contractions can be quite intense and sometimes painful, they usually last only for a minute or two as your milk lets down, and then dissipate.

Nursing is a learning experience for both mother and baby. Sometimes the early road is a bumpy one. The La Leche League, an organization dedicated to providing guidance and encouragement to nursing women, has local chapters in most cities around the country. Finally, many medical facilities have lactation experts, who are trained to help new mothers and their babies become a nursing twosome.

One of the most common concerns of mothers on the first day or two after birth is that their baby might not be getting enough sustenance because their breasts have not yet produced milk. During the first two or three days, your breasts produce *colostrum,* a thick, yellow substance that provides both nourishment and antibodies to the newborn. Your newborn baby doesn't need anything more than the colostrum for the first couple of days. When your baby is ready for more, lo and behold, your breasts will become hard and engorged with milk. Sometimes babies find it difficult at first to put his or her mouth around the nipple correctly. Your lactation consultant can give you and your baby personalized advice to help you succeed.

The thing to do when faced with all of these breastfeeding problems is to relax. It's going to take a little while for all the wrinkles to be worked out, but soon enough, you'll be able to nurse your baby while talking on the phone and cutting up tomatoes for the dinner salad.

TIP

One of the best books about breastfeeding that many new moms consider to be their nursing bible is The Complete Book of Breastfeeding *by Marvin S. Eiger, MD, and Sally Wendkos Olds.*

BREASTFEEDING AND WEIGHT LOSS

Although you need an additional 300 calories or so in your diet when you breastfeed, it is true that the pounds literally roll off some women when they are breastfeeding. However, this is not always the case. In fact, some women's bodies are hormonally primed to conserve energy (that is, to retain fat tissue) to ensure that there is enough for milk production in case of malnutrition. The chances of malnutrition are slight in the Western world, but the body doesn't know that. If you are like these women, it's possible that you will lose weight more slowly than others and may have to wear loose clothing a little longer. You may even have to wait until you stop nursing. But don't despair. You, too, will be able to get your old body back after you've stopped breastfeeding.

TIP

To feel better about yourself until you return to your regular weight, buy a few outfits that flatter your current figure rather than remain resolute in your decision to wear your maternity clothes until you fit into your old wardrobe. Wearing baggier clothing than you need to will only make you feel less attractive and frustrated.

IF YOU CANNOT BREASTFEED

If you cannot breastfeed because you are not producing enough milk or because you find nursing problematic, bottle feeding is a perfectly safe and healthy way to feed your baby, as long as you follow the instructions on the formula for proper use. However, even if you bottle feed, your breasts are going to become engorged with milk. If you are not nursing your baby, the milk production will cease by itself within a few weeks.

BREASTFEEDING AND SEX

According to Masters and Johnson, women who breastfeed their children become interested in renewing sexual relations faster than those who don't. However, women who breastfeed have suppressed levels of estrogen for a longer period of time than those who don't, so although she may be willing, the body often isn't. Because of the low estrogen levels, a nursing mother's vagina may be dry and the lining easily bruised or cracked, making intercourse often more uncomfortable. Luckily, there are lubricants that can be used safely during breastfeeding to relieve vaginal dryness and make intercourse a pleasure again.

Also, women who are breastfeeding may leak milk when they are excited. Some men may be aroused by this; for others, it is a turnoff.

From Our Files

Barbara and Paul were delighted to have their new baby. It was now a month after the delivery, and they had resumed sexual activity. During the height of excitement, Paul lost his erection. They were both terribly embarrassed, and when the same thing happened again twice over the next few days, they thought their sex life was gone forever. They decided to see a counselor. It quickly became clear that during sexual activity, Paul felt breast milk leaking from Barbara's breast. The thought of being intimate with the mother of his baby during the time that she was breastfeeding bothered him, and that was why he was unable to sustain his erections. With counseling and good communication, they both realized that this is a common problem among parents of newborn babies.

With the advice of their counselor, Barbara wore a nursing bra during sexual activity. This prevented Paul from feeling the milk. As a result, their sex life was back on track.

TIP

Some women who breastfeed may be aroused by the baby sucking on their nipples and may even have an orgasm. They may feel disturbed and ashamed of their sexual response and may stop nursing. Our suggestion is to enjoy these sensations without any feelings of guilt. Clearly, you are not thinking sexually of your baby, and if you get this extra kick from breastfeeding, count yourself lucky!

BREASTFEEDING AND CONTRACEPTION

Although breastfeeding may delay ovulation, it cannot be used as a contraceptive. Ovulation and pregnancy can happen while you're breastfeeding, even if you don't get your period. Therefore, you should discuss postpregnancy contraception with your health care provider before leaving the hospital. If you are used to taking oral contraceptives, progestin-only birth control pills are considered safe to take while nursing. Whatever method you choose, be sure to use a contraceptive when breastfeeding if you don't want to get pregnant.

Postpartum Blues and Anxiety

*Postpartum
Blues*

You've had a great pregnancy, delivered a healthy baby, and now you are at home, but you really can't enjoy yourself. Although this is a time to celebrate, you feel lousy. Welcome to the world of postpartum blues, a condition affecting up to fifty percent of all new mothers. Postpartum blues, a mild form of postpartum depression, usually begins during the first weeks after delivery, but may appear anytime during the first year. It affects first-time mothers less than second- or third-time mothers and is usually over in several days. The new mother feels down, can't cope with tasks, and can't enjoy herself or the new baby.

There are many theories about postpartum blues, including rapid changes in hormone levels after birth, exhaustion following pregnancy and childbirth, being overwhelmed by the new responsibilities of motherhood, and feeling inadequate as a mother. If you're feeling blue, we suggest the following to lift your spirits:

- Don't stay in the house all day:
  - Take the baby out for a walk or ride.
  - Go out for a cup of tea with your best friend.
  - Join a new mother's group in town.
  - Go out for a massage.
  - Sign up for yoga classes.
  - Make a date with your husband
  - Visit a museum.
- Talk to your partner about your feelings.
- Order a gourmet take-out dinner instead of the usual pizza.
- Shower twice daily, get dressed up, and put on your usual makeup.
- Rent a movie so that you can pause it as necessary and not miss any of the action.
- Reminisce about the birth.

Whatever you do, keep it simple and undemanding to avoid adding more stress to your life. For instance, it would not be a good idea to invite friends over and frantically try to clean up the house, cook, and entertain. If you want company, ask them to bring in some dinner or go out.

Postpartum
Depression

Some women experience severe postpartum depression, a condition that requires professional treatment. The warning signals are depression that lasts for longer than several days; inability to cope with simple daily activities, such as showering, dressing, or caring for the basic needs of the baby; a lack of appetite; and occasional violent feelings toward oneself or the baby. If you experience signs of severe depression, get in touch with your health care provider immediately, because you will need help right away.

Anxiety

Depression isn't the only emotion that you might have to overcome. Many couples facing parenthood for the first time experience bouts of anxiety as well. It's only natural after childbirth to find yourself lying awake some nights, your mind racing in different directions thinking about all the bills and responsibilities.

ASK DR. RUTH

Q When I pictured being home with the baby, it was always such a nice family scene, with my husband and I taking turns holding and taking care of the baby. Instead it has become a nightmare, with both of us constantly tired and always on the verge of a fight. Maybe the ideal isn't possible, but is there anything we can do to at least keep our relationship from falling apart?

A One word that seems synonymous with a new baby is chaos. Your house gets turned upside down and your schedules get turned inside out. This can drive you both crazy. One solution is organization. If you try to take care of the baby in a haphazard manner, it can become overwhelming. But if you plan your day, leaving plenty of flextime for the unexpected, maybe you can stay in control. For example, the weekend is coming up and you feel the need to go for a long walk. Your partner wants to watch football. Draw up a plan that allows both of you to fulfill both your needs. That way, you'll have something to look forward to before the weekend starts, and you'll be able to look back on it knowing that it just didn't pass without your doing anything that you wanted to. Remember, though, that flexibility is the key. Keep the bigger goals in mind and be ready to adjust other parts of the schedule as needed to make those goals happen. If the baby has been sleeping from 10 AM to 1 PM every day, you can bet that on Sunday, she or he will suddenly change her schedule and sleep later or earlier. You'll need to take advantage of the nap time whenever it occurs and be flexible about changing your plans to accommodate the baby's schedule.

If you experience anxiety to an extent that prevents you from enjoying the baby or yourselves, start by sitting back and taking a deep breath. Put things in perspective. Remember that you are not the first couple to experience life with a new baby. Your parents and billions of people in this world have faced the same daunting experience as new parents. Talk to your parents and friends who already have children, or with members of a parents' group about your feelings and ask how they handled the situation. Most important of all, take your situation step-by-step, one crisis at a time.

Keeping the Family Bonds Strong

Dad Feels Neglected and Mom Overwhelmed

While the mother is going through a variety of emotional and physical transformations, the father will have his own problems to deal with, too. He may feel as harassed or anxious as the mother. In addition, it is not just siblings who feel jealousy toward the new arrival; fathers also can feel neglected. Although they are not being replaced, they are certainly not getting the attention—particularly the nurturing attention—that they received before the birth of the new baby. Sometimes, new mothers devote so much of their attention to bonding with the new baby that they don't have time left over for their partner, who suddenly feels left out in the cold.

Some fathers take a philosophical view. They understand that the situation is temporary and things will go back to normal. Others, however, feel hurt, and when those hurt feelings build up, the relationship can end up in trouble. The sooner you nip the competition for attention in the bud, the better. Fathers, you need to speak up if you're feeling abandoned. Mothers, you need to listen to him, rather than perceive him as one more burden in your life. You both need to commit to finding time to renew your relationship. A weekly (or more frequent) date scheduled in advance with a caregiver can give you the impetus you need to get away and reconnect—even if it means spending the evening talking about the baby.

Sometimes a father who feels overwhelmed by the responsibilities of the new baby will tune out and leave everything to the mother. He may suddenly spend long evening hours at the office or work on weekends. Mom, who is left caring for the infant full time with little adult interaction, will soon start to feel abandoned. As a result, the relationship may soon show signs of strain.

In this case, the mother needs to speak her mind and let the father know that she and the baby need him to participate and not just be a family figurehead. Dad might also need some coaching, particularly if he was raised himself in a traditional family, in which the mom handled the home front and the dad's responsibilities were at the office.

Take Time Off

Of course the best way to restore your relationship is to take time off from caring for the baby, even if it's for only one night. Don't wait until you can get away for a whole weekend. Even if your relationship seems strong, make plans to regularly spend a few hours alone together. These few hours could set the mood for you to cuddle together and watch a movie as soon as the baby is asleep.

If there is no one you feel you can trust with your baby, the next best solution—believe it or not—is to clear the deck for one weekend and just take care of the baby and yourselves. Unplug the television and the telephone, buy enough food to last 24 hours, and spend the time together. Without anyone else demanding your attention, you can adjust your rhythms to work with those of your newborn. When the baby goes to sleep—and a young baby will spend more than half of the day sleeping—you'll be ready to take full advantage of the time to get the rest you need and undo the stress of being new parents.

T I P

Although it is important for parents to spend some quality time together, it may also be just as important for them to spend some sleep time apart. Although sleeping on the couch has become synonymous with being estranged, when a newborn is keeping both parents awake, sleeping on the couch without interruption can be rewarding.

How Do Your Older Children Feel?

If this is not your first child, then you are not the only family members making an adjustment. The reactions of your older children to having a newborn in the house will depend on many factors. Usually, the more involved they are in welcoming the sibling, the better. However, with very young children, you'll have to be watchful that they don't unintentionally (or intentionally, in a moment of pique) hurt the newborn.

There are bound to be some conflicts, especially in the earliest stages when the newborn demands so much parental attention, and these conflicts are bound to affect the family dynamics. However, the baby is not conscious if he or she is receiving more or less attention than the older children, so make sure that you give part of your attention to your older children while still attending to the newborn. Perhaps dad can focus his attention on the older children while mom takes a nap or breastfeeds the baby. Or, you could arrange for a sitter one afternoon a week and go out to the park or other activity with your older children. As your baby grows, he or she will be more demanding of your total attention, so diffuse sibling rivalry at the beginning by sharing your attention.

Your Extended Family

When your baby comes home, you'll love having your parents, in-laws, and immediate family to come to see your new baby. But as the initial excitement wears off and the sleepless nights take their toll, you're likely to cringe every time the phone or doorbell rings announcing another caller.

If you have close relatives who live nearby, it might be a good idea to have the baby's first showing at someone else's house. It's hard to ask people to leave your own home, but it's less difficult to excuse yourselves when you're worn out and retreat to your own quiet home.

If the stream of relatives dropping by becomes overwhelming, you will have to be forthright in letting your family know that you need your privacy to regain your strength and for the two of you to get used to caring for your new baby. If some persistent relatives don't get the message, you can always get an answering machine or an answering service from the local phone company to give you the privacy you need.

Enjoy! Enjoy! Enjoy!

We've talked about all of the ups and downs of the postpartum period, as well as some of the problems that couples encounter that require medical attention. Although it's important for you to know about these unusual problems, we don't want you to be overly concerned. Think about the mothers you know. How many had permanent adverse effects following their labor and delivery? How many went on to have more children after their first? Yes, becoming a mother and father is a challenge, but it's an experience that nature intended. For the great majority of you, it's also one that will bring you great joy and satisfaction.

$\mathcal{K}$EEPING THE ROMANCE ALIVE: SEX AFTER CHILDREN

YOU'VE certainly heard the expression, two's company, three's a crowd, but you probably never thought about it in terms of your own family. It is important to remember that if you are both committed to your relationship, you must keep your love candle burning brightly, no matter how difficult the circumstances. Conversely, if your love life is the lowest priority on your agenda, you'll never make time for it. You'll always allow the duties of raising a family and other matters to take priority.

We're going to offer advice about some specific concerns that arise between partners after they bring their new baby home. Above all else, remember to make your relationship a priority. Be mindful of when it begins to slip too low on your agenda, and, when it does start to slip, take some concrete steps to rekindle the passion.

You don't want the baby to turn your relationship into a sexless marriage. Most couples have difficulty jumpstarting their sex life after the baby is born, and jumpstarting is a very appropriate term because, believe it or not, sex lives are somewhat like car batteries. If you leave the car lights on for an hour, you can still see a dim glow; starting the battery is quick and easy. However, if you leave the lights on overnight and the car battery is completely drained, starting it again is no longer possible. Instead, you have to recharge the battery or buy a new one. If you haven't had sex for a month or so after the baby is born, you shouldn't have a problem getting your sex life in gear again. But, if that sexless period stretches to four, five, or six months, then major repairs to your sex life are going to be necessary.

The stereotype that paints all new mothers as too exhausted to even think about sex is certainly not true. There may certainly be some women who leave their libidos in the delivery room, but a large number of women yearn for sex, even if they are not yet physically ready for intercourse. Doctors no longer recommend any one set time for all women to wait before resuming intercourse after birth. We recommend that intercourse be initiated after childbirth as soon as the healing process is completed. For some women that may be two weeks after a vaginal birth; for others, it may take longer depending on the extent of lacerations or episiotomy.

Does this mean that you both have to remain sexually frustrated until you are completely healed? Absolutely not. Because your partner's penis is being declared persona non grata inside your vagina doesn't mean that your clitoris, the seat of most women's sexual pleasure, is off limits to his tongue or fingers—or, for that matter, your fingers. The clitoris is located at the top of the vagina, where it is well protected during delivery and is not affected at all during birth for most women. And, of course, just because your vagina can't give comfort to your partner's penis yet doesn't mean that you can't satisfy your partner in other ways.

Physiological Considerations

After the baby's birth, scar tissue may form where incisions or tears were made during childbirth. Thus, even when your vagina and perineum are physiologically capable of intercourse, stretching the newly healed tissue may be uncomfortable or downright painful during sex. At first, you need to approach sex delicately. Perhaps you can use extra lubrication, such as K-Y Jelly. The first time, you can also try to gently stretch the tissues with your fingers to make entry more comfortable. Consider trying a different position; you may find one position more comfortable than another. You may require a few weeks of extra healing before you find vaginal intercourse comfortable in any position, but there is no reason why you can't enjoy masturbation or oral sex. These other forms of lovemaking are certainly preferable to not having sex at all.

Once you resume intercourse, you may notice that because the vagina was stretched during birth, it may not be as tight and does not provide as much friction during sex as before your pregnancy. This may diminish your or your partner's pleasure. The Kegel exercises described in Chapter 3 will strengthen the pubococcygeal, or PC, muscle. At first, you might not be able to sense that you're contracting the muscles, but if you repeat the exercises every day, you'll notice a gradual improvement. If you perform the exercise with his penis inside your vagina, your partner will notice the improvement too.

If you've had a cesarean section, you may have vaginal intercourse although your abdominal incision can cause discomfort. In that case, you could try some of the positions you used during the third trimester of pregnancy, in which pressure on the abdomen is avoided.

T I P

If you find that your sexuality cannot be ignited, no matter how many times you and your partner try, call your health care provider and discuss the problem with him or her. The problem may not be in your head, but in your hormones. If your hormones haven't reverted to their normal levels, your libido could remain in limbo for a long time. Your health care provider may be able to give you medication to increase your sexual interest.

Psychological Considerations

Although the physical component is certainly important, the more common problems to resuming intercourse are psychological. You have to be emotionally ready as well, and that's an issue for many women. Rather than looking forward to the day when the doctor gives them the go-ahead to have intercourse, some women prefer to stretch out the asexual period, whether or not they enjoyed sex before pregnancy. Part of the reason for this disinterest is probably the changing levels of a woman's hormones after pregnancy; another factor could be physical exhaustion. In addition, some men find it difficult to adjust psychologically and sexually to their wives as mothers.

You may also find it difficult to make the transition from mother to sexual partner, particularly if you are often interrupted during sex by

Q I had a baby eight months ago, and I feel that since then I've lost all of my sex drive. I think that the main cause is sheer exhaustion. I know my husband must be feeling frustrated, and I am just curious to know what I can do to spice our love life. Is there anything I can do to make myself feel sexy again?

A Exhaustion can also be a key element, and you should definitely look into why you are feeling this way. By now, your baby should be sleeping better at night, even if not eight straight hours, and you should be feeling less sleep deprived. If your baby is still waking up every couple of hours, ask your pediatrician for advice on how to help him or her develop better sleeping habits, for the sake of your sex life. Set aside definite times to spend alone with your husband. Begin by just touching and kissing each other a few times to begin building the excitement. Your natural feelings for each other will take over and do the rest.

---

cries from your baby. It's important to realize that you are a sexual being, even if that side of you is being overwhelmed by the enormous physical and emotional challenges of becoming a mother. It would be a terrible blow to your relationship if you repress your sexuality; it also means you would miss out on one of life's most delicious pleasures. All you have to do is reach beneath the surface and let your sexual self revive. Give yourself a chance to bloom sexually by letting your partner coax a natural response from your body. Once you get your motor going and start moving down the highway, you'll never want to get off the road again!

One factor could be your job. If you have returned to work full time, you and your partner need to share the household and parenting responsibilities. If you are working a full day only to come home and put in another six or seven hours of housework and mothering, it's no wonder you're exhausted. It might be a good idea to make a list of the chores, so both of you are aware of what has to be done and can share the burden more equitably. If the chores are too much for two full-time working parents and you can afford help, don't hesitate to hire someone. This should give you the necessary time to relax or take a long soak in a bath, after which you'll undoubtedly feel restored and ready to rekindle your love life.

Postpartum Blues and Sex

It's difficult to think about having sex if you're not feeling 100 percent either physically or emotionally, but avoiding sex can become a vicious cycle. When you're not sure if you want to have sex, you may avoid it. Your husband may start to feel frustrated and rejected, and may snap at you. This could result in an argument, which may make you feel even worse and less like having sex. If this goes on for a long time, you might become estranged from each other to a point that will be difficult to repair.

Have you ever tried to enter a cool body of water, like the ocean or a lake, one toe at a time? It's a form of torture. The best way to get wet is to just dive right in. The same is true of sex. If you start hemming and hawing and spouting a continuous string of excuses for not having sex, it just makes it harder to begin. On the other hand, if you jump right into it, you can quickly speed up the process of becoming a couple of lovebirds again.

If you're thinking, "But I just don't feel like it. I shouldn't force myself, should I?," our response is, you should definitely force yourself. The longer you wait, the harder it is going to be. And the quicker you and your partner return to your normal sexual relations, the quicker you'll restore the intimacy and closeness that was a part of your relationship before childbirth—and restoring that relationship is an essential part of beginning your new life as parents together. It really is like riding a bicycle after many years. Once you get back on the seat and begin pedaling, it's like you never got off.

Some men have problems getting reacquainted sexually with partners who are no longer just wives, but also mothers. Suddenly, they become turned off by comparing their wives to their own mothers. Other men may remember the birth and are too worried about hurting their partners.

Whether it is the woman or the man who is having the problems with a languishing libido, both must realize that the problem doesn't lie in the genitals, but in their minds—where the sense of arousal is being short circuited. The key to repairing the short circuit might be in the genitals. If you just begin to make love, even if you're not really in the mood, there's a good chance that you'll become aroused. Once that happens, you'll find yourself very much in the mood—and often!

When the issue is deeper than sex, for instance, if your relationship was rocky to begin with, you may try to patch things up on your own. However, you should keep in mind that outside help is available if you aren't having success by yourselves.

Planning for Sex

There are different approaches to planning your sex life. You could have a calendar in the kitchen on which you can write down the word "SEX" in bold red letters on the days you plan to have sex. If you don't like publicizing your sex life, a little subtlety is probably in order. Maybe you can use an innocent expression whose secret meaning only you and your husband know to replace with the word "sex," such as "change bed sheets" or "empty closet." You can let each other know in the morning, with an exchange of winks or a hug from behind that you have plans for some pleasure sharing later in the evening. On the other hand, you don't want to be so subtle that the message gets lost. Work out some agreed signals, and make a point of giving firm answers. Too many "maybe" answers do not set the right tone.

As parents, you will definitely feel different about expressing your intimate feelings. That part of your life will not be exactly as it was before. Although some couples begin to make love right after the baby arrives, they often find that a baby in a crib at the foot of the bed is inhibiting. Maybe one, or both of you, will want to turn the light off or feel the need to make love under covers. You also won't be able to spontaneously watch a movie, stay out for a late dinner, or make love on the living room floor.

But just because your life together—and sex—can't be spontaneous doesn't mean it can't be fun. In fact, by making dates to be with each other, you can prepare for your special evenings and make them memorable. The key word is anticipation. If you know that tonight's the night, you can allow yourself to fantasize in advance—and plan to make some of your fantasies come true. For new parents, such planned time together usually turns out much better than attempting to have sex on a catch-as-catch-can basis.

This is not to say that you shouldn't have spontaneous sex, too. As far as we're concerned, the more the merrier. We just don't think that you should rely on the rare moments when the baby's asleep and both of you are awake enough to think of romance to fulfill your sexual needs.

THE OVERNIGHT VACATION

If you've having serious problems getting your love life going again, one way of stirring up the juices is to take a short vacation away from home, hearth, and baby. You don't have to go for very long. Overnight would be a real treat, but even a few hours might do the trick. All you need is a trusted babysitting service—grandparents are ideal, but anyone with whom you can trust the baby for four or five hours will do—and a nearby motel.

You may feel a little strange checking into a motel for a few hours, but if you use your imagination, it can be quite exciting. Anticipate the meeting and get dressed especially for your tryst. You may want to bring some gourmet tidbits to eat and some wine or champagne to sip. You're not having an illicit affair, so you have no reason to feel as if you're doing something wrong. You just need a change of scenery.

SETTING THE MOOD

From Our Files

One of the reasons that Sam and Cathy knew they were right for each other was that they each had imagined having four children. They realized how unusual it was today to want to have such a large family. Even though they were young—Cathy was only 18 and Sam 19—they wanted to start their life together and were married. They immediately had four daughters.

As you can imagine, Cathy and Sam were constantly busy with one child or another. When the children were old enough to start coming into their bedroom, Sam and Cathy fell into the habit of locking their bedroom door on Friday nights, when no one had to get up early the next morning for school or church. On Saturday morning, the children would be engrossed in Saturday morning television cartoons, so that they wouldn't be interrupted first thing in the morning, which was their favorite time for making love.

When their daughters were grown, they told their parents that they had been aware for some time why their parents locked their bedroom door on Friday nights. Far from being traumatized by the fact that their parents had sex, the daughters said that knowing their parents were still in love enough to lock the door on Friday nights made them feel secure, particularly as they watched so many of their friends' parents divorce.

As your baby matures and, possibly, as you have other babies, your physical and emotional energy will be stretched even further. That is why it's important to give your intimate life the priority it deserves right from the start. Family rules should be set up accordingly.

For example, if your bedroom door is closed, children should know that thay have to knock before entering. You should also have a lock on the door so that you can be assured of having privacy. If a young child accidentally comes into a room when you are making love, try to remain calm. Sex is a natural part of life. After all, your children wouldn't be around without you having had sex in the first place. Young children probably will have no idea what is going on. If it's an older child, don't be afraid to offer a simple explanation the next day.

Locked doors, however, don't completely isolate you. If your child wakes up in the middle of the night, hears you making love, and says something to you about the noises, tell your child that you were sharing something pleasurable. This will prevent him or her from associating the moans or groans of lovemaking with pain. If making noise is one of the pleasures of your sexual interchanges, there's no reason to give it up.

T I P

Don't be afraid to show affection for each other in front of the kids. Toddlers sometimes can be jealous and try to get your attention away from each other. Just tell them that hugging is one of the ways that mommies and daddies show that they love each other.

USING BABYSITTERS

To create the privacy you need during your work-a-day life, use babysitters all through your childrearing years. Grandparents make wonderful babysitters, when they're interested and able, especially if they live close enough. You may send the children over to grandma's, so you can have an evening of romance and privacy. If you have friends who have their own children, perhaps you could swap babysitting services with them. If you want to hire a teenager and go to a motel for a special evening of intimacy once in a while, don't hesitate. Sex is part of the glue that binds you together, so it's definitely a worthwhile investment. The combination of anticipation and memories of those nights of passion is powerful stuff, indeed.

Family Planning

Although we both want to encourage you to have as much sexual pleasure as possible after you give birth, we also want to encourage you to avoid having another baby before you're ready. For practical and health reasons, birth control should be a part of the repertoire of sex after childbirth. In Chapter 2, we discussed the different methods of birth control, with an emphasis on putting them away so you could get pregnant. Now it is time to bring out contraceptives again and review which ones will work best for you. The average woman starts to ovulate within one to two months after birth, although ovulation may be slightly delayed in breastfeeding women. Thus, you can see that planning for contraception becomes essential as soon as you deliver. There are basically five types of temporary birth control—barrier methods (condom, diaphragm, and cervical cap), vaginal spermicides, intrauterine devices, hormonal contraception, and natural family planning. There are two forms of permanent birth control—tubal ligation and vasectomy.

TIP

We want to add a note about the way failure rates for temporary contraceptives are calculated. All failure rates are calculated in "per 100 women years," which means the number of pregnancies that occur either if one woman uses the contraceptive for 100 years or if 100 women take it for one year. With this in mind, note that the failure rate for male condoms is 2 to 20 per 100 women years; for female condoms, unknown (but probably similar to male condoms); for the diaphragm, 2 to 20 per 100 women years (same as for condoms); for the cap (similar to the diaphragm and condom); for vaginal spermicides, over 20 per 100 women years; for IUDs, 2 to 3 per 100 women years (most likely lower now, approaching pills); for pills, fewer than 0.5 per 100 women years.

Barrier Methods

Barrier methods are birth control devices that block the cervix so that sperm cannot penetrate it to fertilize an egg. In addition, barrier methods also decrease your chance of becoming infected with an STD. The most common of these devices are the male condom, the diaphragm, and the cervical cap, while the female condom is used infrequently.

MALE CONDOMS

A male condom is a latex sheath that is placed over the erect penis to collect the ejaculate, thus preventing it from entering the uterus and fertilizing an egg. Not only does it prevent pregnancy, it also protects against the spread of STDs. (Condoms made out of lambskin that provide contraception are too porous to protect against infection with a virus, and thus do not protect against STDs.) You may also use a condom to prevent infection together with another method of birth control, such as the diaphragm or the cervical cap, to prevent conception. Male condoms can be lubricated, textured, tinted, contoured, and equipped with contraceptive gel. Although they come in different sizes, the average condom will fit most penis sizes.

Under ideal conditions, male condoms are highly effective, specifically if they are used in combination with spermicidal foams, creams, or gels. However, condoms can break and leak upon removal. Because condoms may diminish sexual enjoyment, some men may not want to use a condom all the time. It is therefore better to use another form of protection against pregnancy along with the condom.

FEMALE CONDOMS

The female condom is a relatively recent addition to the contraceptive arsenal. A female condom is a latex sheath that is placed inside the vagina. During intercourse, the man ejaculates inside the condom-lined vagina, thus preventing any sperm from entering the cervix. Data on the effectiveness of this recently developed contraceptive are limited. Using a spermicide together with the female condom will further improve its effectiveness in preventing conception. There are drawbacks to the female condom. It is cumbersome to use and may fall out or be pushed up into the vagina during intercourse. There is also the danger of the man inadvertently inserting his penis between the condom and vaginal wall, making the condom ineffective. This device is not yet used widely in the United States.

DIAPHRAGM AND CERVICAL CAPS

To block sperm from going through the cervix, many types of barriers have been placed inside a woman's vagina during intercourse. It has been said, for instance, that the noted lover, Casanova, used hollowed out lemons to cover the cervix of his many sexual partners.

The diaphragm and the cervical cap both cover the cervix, providing a barrier that prevents sperm from entering the uterus. The diaphragm, however, is wider than the cervical cap, and it is easier both to insert properly and remove. Diaphragms need to be fitted to each woman's size. If you used a diaphragm or a cervical cap before your pregnancy, it will need to be refitted after delivery. Proper insertion and positioning of this barrier contraceptive is important to its success, so adequate instruction for its use is important. In this country, diaphragms are in much greater use than cervical caps, which are more commonly used in Europe.

Diaphragms are designed to be used in conjunction with spermicidal foam, jelly, or cream. They must be placed in the vagina together with the spermicide before intercourse, and, once inserted, should stay in place for at least six to eight hours after intercourse. If a diaphragm is inserted with spermicide for more than six hours prior to intercourse, or if a second episode of intercourse takes place within the six- to eight-hour time frame, additional spermicide should be added to ensure adequate protection. If preventing a pregnancy is of utmost importance to you, you should use a different contraceptive method, or you can combine two barrier methods, such as a condom and a diaphragm. When used together, these two methods approach the effectiveness of the birth control pill.

The cervical cap is a barrier similar to the diaphragm. As its name implies it sits tightly, like a cap, on the cervix to prevent sperm from entering. Insertion and positioning is harder with the cervical cap than with the diaphragm. Like the diaphragm, the cervical cap needs to be inserted before intercourse, but it has to remain at least eight hours after intercourse to be effective. The cervical cap may be kept in place for up to 48 hours, and should be removed for at least several hours every other day. Spermicide is applied when the cervical cap is inserted, but does not have to be reapplied for each sexual encounter. Its advantage over the diaphragm is that it can stay in place longer and does not require additional spermicide application, which some women find messy. However, the position of the cervical cap should be checked before having sex to make sure that it is snugly covering the cervix and hasn't changed position.

Vaginal Spermicides	Spermicidal agents, such as foams, creams, and gels, are placed in the vagina before intercourse. In addition to being easy to use and affordable, they provide some protection against some STDs. However, used alone, they are not very effective in preventing pregnancy. They should therefore be used in conjunction with such barrier methods as condoms, diaphragms, or cervical caps to improve their effectiveness.
Intrauterine Devices	An intrauterine device (IUD) is a small plastic device containing either hormones or copper that is inserted in a woman's uterus. It is widely used throughout the world and has been rated by the World Health Organization and the American Medical Association as one of the

safest and most effective temporary methods of birth control for women.

In the 1970s, a single type of IUD (the Dalkon shield) was found to be associated with an increased risk of pelvic infections because of the way the string was made. Since then, IUDs have become much safer and are nowadays considered a very safe choice for contraception for many women. The new IUDs can be used for up to ten years, and they are very effective (over 99 percent).

IUDs can be inserted shortly after delivery or at any time during a woman's cycle as long as the woman isn't pregnant. A woman using an IUD should periodically check to see that the string that hangs from the IUD is palpable in her vagina to indicate that the IUD is in its proper position. If she does not feel the string, she should see her health care provider to ensure that the IUD hasn't moved out of position. The best candidates for the IUD are women who have had at least one child, are in a monogamous relationship, and have no history of previous pelvic inflammatory disease or ectopic pregnancy.

The IUD has also been used as a method of emergency contraception. An IUD that is inserted within five days after intercourse has been known to prevent pregnancy.

Hormonal Birth Control

Hormonal birth control became widely used in the 1960s. This type of birth control artificially alters the production of hormones in a woman's body in a way that prevents conception. There are several types of hormonal birth control available today—the oral birth control pill, the implantable form, and the injectable form.

BIRTH CONTROL PILLS

The birth control pill (BCP), which has been credited with being an instigator of the sexual revolution, continues to be the most reliable form of temporary birth control. The composition of the pill has changed dramatically since it was first launched in the 1950s. The type of pill most often prescribed today contains much fewer hormones, and as a result, the side effects, if any, are also much fewer. There are two types of oral contraceptives: the combined estrogen/progestin oral contraceptive and the so-called "minipill," which contains only progestin.

The combined estrogen/progestin pills suppress ovulation, thereby preventing the release of the egg from the ovary; the minipill does not have this effect. However, both the combined BCP and the minipill make the cervical mucus thick and inhospitable for sperm to penetrate. They also make it difficult for the fertilized egg to implant by changing the lining of the uterus and causing changes in the fallopian tubes. The safety of birth control pills has been well established. In fact, usage of BCP has been found to have important benefits, such as reduced rates of endometrial and ovarian cancer, pelvic inflammatory disease, iron deficiency anemia, benign breast disease, and ovarian cysts. However, there are some women (such as those who smoke over the age of 35 and those with a history of blood clots) who should probably not take combination BCP, but may take progestin-only BCP. Many doctors will prefer progestin-only pills for women who breastfeed. You should discuss your alternatives with your health care provider to determine which pill is most suitable for you.

Birth control pills, if used regularly, are almost 100 percent effective, with the failure rate being tied closely to whether or not the pills are taken as directed. Obviously, if you fail to take your pill every day, especially if it's the "minipill," it is not going to protect you effectively against pregnancy.

Aside from protecting against conception, birth control pills offer other health advantages—they regulate one's periods, diminish menstrual cramping and premenstrual tension, and decrease the likelihood of ectopic pregnancies and pelvic inflammatory disease. BCPs have also been used as treatment for acne and have been known to act as protection against endometrial and ovarian cancer. In addition, women who take the pill have been known to suffer less from iron deficiency.

EMERGENCY CONTRACEPTION

Emergency contraception is also commonly known as the morning after pill. It's important to understand that emergency contraception may be effective not only the morning after, but up to 72 hours after intercourse.

Emergency contraception involves the use of hormonal pills, usually birth control pills. Depending on the type of pill, two to four pills are taken two times, 12 hours apart, shortly after unprotected intercourse during the fertile phase of a woman's cycle. Emergency contraception is not 100 percent effective, and it should be used rarely. You should do a pregnancy test if you miss your period, even if you are taking emergency contraception. If this regimen fails and pregnancy continues, there is no evidence to suggest that the pregnancy will be adversely affected.

HORMONAL IMPLANTS

Some women prefer the convenience of a long-acting contraceptive to a daily pill. There are now implants that can work for several months or even years. Norplant, for example, is supplied in six soft capsules, each about the size of a matchstick, that are inserted under the skin of the upper arm where they continually release the hormone progestin for five years. Norplant is similar to the contraceptive pill, which contains progestin and has similar side effects. If a woman wants to become pregnant before the five years have passed, she can have the rods removed.

INJECTABLE CONTRACEPTIVES

Another long-acting contraceptive contains a progesterone-like hormone and is administered by a single intramuscular shot that is given every three months. It works for about three to four months after the last injection. The efficacy rate of this birth control method is similar to that reported for oral contraceptives.

Natural Family Planning

The term natural family planning, similar to the rhythm method, describes methods of birth control that involve monitoring a woman's ovulatory cycle and anticipating her fertile periods. (For a full discussion of how this is done, see Chapter 2.) To avoid conception, a woman abstains from sex during those periods or may use a barrier form of birth control, such as a condom or a diaphragm.

The simplest method is the calendar method, which involves keeping track of the woman's menstrual period and calculating which days of the month she is most likely to be fertile. Since this is really only a rough guess, this method is not very effective.

Other methods of natural family planning include measuring basal body temperature and checking the consistency of the cervical mucus. This is called the symptothermal method. Although these methods can be very helpful in making a baby because they can reliably indicate when ovulation has taken place, as a method of contraception they have a major drawback: Any sperm deposited shortly before ovulation might still be able to fertilize the egg when ovulation occurs. If a woman has very regular periods, and if she is conscientious about making her calculations, the natural family planning method can be effective. However, because of the effort involved, many couples who rely on this method often have unintended pregnancies.

Permanent
Birth Control

TUBAL LIGATION

Tubal ligation continues to be the most frequently used method of birth control in the world. It involves separation or occlusion of both fallopian tubes, either by tying them, cutting them, burning them, putting a clip on them, or any combination of these methods. This prevents the egg from meeting the sperm. The egg cannot move down the fallopian tubes, and the sperm cannot enter the tubes to meet the egg. Tubal ligation is usually done under a light anesthetic, and one or two small incisions below the belly button are necessary. Women can usually go home the same day, and the complication rate is low. Tubal ligation can be performed right after delivery, especially when an epidural anesthetic was given for childbirth, and you don't have to stay longer in the hospital. Many women, however, prefer to postpone tubal ligation for two to three months after childbirth. This gives the couple enough time to think about their decision and to ensure that the newborn baby is okay. At that time, tubal ligation can easily be done with a special instrument called a "laparoscope."

The failure rate of tubal ligation depends on the procedure performed, but in general is less than one percent. Women who have had tubal ligation have an increased risk for an ectopic pregnancy if they do get pregnant.

VASECTOMY

Vascectomy is a procedure done on men and involves the interruption of the tubes from the testes to the urethra, thus preventing sperm from entering the ejaculate. Its easier to do than tubal ligation, the procedure is shorter, it is cheaper, and there is a lower failure rate (about 2 to 3 per 1,000). Although the failure of a tubal ligation can be detected only if the woman becomes pregnant, the effectiveness of a vasectomy can be tested by doing a semen analysis after the procedure is completed.

Birth Control
after Delivery

The ideal contraceptive has yet to be developed, and you should discuss your options with your doctor or midwife. If you are breastfeeding, the progestin-only methods, the injectable contraceptive, and the IUD are all suitable. If combined with a barrier, these are a desirable option for some women. Nonbreastfeeding mothers can start to take combined oral contraceptives from the third week after delivery.

Myths about Birth Control

Unfortunately, there are many myths about getting pregnant. Some common misconceptions about birth control are given in Table 1.

⬥ TABLE 1 **Pregnancy: Myths and Realities**

Myth	Reality
Pulling out (coitus interruptus) prevents pregnancy.	There is fluid called "pre-ejaculatory fluid" that is filled with sperm and that leaks out shortly before he has his orgasm. Any time the erect penis is inserted into the vagina, you can get pregnant.
Breastfeeding prevents pregnancy.	You can get pregnant while breastfeeding; breastfeeding delays, but does not preclude, ovulation.
You can't get pregnant the first time you have sex.	You CAN get pregnant even if it's your first time. In fact, younger women are more likely to get pregnant than women in their 30s or 40s.
You can't get pregnant if the woman doesn't have an orgasm.	With or without orgasm, you can get pregnant.
You can't get pregnant if you do it standing up or bending over.	Though standing up or bending doesn't improve your chances of getting pregnant, you definitely CAN get pregnant that way.
Douching after intercourse prevents pregnancy by washing sperm away.	Douching does not prevent pregnancy.
He can't make you pregnant because he couldn't get his previous partner pregnant.	The reality is that if his previous partner couldn't get pregnant, it wasn't necessarily his responsibility.
You can't get pregnant because you were infertile before and needed special ovulation inducing medicine to get pregnant.	You could ovulate and get pregnant even without any ovulation inducing medicine now. Spontaneous ovulation could happen anytime.
You can't get pregnant because his sperm count is too low.	A low sperm count may decrease your chances of getting pregnant, but it does not prevent pregnancy all the time.
You can't get pregnant if you are having sex during your period.	You can get pregnant if you have sex during your period, specifically if you have short cycles.
You can never get pregnant again because you had your tubes tied.	Tubal ligation is a great way to prevent pregnancy. But it's not 100% effective. Approximately 1 out of 300 tubal ligations fails. If you had a tubal ligation and miss your period, think you might be pregnant, or have unusual complaints, see your health care provider immediately.

Having a baby is a wonderful experience, but most couples prefer to plan a pregnancy. If you have any questions about any of these methods of birth control, consult with your health care provider or seek advice at a local clinic, such as those affiliated with a hospital or a Planned Parenthood center.

From Our Files

Arlene had heard that breastfeeding prevented ovulation, so when she and her husband, William, resumed having sex, she did not take any precautions. Arlene planned to go back to work for a few years before having another child so that they could save enough money to buy a house. However, two months later, Arlene was pregnant with her second child. Having two young children would will make it difficult for her to go back to work as she'd planned. This meant that she and William would have to live with their two children in their tiny apartment for several years before buying their dream house.

It's true that breastfeeding usually delays the onset of ovulation, but it doesn't prevent ovulation indefinitely. Because ovulation occurs before menstruation, you may not have any indication that you are fertile again and may become pregnant unexpectedly. To prevent an unplanned pregnancy, you need to take proper precautions whether or not you are breastfeeding.

Arlene should, however, enjoy the years she spends with her two young children and should not permit herself to feel guilty or frustrated about waiting to buy the dream house. The children need a loving, supportive, and positive environment from the beginning; the house can come later.

You've Come Full Circle

In this book, we have tried to give advice to expecting and pregnant couples about the joy of sex and the importance of maintaining the spark of excitement. There is a German proverb, which translates as "To BECOME parents is easy, to BE parents is difficult." Before your baby came into your life, you had all the time in the world to be with each other. You could have sex whenever you wanted, wherever you desired.

With the arrival of the baby, your lives have changed tremendously. Now, another person in your house needs most of your attention and time. Your sex life after the baby is not exactly what is was before your pregnancy, but that doesn't mean that you should give up easily. Sex is what brought this baby to life, and sex is what bounds you, as a couple, together.

Eventually, your babies will become children who will grow up and leave the house, and you and your partner will again have more time for yourselves and each other. But, until then, child rearing, love, and sex ought to be essential parts of your lives. Throughout all stages of your life, you will need to make adjustments to your sex life, but the love that brought you together should be sustained throughout pregnancy, parenthood, and, eventually, grandparenthood.

INDEX